Clint Eastwood's Cinema of Trauma

Clint Eastwood's Cinema of Trauma

Essays on PTSD in the Director's Films

Edited by
CHARLES R. HAMILTON *and*
ALLEN H. REDMON

McFarland & Company, Inc., Publishers
Jefferson, North Carolina

ISBN (print) 978-1-4766-6750-8
ISBN (ebook) 978-1-4766-3042-7

Library of Congress Cataloguing-in-Publication Data

British Library cataloguing data are available

Front cover: poster art from *Mystic River*, 2003 (Warner Bros./Photofest)

Printed in the United States of America

McFarland & Company, Inc., Publishers
Box 611, Jefferson, North Carolina 28640
www.mcfarlandpub.com

Table of Contents

Acknowledgments

We want to offer a warm thank you to the contributors to this volume. This project would be just an idea without your excellent contributions. We also thank Ms. Hart and Ms. Miller, two wonderful librarians whose support was so critical at several points of this project. Many thanks go to Ms. Danquah and Ms. Chandler, both of whom proved again the value of a trusted graduate assistant.

Charles R. Hamilton would like to acknowledge Gerald Duchovney, professor, mentor, and friend, for the immeasurable guidance given him during the past ten years. Charles would also like to thank his wife, Judy, who offers her psychological support in everything he does.

Allen H. Redmon would like to extend a special acknowledgment to those courageous students at Texas A&M University Central Texas who pursue an education in the midst of trauma and recovery and everything else. Their courage gave him a reason to enter trauma studies in the first place. This book is a small return on their daring.

Preface

Coady Lapierre

Spartans were known to only put names on tombstones in two cases, if the person died in battle or in childbirth. This example serves as an early acknowledgment of the fact that the traumas encountered in life happen both on and off the battlefield, and that society takes note of exceptional examples in the face of those experiences. Citizens, artists, and historians strive to articulate ways to understand and respond to traumatic events. My work as a research psychologist is focused on better understanding the prevalence and impact of trauma-related psychological issues such as post-traumatic stress disorder. My team is looking for links between common experiences such as cell phone ring tones and extreme reactions in some individuals. Identifying common themes or triggers for memory is helpful as some people don't recognize them as the source of their sudden emotional episodes. Better understanding the process people use to identify themes of violence and loss allows them to better plan their reactions and increase positive outcomes.

The study of traumatic events on humans goes back through history with roots in surgery and dealt with participants in war or work-related accidents. Most formal study of the psychological impact of exposure to death, violence, and extreme injury was based on war veterans, and this focus has shifted in modern times to include other groups that face abuse and violence equal to any battlefield. First responders such as emergency medical technicians, police officers and firefighters often are faced with traumatic deaths or their aftermath. Victims of disasters, both man-made and natural, show similar patterns of behavior in reaction to deaths as soldiers. Philosophically, two camps of thought exist, one that treats all trauma as trauma, and another that holds that the specific details of the trauma should guide treatment and response.

How society views the common reactions to violence determines the ter-

1

minology and classification used. The first term associated with stereotypical reactions to war was in the early 19th century during the Napoleonic wars. *"Vent du boulet"* syndrome or "wind of a passing cannonball" was used to describe soldiers collapsing when cannon fire was close enough for them to feel the wind, but they were not struck (Corcq, M., and Crocq, L., 2000). Goethe described the sound as "quite strange, as if it were made up of the spinning of a top, the boiling of water, and the whistling of a bird." The reaction often included a sense of de-realization or de-personalization, the feeling that what is being experienced is not real, or is not happening to the individual but to someone else and he or she is merely a spectator. These elements are recognized today as part of common reactions to war and trauma.

Every war is different and every participant carries his or her own story that is unique, yet shared with all that have ever engaged in war. The impact of wartime experiences are often profound and life changing and some of the earliest writings on war address the changes it can bring in behavior including the oldest epic of Gilgamesh. Every person brings his or her own history to the unique events of war and responds as an individual. Some people scarred by traumatic deaths in their past may be re-traumatized by seeing the death of others, others may find resilience in having previous experience and context. How a person deals with the sum of his or her experiences and chooses or is forced to incorporate them into a self-concept varies with the individual.

Psychology was slowly growing out of psychiatry and the medical field during the 19th century and the terminology used to describe reactions to war or trauma evolved with it. The term "cardiorespiratory neurosis" was used in France as one of the first well-defined terms and alluded to impact on the heart which carries forward to today. During the American Civil War the term "soldier's heart" was used to describe impaired behaviors and increased heart rates in veterans. Toward the end of the 1800s the term "hysteria" become more commonly used and "combat hysteria" was associated with soldiers' post-war behaviors. Charcot's concept of wartime or traumatic experiences being too much to remember and pushed into the unconsciousness where they did not have to be openly dealt with influenced Freud's approach to psychotherapy in general and set the stage for the next 100 years of treatment approaches to most psychological issues.

The First World War opened the 20th century and artillery was used heavily by most combatants. The term "shell shocked" came into use to describe soldiers who were not physically injured but unable to return to duty. Often exposure to maimed or killed comrades was the determining factor if soldiers developed impairments, which were described as loss of consciousness and weakened physical state. By World War II weaponry had advanced to nuclear bombs, trauma to concentration camps. The civilian survivors of the concentration camps of World War II greatly spurred the incorporation and expansion of formal studies of the effects of trauma on non-military populations (Friedman, M., n.d.). Important work was carried out in post-war Israel whose population included the most impacted individuals. In 1949 in Israel Gerald Caplan and a small staff were charged with providing psychological services to more than 16,000 adolescent immigrants scattered over hundreds of miles in various living centers (Watson, S., and Skinner, C., eds., 2004). Knowing that providing meaningful care to that many clients was impossible, he developed a consultation model that worked with professionals of other disciplines who were referring adolescents for help. By helping doctors, social workers, teachers, and other professionals working with this group develop effective and supportive responses to psychological needs, they were able to multiply the services provided several fold. This approach to psychological consultation is largely used today and drives most other models in the field. Psychologists haven't cornered the market on helping; every other professional field of study has something to offer in either practice or theory.

Post–World War II work on trauma by psychologists in the United States shifted to the concept of and term "exhaustion." Armies found treatment for soldiers showing disabling behaviors was best accomplished in the field as soldiers removed from battle were often understandably hesitant to return. The term "exhaustion" allowed the treatment to be rest, not removal from the battlefield unless the behaviors were extreme. At the end of World War II, the term "physioneurosis" came into use, again linking the physical and behavioral aspects of common reactions to war trauma. The United States Air Force maintained the term "operational fatigue" well past the war years. Shortly after the war the Veteran's Administration produced a manual attempting to classify trauma reactions and other issues requiring care. This approach of technically defining specific categories was intended to standardize the variety of treatment approaches used in different parts of the country and world. The American Psychiatric Association produced the first edition of the Diagnostic and Statistical Manual of Mental Disorders (DSM) in 1952 which began the process of standardizing both diagnosis and treatment approaches. The manual included "gross stress reaction" as a diagnosis for both civilian and military populations but noted that the condition should be short-term and if problems continued past a few weeks another diagnosis should be made. The condition was considered a healthy reaction to a stressful event and was normal behavior. By the time the second edition of the DSM was published in 1968, "gross stress reaction" was dropped with no replacing diagnoses offered.

While almost all Americans were impacted by World War II, there was a surprising resilience to or a large suppression of psychological consequences of wartime experiences. There has been much debate as to why this occurred. Some point to the extended time it took to withdraw the troops, with many remaining in Europe for six or more months before being returned home. It is possible that this time allowed soldiers to process what they had experienced with others who shared the experience which allowed for a collective, more positive understanding. Another theory focuses on the nature of warfare during that time, which was largely with ranged weapons against a uniformed enemy. Some studies indicate that urban fighting with civilian casualties poses a greater psychological risk than other forms (Lawson, N., 2014). Psychosocial theorists often look to the levels of support given to war efforts and note the almost unified public response to the war effort during World War II compared to the civil disobedience that accompanied the Vietnam War.

The Vietnam War generated large numbers of soldiers seeking help for psychological issues related to wartime experiences and in 1980 the term "post-traumatic stress disorder (PTSD)" was added to the third edition of the DSM. The fourth edition text revision of the DSM published in 2000 included the requirement of a strong emotional reaction at the time of the traumatic event. This was later dropped largely in response to combat veterans often reporting they were unable to emotionally respond at the time of the event due to combat responsibilities. The fourth edition included people having a delayed reaction to traumatic events where problems connected to the event start up to six months after the event is over. This pattern is known as a delayed onset and often means more serious impairment. Conversely, if individuals show impaired responses immediately after the event, they are diagnosed with "acute stress disorder." Research has shown that roughly half of individuals exposed to a traumatic event will be able to recover within three months or "spontaneously remit" as the disorder goes away on its own. The other half tend to deal with aspects of the trauma for the rest of their lives. One of the few prognostic signs to indicate which path the disorder will go is if the person experiences de-personalization or de-realization at the time of the event. Denying the reality of the experience is an unsuccessful strategy.

The criteria used to define the term better known by the acronym PTSD have evolved slightly from the fourth edition to the DSM 5 but remains largely based on the same following core concepts (American Psychiatric Association, 2013).

Exposure to actual or threatened death, serious injury, or sexual violence. To meet this criteria the individual has to have directly witnessed in person traumatic events as they occur to others, or learned of an event occurring to people close to the individual, or have been exposed to repeated aversive details of traumatic events such as first responders in their line of work. The

DSM makes an exclusion for those exposed to trauma through media unless the exposure is work-related such as reviewing evidence in a criminal case.

Intrusion symptoms associated with the traumatic event(s). The criterion evaluates if the person has recurrent, involuntary and intrusive distressing memories, dreams, or flashbacks. It also examines if the person has intense or prolonged psychological distress or extreme psychological reactions to either internal or external cues related to the trauma. Internal cues are often thoughts or emotions that are linked to the trauma in some way for the individual, where external cues are environmental and can be sounds, smells, sights, tastes or textures.

Avoidance of things associated with the traumatic event. As cues and reminders of trauma are disturbing, the individual seeks to avoid contact with anything that reminds him or her of the event(s). The criterion used by the DSM examines efforts to avoid memories, thoughts, or feelings, or efforts to avoid external reminders such as people, places, conversations, activities, objects or situations. This avoidance often hinders progress as the person doesn't allow himself or herself opportunities to learn to deal with the unwanted memories.

Negative altercations in cognitions and mood associated with the traumatic event(s). This criterion can be met a number of different ways. One is assessed by looking for an inability to remember important aspects of the event(s) that cannot be explained by head injury, drugs, alcohol, or dissociative amnesia. Persistent and exaggerated negative beliefs or expectations about themselves, others or the world is another element of this criteria. People perceive themselves as broken, or bad, and perceive others in the same light. They also can show distorted beliefs about the cause or consequences of the event(s) that lead to self-blame that may not be assigned by others. This shame or guilt can lead to a persistent negative emotional state and lead to detachment or estrangement from others who could be sources of support. All of these can lead to a diminished interest and participation in significant activities such as work, school, or social events. Some individuals report an inability to feel positive emotions such as happiness or love.

Marked arousal and reactivity associated with the event(s). Individuals are often irritable or angry which leads to verbal or physical aggression toward people or objects. Some show reckless or self-destructive behavior. Another classic signature of this classification is the hypervigilance and/or exaggerated startle response. Awaking from dreams can lead to angry and possibly violent episodes. Sleep is often impaired with difficulty going to sleep and restless sleep, which may contribute to problems concentrating and being fully awake during the day. This arousal can be triggered in a wide variety of ways; the bright flash of a traffic camera, the sound of a ring tone, or the popping of a balloon.

These problems last at least a month and interfere significantly with the person's life. Clinicians have to ensure the problems are not explained by another disorder; however, depression as well as substance use and abuse is often associated with PTSD. People dealing with traumatic events impact the lives of those around them. Spouses are known to be at risk from vicarious trauma, horrified by the experiences related by their spouse while dealing with a partner in need of support (Galovski, T., and Lyons, J., 2004). Therapists are also at risk working with these issues and are encouraged to seek their own mental health supports to deal with the horrors of others.

Today many clinicians who work with veterans avoid the use of the terms of the DSM as they are deficiency-based definitions. There is stigma involved in the term PTSD and the term implies a dysfunctional reaction to a traumatic event, and implies a disability or injury. As this can make soldiers ineligible for duty, the term "consequences of war" has gained popularity as has the term "PTSS" for "Post-Traumatic Stress Symptoms." These terms normalize reactions to extreme events and assume healthy status in the people dealing with them. Reframing re-experiencing traumatic memories as conditioned fear in a rational actor rather than an illness expressed by an injured soldier can validate emotions and help people organize experiences into manageable, understandable narratives.

Narratives are extremely important for people both cognitively and culturally. Narrative therapy seeks to help people organize their thoughts and emotions into a storyline. Translating experiences to a story serves both to remember the traumatic events, and remove them from working memory. The avoidance of reminders of the traumatic events creates a bit of a paradox as we do not like unfinished tasks. Avoiding dealing with the painful memories and emotions demands a constant vigilance against those reminders, which takes effort and keeps the task on our "to-do" list. Creating a narrative that addresses all the disjointed emotions and facts of the events allows us to complete the task, to be done with it. It also allows us to share the story with others in a contained and rehearsed way minimizing cognitive and emotional effort, and helps others make sense of the experience.

WORKS CITED

Andreasen, N. 2010. "Posttraumatic Stress Disorder: A History and a Critique." *Annals of the New York Academy of Sciences* 1208, 67–71.

Corcq, M., and Crocq, L. 2002. "From Shell Shock and War Neurosis to Posttraumatic Stress Disorder: A History of Psychotramumatology." *Dialogues in Clinical Neuroscience* 2(1), 47–55.

Friedman, M. n.d. "U.S. Department of Veteran's Affairs PTSD History and Overview." http://www.ptsd.va.gov/professional/PTSD-overview/ptsd-overview.asp.

Galovski, T., and Lyons, J. 2004. "Psychological Sequelae of Combat Violence: A Review of the Impact of PTSD on the Veteran's Family and Possible Interventions." *Aggression and Violent Behavior* 9(5), 477–501.

Lawson, N. 2014. "Posttraumatic Stress Disorder in Combat Veterans." *Journal of the American Academy of Physician Assistants* 27(5), 18–22. doi: 10.1097/01.JAA.0000446228.62683.52.
American Psychiatric Association. Diagnostic and Statistical Manual 5th ed.
Watson, S., and, Skinner C., eds. 2004. *Encyclopedia of School Psychology.* Dordrecht: Kluwer Academic/Plenum.

Introduction

CHARLES R. HAMILTON
and ALLEN H. REDMON

Sueng-hoon Jeong and Jeremi Szaniawski's edited collection, *The Global Auteur* (2016), contends that discussions of the auteur are as relevant today as they ever have been. Backed by the work of "scholars who weave auteurs into a systematic web of critical ideas," some directors achieve the status of auteur and, in so doing, accumulate a vibrant political immanence (4). The critically created and widely recognized auteur begins to isolate "a mini-network ... of ... sociohistorical ideologies, cultural voices, and technological conditions" that engages political issues that re-informs each of those socially constructed realities (5). In this way, the auteur becomes "a causative force ... able to ... sustain critically meaningful or artistically transformative stances" on a range of political issues (6). While not one of the examples examined in *The Global Auteur*, Clint Eastwood certainly does support the book's premise. The esteemed director is one of the most recognized filmmakers in the history of cinema. Critics consistently reveal the ways in which his films enter political debate and on a range of social issues. David Sterritt (2014), for instance, contends that Eastwood's distinguished directorial career has been marked by "his political views as reflected and refracted in his films" (2). Richard T. McClelland and Brian B. Clayton (2014) identify a range of philosophical debates Eastwood enters, even noting the ways that Eastwood's revisions of popularly conceived genres tends to shift attention to the victimization and injustice implicit in so many popular forms of story telling. Leonard Engel (2007) continues this line of thought by showing the ways that Eastwood's films have long explored "issues of violence and vengeance, [and] the portrayal of gender" (14). Critics have shown the ways in which Eastwood has engaged a number of socially constructed and institutionally accepted realities.

Eastwood's exploration of violence deserves particular attention, and especially as it develops into one of the most sophisticated and sustained studies of PTSD and more general forms of trauma in popular film. Eastwood's connection to violence appears with his first roles as an actor. His long-standing portrayal of Rowdy Yates on the TV series *Rawhide* (1959–1965) places him in one type of mythic violence. His roles in Sergio Leone's Spaghetti Westerns *A Fistful of Dollars* (1964), *For a Few Dollars More* (1965), and *The Good, the Bad, and the Ugly* (1966) positions him in another. Together, Eastwood's work as actor, even early on, associated him with characters that rely on violence as a means to sustain social order and to survive. This same association continues in subsequent roles in *Hang 'Em High* (1968), *Coogan's Bluff* (1968), and *Two Mules for Sister Sara* (1970). By the time Eastwood arrives at his most definitive and controversial early role in *Dirty Harry* (1971), his persona as a man dependent on violence was already fully formed.

More interesting than the persona that develops around these roles, though, is the way Eastwood begins to take an active role in the shape of the story and especially the violence in the Dirty Harry films, beginning with the first film. In A&E's 2005 *Biography: Clint Eastwood*, Eastwood discusses his concerns with what he saw as the lack of justice for the victims of violent crime, and how he worked to bring that concern into the early "Harry" films. Eastwood explains, "There weren't too many movies at that time that were concerned about the victims of violent crime. They were more interested in the perpetrator.... *Dirty Harry* ... was about a guy that was obsessed about the victim, and that, to me, made it appealing." Scholars have connected Eastwood's concern for the victim to a more general interest in the victim during the early 1970s. Akiva Gottlieb (2009), for instance, suggests that Eastwood's concern sprang from court decisions like *Miranda v. Arizona* and *Escobedo v. Illinois*. The nation as a whole began to develop a concern for "a justice system that affords the criminal more rights than the victim" after these court cases.

Eastwood has shown over the last 40 years that his interest outlasts the more general concern felt in the early 1970s. Eastwood's films, and especially his directorial efforts, demonstrate a recurring interest in stories about victims caught in particular forms of trauma. Eastwood returns to stories that challenge accepted notions of social justice, that identify those victimized by efforts to create such justice, and that expose the extent to which society tolerates instances of violence that victimize individuals all deserve some attention if Eastwood's directorial career is going to assessed properly. The ways in which these interests appear in early films should be of particular interest, as these appearances counter an accepted assessment of Eastwood's story that has him making a turn toward something more socially responsible in

Unforgiven. The truth is, as the authors in this collection reveal, Eastwood's interest in the above issues begins to form into coherent statements in films as early as *The Beguiled* (1971) and Eastwood's directorial debut, *Play Misty for Me* (1971). Both films fashion stories that depend on violence, but the results of that violence are not as clean as they were in Leone's films. By adopting contemporary settings, the films began to explore at least tacitly sociological factors that did not exist in Leone's genre films. More to the point of this collection, they demonstrate Eastwood's willingness to recognize and identify with the plight of groups caught between the extremes of politics. Laurence Knapp (1996) discusses this point in his study of Eastwood's characters that he says cannot escape the violence they inflict or that is inflicted upon them: "None of his characters walk away from a violent encounter unscathed. Exposure to violence can compel an Eastwoodian character to go into spiritual, emotional, and psychological paralysis or experience a spiritual, emotional, and psychological rebirth…. On the whole, violence can be a source of redemption and/or damnation" (14). Knapp concludes that Eastwood's characters tended to suffer the latter. Their violence left them damned rather than redeemed. This decision to reveal the ways violence leaves even those who survive as "lifeless" proves to be a more important point than has been recognized. Eastwood refuses the sense of satisfaction the myth of redemptive violence, to use Walter Wink's (1992) term, should expect. In so doing, Eastwood shifts the attention from violence for violence's sake to the effects of violence, which can be portrayed as a shift toward an interest in victims and trauma.

The films Eastwood directs during the 1980s can be shown to develop this shift in profound ways. These films continue to show that no violent act occurs without comprehensive consequences, and that those consequences revisit and impact those who enact and witness it. This point is particularly important by the time Eastwood directs *White Hunter, Black Heart* (1990), the film adaptation of Peter Viertel's *roman à clef.* Violence remains in that film, but the violence has no semblance of spectacle; the violence is more revelatory. The fight scene during the film between Wilson (Eastwood) and a racist maître d' in a Belgian Congo restaurant especially marks the difference between violence as spectacle and violence as revelation. Wilson knows his younger and more athletic adversary will get the best of him, but he enters the fight and takes the beating he does anyway. The act reveals, if nothing else, that some other set of principles exists than those framing the contest. Luis Miguel Garcia Mainar (2002) recognizes this turn and the way in which Eastwood's *White Hunter* begins to mark a revision or at least clearer articulation of Eastwood's views on violence. Mainar refers to the film as a "revisionist, a self-conscious commentary on itself, disclosing an auteur who has a conscious concern with the meanings he represents" (29). Maynard,

Kearney, and Guimond (2011) agree, describing that new consciousness as an outright rejection of "the myth of redemptive violence" theologian Walter Wink (2007) claims "originated mainly in the popular mass media, [and] has furnished America with a vision of itself as a nation of 'vigilante superheroes'" (xii). Maynard, Kearney, and Guimond claim that Eastwood uses films like *Unforgiven* (1992), *Mystic River* (2003), and *Gran Torino* (2008) to critique the very notions of vigilante justice critics assumed earlier films meant to reinforce. The conclusion of *Gran Torino* actually re-performs Wilson's surrender to violence in the barroom to suggest one way to end the violence that can only traumatize those it touches. In keeping with Annalee Ward's (2011) review of *Gran Torino*, Walt's (Eastwood) final act "rejects a *Dirty Harry* vigilante solution" in order to propose another means to achieve social justice (387).

One might best account for this shift by placing Eastwood's films within the interests of contemporary trauma studies. Nancy K. Miller and Jason Tougaw (2002) begin the introduction of their book *Extremities* with the declaration that 21st-century citizens live in "the age of trauma" (1). The experience of trauma is no longer experienced on the fringes of society or during specific periods of history. Contemporary citizens live "in the wake of the atrocities brought by war and genocide, in the long shadow cast by their prolonged aftermath" (1). Aware of this shift, those who offer the word "trauma" as a descriptor of human experience have expanded its referential reach to describe more than the term originally described. No longer reserved for those relatively narrow populations of women experiencing hysteria or men struggling with shell shock, the concept of trauma now serves as something of a "portmanteau" able to lug within it a range of personal and social issues and injuries under its covering (2). Eric Wertheimer and Monica J. Casper (2016) suggest that the expanded referential scope has led to the formation of a new register of human experience, a modality wherein we might more properly assess our "understandings of ourselves, our actions, and the things that are done to us (and that we do to others)" (5). Wertheimer and Casper further contend that the "social and cultural classification[s]" of the past no longer work within this register (6). These classifications are overturned and replaced by new forms of categorization. So, too, are the stable identities that once existed within these systems. The register of trauma, then, brings new groups of people into focus. Wertheimer and Casper assert that those who once existed "at the edges," and raises new questions "about our relationships with one another, the 'natural' world ... and with the very terms of our existence" (6). New ways of being and new ways of knowing emerge.

The essays in this collection assume that many of the films directed by Clint Eastwood can unequivocally contribute to these new ways of being and knowing. They acknowledge the ways in which Eastwood has long directed films that adopt a broad understanding of trauma. His films have often focused on characters marginalized by trauma. They have consistently exposed the social conditions that tolerate or trigger that traumatization. More recently, his films have even begun to imagine a way through these traumas, both individually and collectively. This last development is particularly important if only because it challenges the ideas reiterated in criticisms against Eastwood's films. For some, Eastwood's directorial career is little more than an extension of the violent men he first played as an actor. These critics take the persona Eastwood played in the Spaghetti Westerns with Sergio Leone or in the Dirty Harry series with Don Siegel to be Clint Eastwood. They extend that persona into the directorial vision they comprise from his films. The characters in those films become extensions of Eastwood's own characters. Josey Wales, the hero of *The Outlaw Josey Wales* (1976), exists as a mere extension of Joe, the character Eastwood plays in *A Fistful of Dollars* (1964), or Monco, Eastwood's character in *For a Few Dollars More* (1965). Ben Shockley in *The Gauntlet* (1977) surfaces as a crude continuation of Harry Callahan. The essays in this collection propose a different starting point and significance for these characters and they do so by showing that Eastwood's directorial vision differs from the characters he plays in the early part of his acting career. To be a director can be, after all, something different than being an actor in another director's film.

The essays in this collection also move beyond the idea that Eastwood chooses the stories he does simply to profit in some market of trauma. The narrative arcs and stylistic choices in his films provide too much sensitivity and awareness of the victim and the trauma s/he suffers to see Eastwood's films as mere exploitation. A return to Miller and Tougaw can mark the difference: "Literary works ... recently and in great number have turned to narratives that record for public consumption the personal strain on the body and the mind produced by certain kinds of extreme suffering.... We've become accustomed in American culture to stories of pain, even [become] addicted to them; and as readers (or viewers), we follow, fascinated ... the vogue   of emotion and shocking events" (2). It would be easy to lump Eastwood's directorial efforts within this trend, but it would also be inaccurate. Eastwood's attention to Byron Sullivan's (Harvey Keitel) grief in *Vanessa in the Garden* (1985) intends to do more than simply watch a man suffer. His decision to make a film like *Absolute Power* (1997) delivers more than another representation of some shocking and brutal sexual encounter and murder. The film refuses, in fact, easy consumption. It, as so many other films discussed in this volume, pushes audiences to understand anew what events count as traumatic events, what it means to be traumatized, and how those in that state move through their trauma. In this way, trauma becomes more than a plot point for Eastwood: it becomes *the* point.

Admittedly, the majority of the essays included in this volume do tend to ground their understanding of trauma in formal understandings of post-traumatic stress disorder (PTSD), which does present some challenges. Some readers will arrive to these pages with a popularly conceived notion of PTSD in place. These readers may find some unexpected uses of this particular term or accounts of trauma more generally. This is to be expected, and, honestly, it is one of the rewards of this collection. PTSD is but one version of trauma and, even though the most widely recognized form of trauma, it is also likely the most misunderstood form. The misunderstandings surrounding PTSD have led clinicians like Bessel van der Kolk and Judith Herman to ask for more specific forms of trauma to be added to the Diagnostic and Statistical Manual of Mental Disorders (DSM). Doctors cannot treat patients properly when they are forced to use too general diagnoses. Theorists like Ruth Leys (2000) have a similar concern over a too generally conceived notion of trauma. Interpreters cannot generate the most meaningful accounts of trauma in the stories they read if they begin with an imprecise understanding of the term. In both situations, greater attention needs to be paid to the ways PTSD is socially constructed, "glued together," in the words of Allan Young (1995), "by the practices, technologies, and narratives with which it is diagnosed, studied, treated, and represented by various interests, institutions, and moral arguments that mobilized these efforts and resources" (5; quoted in Leys 6). Narrative and stylistic choices made by Eastwood in films like *Midnight in the Garden of Good and Evil* (1997) or *Mystic River* (2003) can help society expand its understanding of PTSD. Just as importantly, they can help those who watch them develop a way to recognize the societal forces that contribute to the admittedly temporary but telling social arrangements that support that understanding.

As a more precise notion of PTSD and trauma more generally is still under development, and as trauma has been one of the least examined aspects of Eastwood's films, the scholars in this volume have routinely had to develop their own language for discussing PTSD in Eastwood's films. Scholars have mentioned PTSD and trauma in Eastwood's films, but these comments have been sporadic and peripheral to other interests. For instance, to return to Sterritt again, one finds Eastwood describing *Unforgiven*'s (1992) central character, William Munny (Clint Eastwood), "in the language of PTSD": "[Munny's] constantly pursued by the visual image of what he's done in the past. Or images he's seen. Like for a guy who's been at war. Like for a guy who's seen the Lt. [William] Calley massacre [the My Lai massacre] in Vietnam" (169). The comment is interesting, as it provides a pivot toward a more thoughtful form of violence in *Unforgiven*, something critics and reviewers suspected in the film. The comment is little more than a passing interest for Sterritt, though, who does not use this framework as a means to interpret other aspects of the film. Likewise, John M. Gourlie (2012) offers the structure of *Flags of Our Fathers* (2006) as a means to show audiences "in terms of memory, nightmare, and PTSD flashback—[Iwo Jima] as it lives on in the minds of the Marines who experienced [that battle]" (249). Gourlie even recognizes the ways in which *Flags* represents PTSD in "varying degrees," but he uses this recognition as a way to explore Eastwood's notion of a hero rather than a means to understand trauma (252). Gourlie's contention reverses the path Roland Atkinson (2006) pursues. Atkinson lists *Flags* as one of the most meaningful representations of "stress disorders and postwar adjustment problems," deserving to be placed alongside the best films for representing stress disorder, films like *All Quiet on the Western Front* (1930), *The Best Years of Our Lives* (1946), *Coming Home* (1978), *The Deer Hunter (1978)*, *Mrs. Dalloway* (1997), *The Thin Red Line* (1998), and the relatively recent Danish film, *Brodre* (2004) (74). *Flags'* most meaningful contribution as Atkinson sees it is a willingness to show more than one form of PTSD. Ira Hayes (Adam Beach) immediately exhibits the symptoms associated with PTSD, making him a relatively easy mark for PTSD; Doc Bradley (Ryan Phillippe), on the other hand, only comes to experience the symptoms of PTSD when he faces "failing health [and] other losses" (web). Those who look beyond the traumatized in *Flags* and its companion film, *Letters from Iwo Jima* (2006), can find an even more comprehensive account of PTSD. The features of *Flags* and *Iwo Jima* suggest that Eastwood is just as interested in exploring those responsible for PTSD as he is showing another story of extreme suffering.

The authors in this volume reveal that Eastwood seems especially open to exploring the unacknowledged and dismissed aspects of PTSD if not trauma more generally, and, most recently, to imagining a way through this disorder. In this way, Eastwood's films refuse to be understood as an instance of what Janet Walker (2001) labels "trauma cinema": "To think in the terms of 'trauma cinema,' therefore, is to think of certain Vietnam or World War II–themed movies including Francis Ford Coppola's pioneering *Apocalypse Now* (1979), Oliver Stone's *Platoon* (1986) or the opening of Steven Spielberg's *Saving Private Ryan* (1998), in which fragmented editing and the use of extreme camera angles create in viewers a sense of disorientation and moral ambiguity designed to echo the experience of combat trauma" (215).

Eastwood prefers a simpler approach, somewhat surprisingly, even in his combat films. The battle scenes in *The Outlaw Josey Wales*, *Flags of Our Fathers*, *Letters from Iwo Jima*, or *American Sniper* (2014), for example, routinely avoid the extremes Walker mentions. They place the battle scenes they deliver within a clearly constructed linear plot that clarifies rather than obfuscates their meaning or purpose. Eastwood prefers the same approach in films that involve PTSD but do not deliver battle scenes, films like *Gran Torino* (2008), *Invictus* (2009), or, most recently, *Sully* (2016). Eastwood's willingness to simplify the visual and narrative elements of his films at moments that other directors might complicate their image provides space for spectators to contemplate the meaning the narratives and images Eastwood amasses as his films progress. His choice allows contemplation and understanding to replace rumination and exploitation.

Van der Kolk and McFarlane (1996) contend, "The news media play a pivotal role in the ways that societies deal with traumatized individuals" (42). They offer the United States' coverage of the Vietnam or Gulf War as examples. In the case of the former, citizens saw through the media "the mutilation and horror of war"; in the latter, they saw what might look more like "a computer game than like the intentional infliction of mass death" (42). In both cases, the opinions of a populace were negotiated through the images surrounding these conflicts. These images further make space for the victim to be seen or ignored. Van der Kolk and McFarlane offer that "most television images gloss over the immediate impact of trauma on its victims, and give no indication whatever of the long-term effects" (42). Set in this context, Eastwood's moving images stand as a kind of corrective. His stories and the films that project them embrace rather than avoid the impact of trauma. One finds this embrace in Eastwood's earliest directorial efforts, too. By noticing this early embrace of more sophisticated constructions of trauma, one can find an unmistakable interest in trauma throughout Eastwood's directorial career, an interest that matures into a profound examination of trauma and film's ability to participate in the overcoming of trauma.

The essays in this collection are arranged to demonstrate this maturation and examination. Sydney Sian Walmsley traces trauma as it extends across *The Outlaw Josey Wales* (1976). Walmsely shows that Eastwood utilizes a variety of constructs of trauma to establish not only the film's titular character, but also those he takes as his surrogate family. Walmsley takes particular interest in the fact that none of these traumas emerge from directly from the war. They are "civilian traumas," a point considered again in Alison S. Wallace's essay. For Walmsely, the fact that Josey's (Eastwood) trauma springs from his seeing his wife and child brutally murdered by an outlaw gang of ex-military marauders is particularly important. Wales first deals with his trauma by becoming an outlaw himself, and only begins to recover from his trauma once he surrounds himself with others who have been displaced by the consequences of war and violence. Wales is unable to remain with these others, which suggests he does not begin to recover. The attention to his life with trauma proves an important first instance of Eastwood's study in trauma and PTSD in places one might not expect to find it.

Andrew Grossman turns his attention to *The Gauntlet* (1997), which brings together two trauma victims, police officer Ben Shockley (Eastwood) and Gus Mally (Sondra Locke). Grossman attends to the self-preservative but anti-heroic actions these characters exhibit throughout their life-threatening experience. Their feat defies the odds as they make their way through a constant barrage of gunfire, in what many critics decried as Eastwood's worst film of his young career. Grossman offers that Eastwood's attention to the effects of trauma can be a reason to return to the film. Of particular interest is the way that these characters can only temporarily conquer their traumas and only to the extent that they serve as reliable therapists for each other. The temporality of their healing, and especially Shockley's, can be most clearly caught in that character's struggle to re-gain his masculinity, which he will lose again once the smoke clears. In this way, Grossman's analysis provides an early example of how Eastwood explores violence through a representation of masculinity. This same idea will appear again in Fernando Gabriel Pagnoni Berns and Canela Ailén Rodriguez Fontao's essay.

Alison S. Wallace explores three films—*Unforgiven* (1992), *Midnight in the Garden of Good and Evil* (1997), and *Changeling* (2008)—that look at PTSD following civilian trauma. The three-part arrangement is particularly rewarding as it shows Eastwood's study of trauma as it moves from more generic stories to more contemporary even if peculiar environs. The point throughout Wallace's essay is the efforts Eastwood makes to remind audiences that the characters in these films are ordinary people left to face extraordinary violence. Wallace uses this emphasis on the civilian as a way to trace Eastwood's outline of pre- and post-trauma conditions. Taken together, the two representations mark the ways in which trauma changes a person, and, just as importantly, how the effects of trauma differ for different people. Wallace's essay uncovers the extent to which Eastwood insists that PTSD is as much a civilian matter as it is a disorder to be experienced by military or law enforcement. This idea returns again in Charles R. Hamilton's essay, and certainly impacts the conclusions articulated in the final essay.

Mária I. Cipriani turns to the ways Eastwood contrasts and compares the causes, symptoms, and depictions of recovery responses in *In the Line of Fire* (1993) and *Absolute Power* (1997). The essay contrasts versions of trauma represented in films starring Eastwood as the lead actor and in those he later directs. The juxtaposition reveals the extent to which Eastwood further develops attitudes toward trauma only mentioned in the acting roles. As it relates to Cipriani's essay, Eastwood's *Absolute Power* finds a way to recovery that *In the Line of Fire* refuses to offer. In this way, Cipriani concludes that Eastwood finds a more nuanced, multifaceted exploration of trauma in the directed film than he found in his acting role. *Absolute Power* explores, as *The Outlaw Josey Wales* had before it and *Invictus* and *Sully* will after it, the importance of meaningful relationships to help heal from the symptoms of PTSD.

This same idea marks the next essay, albeit in a more politically charged way. Fernando Gabriel Pagnoni Berns and Canela Ailén Rodriguez Fontao explore the ways in which *Blood Work* (2002) completes a cycle of trauma that can only frustrate the hero in *Vanessa in the Garden* (1985). As Pagnoni Berns and Rodriguez Fontao reveal, Eastwood leaves *Vanessa's* hero in a state of melancholia, while the hero of *Blood Work* better represents first mourning and then recovery. The surprise is the extent to which both states arise from a sense of wounded masculinity as much as some overt form of trauma causing violence. Both films focus on male characters caught in the midst of trauma precisely because they must renegotiate their culturally constructed notion of masculinity. Rather than being the point of either film, this renegotiation clarifies Eastwood's interest in trauma and how PTSD in particular relates to notions of masculinity.

Charles R. Hamilton reframes the violence in *Mystic River* (2003) so that the film begins to trace the effects of trauma on an entire community rather than being merely a violent story. The key point for Hamilton is the ways in which Eastwood emphasizes the circularity of violence in this community, and how that circularity is at the root of their personal and communal traumas. Within this small, enclosed neighborhood, history is not forgotten, and the victims of past trauma are constantly reminded, through recurring exposure to those who endure, and to the exposure to ongoing violence, that violence has become a systemic way of life in this community. Eastwood encourages audiences to see this circularity by framing the film's contemporary moment of violence with the kidnapping and sexual molestation of one of the characters years earlier. The event is never forgotten, even though the boy is released and reunited with his family. By all accounts, Dave is "damaged goods." Eastwood's narrative framing allows audiences to see the ways in which the entire community is "damaged goods," at least as long as it resolves its crises through violence. In this way, Hamilton shows the rather comprehensive view of violence and PTSD *Mystic River* provides audiences.

Kathleen A. Brown and Brett Westbrook describe an equally all-encompassing look at PTSD in three war films—*Kelly's Heroes* (1970), *Flags of Our Fathers* and *Letters from Iwo Jima* (both 2006). All three films offer audiences examples of traumatized characters, but Brown and Westbrook claim that Eastwood's primary interest in these films is who is to blame for these instances of trauma. Brown and Westbrook accomplish this shift by tracing the ways in which Eastwood explores the extent to which military and civilian authorities put combatants at risk, which is the reason for the moral injuries these combatants suffer. In other words, rather than simply noting that moral injuries occur in war, Brown and Westbrook expose the efforts Eastwood makes to show that a world at war is doomed to suffer traumas. Military leadership will fail. Politicians will manipulate the stories. In these ways, PTSD becomes an institutional rather than personal issue as it is most often described.

James F. Scott continues the reassessment of military-related PTSD. Scott examines the trauma of Walt Kowalski (Eastwood), the Korean War vet who is the focal point of *Gran Torino* (2008), to bare Eastwood's insight that the battlefield offers but one instance of trauma. The alienation and estrangement from the society that sent them to war provides another. Scott claims that the latter is the real interest in *Gran Torino*, and audiences can realize this by approaching the film through the insights disclosed by Walt's renegotiation of neighborhood and his own masculinity. Following Scott, Walt's final sacrifice in the film reveals more about his evolution as a traumatized character than it does some commitment to violence. Scott views Walt's denial of himself as evidence the character can evolve even after years of separation from his own identity or the world around him that left him in that identity. In this way, the trauma in *Gran Torino* is less personal than it first appears.

Laurence Raw shows the extent to which one may not ever be able to read trauma as something personal. Raw reads *Invictus* (2009) as a study of how South Africa begins its journey to freedom through sports after the trauma of apartheid. Both the trauma and the recovery exist on a national level. Raw contends that Eastwood builds the basis of *Invictus* around then–President Nelson Mandela's plan to use the 1995 Rugby World Cup final match between South Africa and New Zealand's All Blacks as a way to overcome a long history of racial segregation. Mandela's bet was that the rugby team's international success could unite South Africa in ways that little else could. Raw shows how Eastwood highlights not the sources or trauma associated with PTSD, but how, through universal and personal support, an entire country takes major steps on the road to PTSD recovery.

Allen H. Redmon draws comparisons between Eastwood's *American Sniper* (2014) and *Sully* (2016). Redmon works to show how Eastwood makes narrative and stylistic choices in both films that actually perform a means to recover from trauma. In the case of *American Sniper*, Eastwood prefocuses the entire narrative through a flashback that becomes the one authoritative moment in the film's hero's life. Eastwood uses this moment throughout the film to limit what the audience can and cannot accept as the reality of that character. *Sully* performs a similar trick, albeit in a different manner. Rather than begin the film with a definitive moment, *Sully* sorts through a series of proposed accounts before finally settling into the authoritative one. In both cases, these two films can be taken not only as an example of recovery from trauma, but as a demonstration of how film can perform such recovery.

The book ends with a final essay by Hamilton and Redmon meant to uncover what the whole of this collection suggests, that Eastwood's artistic vision provides society a way to and through various forms of trauma. Eastwood is not so naïve to imagine a world where trauma does not exist or where violence can respond to that trauma. He does imagine a world where those who are being victimized are recognized, where those who are victimizing are aware of their actions, and where both can find a way through the trauma either position creates. Eastwood seems to accept van der Kolk and McFarlane's (1996) suggestion that a certainty in life, as certain as death and taxes, as the saying goes, is some exposure to "terrible events" (3). These authors say, "What distinguishes people who develop PTSD from people who are merely temporarily stressed is that ... the former ... start organizing their lives around trauma" (6). Eastwood's films refuse to leave audiences in the midst of terrible events. He does not pretend that violence will solve their problems. He does show them the way through their traumas, though, a way that begins with recognition, that continues with honest discussion, and that insists some recovery is possible for those who can find a community that can support them. We hope this book helps create such a community.

Works Cited

Absolute Power. 1997. Directed by Clint Eastwood, performances by Clint Eastwood, Gene Hackman, and Ed Harris, Castle Rock Entertainment.

All Quiet on the Western Front. 1930. Directed by Lewis Milestone, performances by Lew Ayres, Louis Wolheim, and John Wray, Universal Pictures.

American Sniper. 2014. Directed by Clint Eastwood, performances by Bradley Cooper, Sienna Miller, and Kyle Gallner, Warner Bros.

Atkinson, Roland. 2006. "Postcombat PTSD in the Movies." *Clinical Psychiatry News* 34:12: 74.

The Beguiled. 1971. Directed by Don Siegel, performances by Clint Eastwood, Geraldine Page, and Elizabeth Hartman, Malpaso Company.

The Best Years of Our Lives. 1946. Directed by William Wyler, performances by Fredric March, Dana Andrews, and Myrna Loy, Samuel Goldwyn Company.

Biography: Clint Eastwood. 2005. A&E Home Video.

Brodre. 2004. Directed by Susanne Bier, performances by Ulrich Thomsen, Nikolaj Lie Kaas, and Connie Nielsen, Two Brothers Ltd.

Casper, Monica J., and Eric Wertheimer. 2016. *Critical Trauma Studies: Understanding Violence, Conflict, and Memory in Everyday Life.* New York: New York University Press.

Coming Home. 1978. Directed by Hal Ashby, performances by Jane Fonda, Jon Voight, and Bruce Dern, Jerome Hellman Productions.

Coogan's Bluff. 1968. Directed by Don Siegel, performances by Clint Eastwood, Lee J. Cobb, and Susan Clark, Universal Pictures.

The Deer Hunter. 1978. Directed by Michael Cimino, performances by Robert De Niro, Christopher Walken, and John Cazale, EMI Films.

Dirty Harry. 1971. Directed by Don Siegel, performances by Clint Eastwood, Andrew Robinson, and Harry Guardino, Warner Bros.

Engel, Leonard. 2007. *Clint Eastwood, Actor, and Director: New Perspectives.* Salt Lake City: University of Utah Press.

A Fistful of Dollars. 1964. Directed by Sergio Leone, performances by Clint Eastwood, Gian Maria Volontè, and Jolly Film.

Flags of Our Fathers. 2006. Directed by Clint Eastwood, performances by Ryan Phillippe, Barry Pepper, and Joseph Cross, DreamWorks.

For a Few Dollars More. 1965. Directed by Sergio Leone, performances by Clint Eastwood, Lee Van Cleef, and Gian Maria Volonte. Italy.

The Gauntlet. 1977. Directed by Clint Eastwood, performances by Clint Eastwood, Sondra Locke, and Pat Hingle, Warner Bros.

The Good, the Bad, and the Ugly. 1966. Directed by Sergio Leone, performances by Clint Eastwood, Eli Wallach, and Lee Van Cleef, Produzioni Europee Associati.

Gottlieb, Akiva. 2009. "Last Man Standing: On Clint Eastwood." *The Nation*, 13 May, https://www.thenation.com/article/last-man-standing-clint-eastwood. Accessed 4 January 2017.

Gourlie, John M. 2012. "Eastwood's Flags of Our Fathers and Letters from Iwo Jima: The Silence of Heroes and the Voice of History." *New Essays on Clint Eastwood*, edited by Leonard Engel, 249–265.

Gran Torino. 2008. Directed by Clint Eastwood, performances by Clint Eastwood, Bee Vang, and Christopher Carley, Matten Productions.

Hang 'Em High. 1968. Directed by Ted Post, performances by Clint Eastwood, Inger Stevens, and Pat Hingle, Leonard Freeman Production.

Herman, Judith. 1992. *Trauma and Recovery*. New York: Basic Books.

Invictus. 2009. Directed by Clint Eastwood, performances by Morgan Freeman, Matt Damon, and Tony Kgoroge, Warner Bros.

Jeong, Sueng-hoon, and Jeremi Szaniawski. 2016. *The Global Auteur: The Politics of Authorship in 21st Century Cinema*. New York: Bloomsbury Academic.

Knapp, Laurence. 1996. *Directed by Clint Eastwood: Eighteen Films Analyzed*. Jefferson, NC: McFarland.

Letters from Iwo Jima. 2006. Directed by Clint Eastwood, performances by Ken Watanabe, Kazunari Niomiya, and Tsuyoshi Ihara, Dreamworks.

Leys, Ruth. 2000. *Trauma: A Genealogy*. Chicago: University of Chicago Press.

Mainar, Luis Miguel Garcia. 2002. "Genre, Auteur and Identity in Contemporary Hollywood Cinema: Clint Eastwood's *White Hunter, Black Heart*." *Miscelánea: A Journal of English and American Studies* 26: 21–37, http://www.miscelaneajournal.net/images/stories/articulos/vol26/Mainar.pdf. Accessed 4 January 2017.

Maynard, Katherine, Jarod Kearney, and James Guimond. 2010. *Revenge Versus Legality: Wild Justice from Balzac to Clint Eastwood and Abu Ghraib*. London: Cavendish.

McClelland, Richard T., and Brian B. Clayton. 2014. *The Philosophy of Clint Eastwood*. Lexington: University Press of Kentucky.

Midnight in the Garden of Good and Evil. 1997. Directed by Clint Eastwood, performances by John Cusack, Kevin Spacey, and Jack Thompson, Warner Bros.

Miller, Nancy K., and Jason Tougaw. 2002. *Extremities: Trauma, Testimony, and Community*. Urbana: University of Illinois Press.

Mrs. Dalloway. 1997. Directed by Marleen Gorris, performances by Vanessa Redgrave, Natascha McElhone, and Michael Kitchen, First Look International.

Mystic River. 2003. Directed by Clint Eastwood, performances by Sean Penn, Tim Robbins, and Kevin Bacon, Warner Bros.

The Outlaw Josey Wales. 1976. Directed by Clint Eastwood, performances by Clint Eastwood, Sondra Locke, and Chief Dan George, Warner Bros.

Play Misty for Me. 1971. Directed by Clint Eastwood, performances by Clint Eastwood, Jessica Walter, and Donna Mills, Universal Pictures.

Spielberg, Steven, and Joshua Brand, creators. 1985. *Vanessa in the Garden*. Universal Studios.

Sterritt, David. 2014. *The Cinema of Clint Eastwood: Chronicles of America*. New York: Columbia University Press.

Sully. 2016. Directed by Clint Eastwood, performances by Tom Hanks, Aaron Eckhart, and Laura Linney, Flashlight Films.

The Thin Red Line. 1998. Directed by Terrence Malick, performances by Nick Nolte, Jim Caviezel, and Sean Penn, Fox 2000 Pictures.

Two Mules for Sister Sara. 1970. Directed by Don Siegel, performances by Clint Eastwood, Shirley MacLaine, and Manolo Fábregas, Universal Pictures.

Unforgiven. 1992. Directed by Clint Eastwood, performances by Clint Eastwood, Gene Hackman, and Morgan Freeman, Warner Bros.

Walker, Janet. 2001. "Trauma Cinema: False Memories and True Experiences." *Screen* 42:2: 211–216.

Ward, Annalee. 2011. "Gran Torino and Moral Order." *Christian Scholar's Review* 40:4: 375–392.

Warren, Charles Marquis, creator. 1959. *Rawhide*. Columbia Broadcasting Systems.

Wertheimer, Eric and Monica J. Casper. 2016. "Within Trauma: An Introduction." *Critical Trauma Studies: Understanding Violence, Conflict, and Memory in Everyday Life*. New York: New York University Press, 1–16.

White Hunter, Black Heart. 1990. Directed by Clint Eastwood, performances by Clint Eastwood, Jeff Fahey, and Charlotte Cornwell, Malpaso Productions.

Wink, Walter. 1992. *Engaging the Powers: Discernment and Resistance in a World of Domination*. Minneapolis: Fortress Press.

_____. 2007. "Facing the Myth of Redemptive Violence." *Christian Peacemaker Teams*. 16 Nov. Web. 21 May 2012.

van der Kolk, Bessel A., and Alexander C. McFarlane. 1996. *Traumatic Stress: The Effects of Overwhelming Experience on Mind, Body, and Society*. New York: The Guilford Press.

Civilian PTSD
in The Outlaw Josey Wales[1]

SYDNEY SIAN WALMSLEY

Clint Eastwood's *The Outlaw Josey Wales* (1976) is based on Forrest Carter's book *Gone to Texas* (1973). Textually, the two seem similar until the end where the resolutions diverge vastly. *Gone to Texas* resolves the plot with the protagonist's return to society vis-à-vis a familial resolution. Carter elects to focus almost entirely on the tensions of war, the need for revenge, and the possibility for the hero's ability to reconcile with his society. The book avoids a number of larger societal issues, including the underlying racial issues of a Civil War period. Carter omits blacks from his story entirely and only alludes to tensions with Native American issues. Eastwood and screenwriters Philip Kaufman and Sonia Chernus change the focus of the novel by relocating the various tensions from Carter's story to the mind of the film's protagonist, Josey Wales (Clint Eastwood), and by setting those tensions within larger social issues. Rather than allow the social issues to dominate the film, these changes create a series of characters, who, like Wales, go through their own mental suffering. In this way, Eastwood and his screenwriters turn a story that might be best summarized as a political allegory intent on showing the external conflicts inherent in a given time of history into a story of civilian trauma. For all of the external action the film delivers, the very types of action that will mark the next 40 years of Clint Eastwood's directorial career, this early film prioritizes the internal struggles and shifts each of his characters makes throughout the film. In this way, the film develops an unexpected dimension that should interest those interested in Eastwood's representations of psychological trauma.

Though set in the American Civil War, Eastwood's Wales is apparently immune to the traditional polarity of North versus South when the film begins if not throughout it. The reserved man lives on a farm with his wife and son. He refuses to pick a side in the conflict that surrounds him. He imagines himself to be entirely removed from the war until he is forced to hear and then see his family massacred. He responds as almost anyone would, and as most anyone aware of post-traumatic stress disorder (PTSD) would expect one to respond, namely, by giving himself over to a dissociative state that begins in earnest during the burial scene. Wales' only thoughts are on retribution. He begins to teach himself marksmanship, even to the point of self-harm. Once proficient in his new craft, Wales joins the first group that can provide him an opportunity to avenge his family's murder. It is particularly significant that Wales' willingness to join a group is not a choice for a side in the larger war. The war is secondary to Wales. He is guided by his own desire for retribution and, perhaps, self-destruction. It is even more interesting that Eastwood frames these desires in the symptoms commonly associated with PTSD even before this disorder had entered the public discourse as it has today. Eastwood does not miss a chance to show Wales' anxiety, often through flashbacks that occur when he faces something that he associates with his original trauma. This stylistic choice suggests that audiences see Wales as a sufferer of both acute PTSD and chronic PTSD. Some discussion of each form of PTSD can clarify the extent to which Eastwood presents Wales through these two aspects, and moves Carter's original story into the mind of the titular character.

Steve Bressert (2016) explains that acute PTSD occurs when subjects "experienced, witnessed, or were confronted with (e.g., can include learning of) an event or events that involved actual or threatened death or serious injury, or a threat to the physical integrity of self or others." Eastwood begins his film in just such a scene. Wales hears and sees his family murdered early in the film, which would certainly fit Bressert's criteria for acute PTSD. Following Bressert further, those familiar with this diagnosis would expect Wales to disassociate from his initial experience in just the way he does. The potential surprise is the extent to which Eastwood's Wales also begins to exhibit the traits associated with chronic PTSD, which Bressert describes as something that exists when a subject faces "a prolonged period (months to years) of chronic victimization." This victimization may be, as it would appear to be for Wales, a replaying of the original trauma. Wales certainly does this. Wales associates his original trauma and otherwise unrelated events throughout the film. Each association leaves Wales seeing or hearing the slaughter of his family anew. Admittedly, Carter's Wales exhibits some of these same tendencies. By the end of the two stories, Carter's Wales and Eastwood's begin to distinguish themselves. To understand the significance of this difference, it is worth looking at some of the seemingly less impactful differences between the book and film.

One might be tempted to focus on the similarities rather than the differences between the book and film. The similarities are overwhelming. The only real difference is in the attention to detail. The book has Wales maintaining a certain distance from his family. His son is a mere toddler. His wife appears to be a passing whim to him. The reader learns about both of these characters and the family the three characters comprise from a distance. Most readers might even feel more connected to the scenery than to the people. Wales' farm looks and feels like a safe haven from the War Between the States. The prominence of the mountains certainly contributes to this feeling as they create a clear barrier between Wales and the rest of the world. They allow Wales to enjoy a sequestered and quiet life.

This feeling changes when Wales' homestead is attacked. Carter does not indicate that it is in danger until the attack has already happened. The surprise, it seems, is part of what Carter wants to create, and he extends this surprise even to Wales. The text says, "It was a long time before Josey Wales saw the smoke rising," and when he sees it, he responds with a clear panic. The description of Wales' response leaves the reader almost feeling Wales' frantic haste and numerous falls as he races back to the house. The reader has every reason to suspect some sense of ongoing trauma. Carter's description forces readers to see the most traumatic aspects of the story, too: "They had fallen near the door, and the blackened skeleton arms of the baby boy were clinging to his mother's neck. Numbly, mechanically, Josey had gotten two sacks from the barn and rolled up the charred figures in them" (Carter 8). Carter concludes this scene with a line that underscores the traumatic response of the scene: "it was the last time Josey Wales would cry" (8). The one thing that does not change before and after the attack is Wales' perceived emotional distance from his family.

Eastwood's filming of this scene is not so terribly different. The only real difference is the extent to which Eastwood emphasizes the family unit that exists before the attack. Wales' wife and son seem to extend from Eastwood's hero rather than merely cohabit with him. For example, Eastwood chooses to show the child plowing the fields with his father. The boy is old enough to play with his father and to learn to help in the fields, even if he is not old enough to do these things on his own. Eastwood shows this by having Wales direct and push the plow as he carries his son between his arms. These sequences certainly suggest some emotional connection between the two characters. The same thing happens with the wife. She remains nameless in the film, but she plays a more maternal role, calling her husband and son to dinner, for instance. Wales would seem to enjoy a relationship with his family rather than just have them as some social obligation, which is the implication in the novel. Eastwood continues to establish this point by having Wales playfully chase his son toward the house before returning to his work in the field to take advantage of the sunlight. Wales only stops his work when he sees the smoke and hears the screams coming from his home. The husband and father reaches the house just in time to see Red-leg's forces leaving his house in cinders. He tries to rush into the house, but Red-leg slashes Wales across the face, which prevents him from entering his own house and saving his family. Eventually, he arrives to see his son's charred body still clinging to his mother. The image is as gruesome as it can be and it certainly justifies almost any reaction that follows.

Through these choices Eastwood fashions the audience's understanding of Wales as something of a dedicated family man. The burial scene continues this impression. Wales buries his son and wife in burlap sacks, just as he does in the book, but, in the film, Wales gives the two slain members of his family more individual attention. He buries the two bodies in separate graves and marks their gravesites with individualized makeshift crosses. Wales cries and then clearly hardens himself. He leaves this scene with the same disassociation with which Carter marked Wales in his novel. Eastwood and Kaufman indicate the mental shift that Wales makes in this moment and after it, in part, by following the burial with a scene that places Wales sitting in front of the rubble. He retrieves his six-shooter from the ashes and resolves to become a better sharpshooter. The scene replaces Carter's confused Bible verse in this moment that talks about turning from revenge with a scene that marks Wales' turn to vengeance.

One could construe that Eastwood has reduced his Wales to the basest response one could have to trauma, and that might be so. Eastwood admits the appeal of simple characters that think in simple terms in an interview: "a man who thinks on a very simple level and has very simple moral values, appeals to a great many people" (Gentry). Wales would appear to be one of Eastwood's simple men, but there is good reason to push to see him through the entanglements of trauma rather than the simplicities of basic human response. Wales is filled with a clear sense of right and wrong, but that sense of right and wrong is deeply personal to him. The Red-legs are wrong and they must pay for the wrong they have done. Wales is right to pursue them. There is an unmistakable kind of escapist appeal to such a response, and Eastwood admits as much in the above interview. Other scholars writing about Eastwood's *Josey Wales* have picked up on this line of thought. Karli Lukas (2004), for instance, focuses on the escapist mentality in the film: "[F]rom the film's very first shot[,] Eastwood is rendered immortal ('good') by the streaks of summer haze that set the scene aglow by the sun's heavenly backlight. He's seen ploughing a field with his son, notably referred to as 'Little Josey'—a smaller, equally humble, noble, and physically similar, version of Eastwood himself. They are so similar they don't even need to exchange words to communicate. The wordless relationship between Josey and Little Josey heightens the definite impression that the person [the audience has] been introduced to is *not* the vengeful/'bad' Eastwood-as-Star, but the wholesome Eastwood. Clearly, the *mise en scène* is telling [the audience] that what [they] are seeing is a storybook version not just of the pastoral West, but also of the legendary Eastwood." But is Eastwood's film a storybook version of the world? Or might it be an honest depiction of civilian trauma?

Eastwood creates a sharp contrast between the storybook setting found at the beginning of the film and just about every aspect after the burial scene. The storybook version of the world exists only before the opening credits of the film. Any sense of innocence and hope is destroyed for Wales when the Red-legs attack his homestead. Eastwood might permit Wales to exist as something of a Christ figure, but he is a crucified Christ, and this point is literally placed on the screen. Eastwood has Wales fall on the cross he makes for the burial plot. The image creates an interesting contest between Christ as a lion or a lamb. For a moment, Wales lies on the cross as a sacrificial lamb, but he rises as a retributive lion. The horrors enacted upon him justify this shift, but the rest of Eastwood's film urges the audience to refuse to entirely accept this shift. No matter how understandable Wales' response is, Eastwood does all he can to reveal it to be the response of a traumatized rather than rational person. Eastwood's Wales desires "right," but it is a right that exists because of Red-leg's wrong. Without Red-leg's act, this right would not exist. Wales never gets to drop his role as family man, nor does he get to leave his original family, or the trauma he experienced. The flashbacks to the earlier scenes function as psychological echoes that jar the audience into remembering the catalyst for everything they watch. Josey is what he is because of that initial event. He never moves beyond it. The premonitions and flashbacks he experiences appear as evidence of ongoing PTSD.

The end of the film and the book likewise differ, reflecting Wales' mentality and typology of PTSD presented. In the book Wales is offered a personal salvation and an opportunity to forget his trauma by living with Laura Lee. She becomes not only a surrogate representative of the sexually viable and socially acceptable woman, but she becomes a replacement for Wales' immolated wife. Laura Lee even bears Wales a new son. Eastwood refuses to bless Wales in this way. Wales is permitted only one sexual encounter with Laura Lee (Sondra Locke), but that sexual encounter sets within Wales a series of flashbacks, night terrors, and an intense desire to flee. Eastwood suggests the illusory nature of this encounter by shooting it in a soft light that is not like any other scene in the film. The choice suggests that any promise found in Laura Lee is but an illusion for Wales. The temptation of a new wife and child will only trigger the original trauma. Rather than establish a new home, this one intimate event reminds Wales of the home he has lost. Rather than be given a new son, he is forced to hear his son's dying screams. Wales has no real choice but to disavow the potential of moving onward with his life. In this way, Eastwood uses this scene to reveal the full extent of Wales' trauma, by showing that he suffers from both acute and chronic PTSD, and so much so that he will not be able to realize the resolution Carter finds for his main character.

Eastwood denies Wales the opportunity to move forward even though his admitted source text permits its hero this break. Eastwood marks his Wales with a type of survivor guilt that prevents him from moving forward. He becomes a near static character stuck in a perpetual state of fear, guilt, and trauma. Any progression Eastwood allows Wales to make with his potential surrogate family—Grandma Sarah (Paula Trueman), Laura Lee, Lone Watie (Chief Dan George), and Little Moonlight (Geraldine Keams), is immediately redacted by the terms of his trauma. This disallowance fits the expectations of PTSD as they are presently understood. Eastwood's Wales would be a textbook example for PTSD. What makes the film so compelling so many years later is the fact that Eastwood was ahead of his time in his understanding of PTSD. Not only does he present Wales in a contemporary notion of PTSD, but he allows this trauma to exist in a range of civilians rather than veterans, which is also a more contemporary allowance. In truth, there are many who might still consider PTSD, either acute or chronic, as a soldier's issue. Civilians, it would seem, do not suffer this disorder. Eastwood's film corrects this idea. Wales' trauma stems from what happened to him on his farm rather than on the battlefield. He exhibits the symptoms associated with soldiers, but the cause of those symptoms does not emerge in that predicted place. Eastwood allows audiences to see this difference by assigning Wales a different reason to even by on the battlefield. He is not fighting for an ideal. He simply wants revenge on those who killed his family. A number of moments support this idea, too. The first moment appears during Wales' attempt to save "his" battalion from an entire camp of Union soldiers with just two six shooters. His action has little to do with the goals of his unit or some bond with his men. Wales simply refuses to surrender to Red-leg. Wales is motivated by a trauma that does not answer to the prescribed responses of war. Wales refuses to release his hatred for those who burned his wife and son. He cannot accept Fletcher's (John Vernon), or anyone else's, request for surrender. His battle is one to satiate his hatred from those who burned his wife and son.

It is worth noting that Eastwood places his audience in the same detached place so all see what his main character occupies. The montage Eastwood creates to show the carnage Wales creates shows the results of the Outlaw's violence, but without any of the personal involvement. Viewers see carnage from the battles, but they do so from an emotional distance. No viewer sees any particular amount of gore, any particular battle, or any particular person with whom to identify. War becomes a generalizable act that is unable to set clear priorities. One could attribute this distance to the feelings some in Eastwood's original audience might have had toward the Vietnam War, but Eastwood seems more interested in exposing Wales' detachments than commenting on that conflict. By causing the audience to feel some of the dissonance Wales feels, Eastwood allows the viewer to connect and feel for Wales without every fully feeling his trauma. Eastwood is content to present his trauma. The audience gets to play the part of voyeur to this highly private response. Eastwood inserts his motifs that indicate more specific things: haste editing to simulate numbness from trauma, drums for heated desire for retribution, and blue for numbness from a dissociative state within the first 15 minutes. But the focus is always to see how every event brings Wales mentally back to his original trauma.

The audience is forced to see aspects of the original scene over and over again. The story returns to associations of Wales' son working with him and then being called back to the house by his mother. But the voyeur never sees her. The viewer only hears her screams and sees Wales race back to the house. Wales becomes the only point of identification, and this point continues throughout the film. This is what audiences see during what could have been an emotional moment for Jamie (Sam Bottoms). Wales attempts to save Jamie, but only, or at least primarily, as a response to his inability to save his own son. Upon seeing Jamie's wound, he can only respond with "You dumb kid." Jamie replies, "I gotta tell you somthin'. I'm scared to die, Josey." The comment shifts Wales' motives at least in the scene itself. He leaves the battle to help Jamie escape. The shift is a sharp contrast to the wild actions that occurred while Wales was at the center of the battle firing the Gatling gun. During that scene, Jamie had yelled out, "You can't get 'em all, Josey," to which Wales responds, "That's a fact." The implication is that he will get as many of them as he can for as long as he can. In the final moments, though, Wales' priority shifts. He suddenly wants to save Jamie. For at least this moment, Wales' desire to protect the living supplants his need for revenge. Audiences could mark this shift as a kind of cure, but Eastwood forces Wales to suffer in the midst of this choice as he does before it. He is no better. He just opens himself for a moment to protecting those he can for as long as he can, at least from some emotional distance.

This distance is two-fold. In one way this distance exists because of the emotional distance Wales feels in any given scene. His actions seem more practical than emotional. In a deeper sense, though, Eastwood leaves Wales at the distance he does so that the director can show his audience the extent to which Wales is never in the moment on screen. He is in his original trauma. The scene with Jamie is no different. It serves as a trigger, or what Shea et al. (2004) call an adrenal intensifier: "During acute stress, adaptive biochemical responses occur, which include increased adrenocortical secretion of hormones, primarily cortisol" (2–3). These intensifiers "help an individual to cope with the stressor, but may be detrimental when stressful experiences are extreme or chronic, particularly when these experiences occur early in life" (3). In other words, these intensifiers create a dissociation that alters the way Wales' brain would work. Following Kim et al. (2016), those who experience PTSD may block normal brain function. Cortisol levels hedge adrenaline and hypothalamus reactions, but trauma and stressors or triggers inhibit cortisol production and amplify adrenaline production. As this brain chemistry becomes the new normative, the brain responds with a naturally lower cortisol level and higher adrenaline level, making the person sit in a constant state of heightened awareness, readiness, and edginess. The more stressors or triggers presented the more traumatized the person becomes. In this way, acute and chronic PTSD, cooperate to prolong one's traumatic experience. Had Wales only suffered the, albeit tragic loss of his family, his PTSD may have remained acute and only lasted for a fraction of the time it did. His decision to seek revenge and face the triggers that brought him back to that original trauma, things like his loss of Jamie, kept his trauma alive. Given enough time, given today's clinical insights, one would expect a permanent alteration of his brain.

Jamie is persistent in his upbeat attitude and flight from the fight and toward the Indian territory. It is through this denial that Jamie's PTSD begins to emerge as clearly as Wales.' The difference is that Jamie's PTSD is more one dimensionally acute. It is, after all, born in war and some resolution to the war would seemingly offer some consolation to his condition. The war is his trigger. The whole world is a trigger for Wales. As the two cross the Missouri River, Jamie laughs at every avoidance of every pursuant—particularly when Wales gives Red-leg and Fletcher a "Missouri Boat Ride" by shooting loose the ropes that pull the ferry. Jamie's smile encourages Wales, but as Jamie begins to disintegrate, he becomes frailer. Jamie feigns hallucinations about his father and pretends to have gold, forcing the gunmen's attention to him. The diversion allows Jamie to shoot one of his assailants and to maintain the attention of the other while Wales shoots him with his waist-gun. This endears Jamie to Wales more, though no emotion is shown. Wales could have been killed, but he ignores this risk to save Jamie. The relationship between Jamie and Wales seems like it will benefit both characters, but Jamie dies, which begins a new cycle of loss for Wales, albeit one that reminds the outlaw of the earlier loss of his son as much as anything else. The first inkling of a surrogate family is denied him, and he suffers that loss and his original loss again.

After this failed reconciliation, Eastwood's *Josey Wales* begins to accumulate traumas. Laura Lee, for example, goes through her own trauma when her family is attacked by the Comancheros. The group kills the men, beats the grandmother, and tears her clothes in preparation to rape her. Interestingly, Laura Lee moves through her trauma more successfully than Wales. She latches on to Josey despite his outlaw status, and begins to heal under his protection. She even becomes sexually attracted to him, if not simply infatuated. One could argue that she uses this infatuation to sublimate her own trauma. The real impact of her story, though, is the way she adds another instance of civilian trauma to the larger story of *The Outlaw Josey Wales*. Laura Lee becomes a way to establish the extent to which mere existence in the world of the film is enough to experience real trauma. The presence of Little Moonlight reiterates this point. Little Moonlight is also nearly raped in one scene, this after being raped off screen in an earlier moment. These two moments are important because they explain her numbness during the attempted rape scene Eastwood places on the screen. She, like Wales, has dis-associated herself from her experiences. Her inability to feel or act leaves her vulnerable to the same chronic PTSD that Wales experiences. Eastwood's film seems intent on gathering a group of people who arrive at the same traumatized place even if their way to that place differs.

Laura Lee and Grandma Sarah are also nearly raped and killed. The Comancheros decision to spare Laura Lee and Grandma Sarah actually begins a second round of trauma rather than end one. The Comancheros only keep these two women alive because the group believes they may have potential trade value as sex slaves for Ten Bears' (Will Sampson) tribe. The thought disgusts Grandma Sarah and she revolts against the idea even if she keeps to the socially prescribed strictures of the feminine role in her era. She largely avoids any personal assault, at least when compared to the rest of her family, but she is traumatized nonetheless. Not only does the thought of her potential role as a sex slave exist as a kind of trauma, but so, too, does the fact that, like Wales, she has witnessed the death of so many in her family. No matter how together she seems, Eastwood ensures that Grandma Sarah is framed by the horrors she has witnessed on screen, and those that precede the beginning of this particular story. References to her life during the War of 1812, the Civil War, the death of her son, and potentially other unknown traumatic experiences all create a clear picture of a repeatedly traumatized woman. Grandma Sarah denies being traumatized, but her denials are made before the attack; she spews vitriol about Ohio and Wales before the outlaw saves her (and more so after as well). It is only after Wales proves his value in a more familial fashion, namely through his willingness to re-build the homestead and to protect the women from Ten Bears, that Grandma Sarah begins to accept him. Eastwood's version of the story even has Grandma Sarah embrace Wales' way of life before the film ends, a point seen most clearly when she begins to fire through the cross-cuts in the windows as Red-leg approaches. This last act is less about revenge and more about defending the home she has reestablished, which means that it is not exactly like Wales' trauma.

Eastwood places the shift in Grandma Sarah somewhat above the stages of trauma available to Wales. Wales aligns more with Lone Watie and Ten Bears than Grandma Sarah. Eastwood actually places Wales, Lone Watie, and Ten Bears in three different stages of Chronic Traumatic Stress. Lone Watie had lost his family on the Trail of Tears, a horrific show of social force by the United States in the early 19th century where thousands died from starvation and disease. One might expect that enough time had passed for Lone Watie to recover from this tragedy before the film opens, but his own words suggest something else: "The White Man's been sneaking up on us for years ... they took away our land and they sent us here. I had a fine woman and two sons, but they all died on The Trail of Tears. And now the White Man is sneaking up on me again." Not only does Lone Watie reveal in these words his sense of loss, but he also shows the loss of his people. In this way, Lone Watie carries a double burden that can cause psychological damage irreparable by any standard or time. His hiding away in a secluded cabin indicates a chronic diagnosis, per de-socialization.

It would be easy to look for ways that Eastwood's film hints that Lone Watie's burden of guilt has eased, but none of these hints stabilize themselves enough to warrant leaving the film thinking this is the case. Lone Watie still holds steadfast to his hatred of the American institution when the film ends, an institution that he feels killed and alienated his family. But the story makes plain that while his hatred of this institution remains, he has begun to limit those he associates with that institution. This is best captured in his revised attitude toward Wales. Lone Watie initially is obviously wary of Wales. Things change when Wales announces his own hatred for The Union. Lone Watie begins to recognize a kindred spirit in this man he would have initially thought an enemy. Even without any mention of Wales' past, Lone Watie realizes that this man has suffered tremendous loss and at the hands of Lone Watie's stated enemy. Having come to this awareness, Lone Watie chooses to ride with Wales, at least initially. The two might have rode together indefinitely had they agreed on their destination. Lone Watie wants to ride to Mexico so that he might never see a Union solider again. Wales is still hungry for retribution. This difference identifies a gap between these two men that places them in different stages of Chronic Traumatic Stress.

Ten Bears, the chief of the Native American tribe near the new home Wales' temporary family finds, occupies another place in the three stages of trauma. Ten Bears' trauma may not have even reached its peak when the film ends. Ten Bears' people remain in a precarious place, one that will only grow worse, and Ten Bears seems to know this. He remains willing to fight even though he knows that neither he nor his people will succeed. Ten Bears laments what he has lost and what he might lose later, but he will not stop the fight. Ten Bears' land is in the new United States' territories, where "Manifest Destiny" has pushed U.S. citizens to find their futures on tribal land. Ten Bears tells Wales at their detente that he will be forced no farther west nor allow any more land to be stolen from him.

Wales identifies with Ten Bears in his defiance, as he had with Lone Watie earlier. All three men share the same enemy. Because of this, they also share a common bond. In the case of Ten Bears and Wales, this kinship prompts them to draw their knives, cut their flesh, and lock hands to promise fellowship upon the soldier's arrival. Wales' commitment further prompts Ten Bears to reveal his own awareness of the never-ending nature of this fight, but Ten Bears says he will not relent. Ten Bears indicates the same mindset that audiences have seen guide Wales toward retribution throughout the film. No matter how commendable this fighting spirit is, it is plain by the end of Eastwood's film that every fight forces these men to relive their earlier traumas, and add to them. To continue the fight, Ten Bears must simultaneously remember and forget; the memories force him onward but they cannot yet free him from the cycle he is in like they had Lone Watie.

Wales is destined to suffer the same fate. While the formation of a surrogate family creates some hope for him, Eastwood makes it clear that this new family presents an awkward obligation rather than opportunity for Wales. He does not want a new family. He cannot watch it be decimated, as that would ask him to relive the initial modality of trauma in a literal way. This realization forces Wales to tear himself from this new family structure just as it begins to cement. Wales' flashbacks and survivor's guilt will not let him "replace" his deceased wife and son. Every encounter must be with them. At first with the rejuvenation of the farmhouse, there appears to be hope with the forceful Grandma Sarah, quiet young Laura Lee, old Native American "Cheif," Chief's new "non-civilized" Moonlight, and randomized townspeople who initially latch to the enclave because they have alcohol but learn to adore them equally. Eastwood's camera angles change. Filters and light shift to create a lighter hue. The background tempo alters, as the wildlife settings attempt to return to pastoral overtones found in Wales' first homestead. There is even a brook and heads of steer, which promise ongoing sustenance. The outside of town almost seems the picturesque escape Grandma Sarah had read about in her son's letters. But even a few flirtatious moments with Laura Lee and an eventual sexual encounter with her is not enough to silence the screams Wales hears in his head. Wales must reject the one act that could create new life. Wales is not permitted the escape Lone Watie finds, nor is he given a fight to continue like Ten Bears. Wales simply sits in the midst of his trauma, which forces him to leave.

This is Wales' only form of semi-catharsis, and Eastwood's reflective form of paralleling the instigating moment of trauma and the moment of retribution: two moments of blood with Red-leg's sword. Thus far, the audience has seen only two moments of Wales being injured. The first occurs when Red-leg slashes Wales' face. The second occurs in this final battle scene. Red-leg delivers both injuries. The final attack sequence begins with Wales attempting to leave his surrogate family as a means to protect them if not to sequester himself with his trauma and survivor's guilt. Those hunting Wales ride up as he attempts to make his escape. His potential family arms themselves as they would if Wales was with them. They engage Red-leg's men and battle back war-hardened hunters. Wales rides off, attempting to draw the gunfire away, but the battle sequence ends with a solitary standoff between him and Red-leg.

This stand-off allows Eastwood to play a trauma soundtrack rising quietly and steadily over a cut to shots of Wales' burning home, an otherwise silent and abandoned pueblo, as a bleeding Wales approaches a similarly wounded Red-leg with an unknown number of bullets. Eastwood raises the tension in this scene by giving Wales multiple six-shooters and enough room to march upon the man who killed his family, slowly having Wales pull the hammer and trigger for each chamber until they both discover all chambers are empty in all four guns. During this approach Wales seems to buffer against the terror of the trauma, allowing his adrenaline to be used as fuel instead of creating a hyper-sensitivity. When Red-leg realizes all chambers are empty, though, he draws his blade, the same one that cut Wales' face before the opening credits. Wales turns the weapon on Red-leg, though. He forces the blade through its owner. The soundtrack is filled with drums of war, which causes the audience to feel the sense of relief, of catharsis Wales has extended in this moment. The sense of relief dissipates even more quickly than it emerges. Eastwood refuses to allow the parallel structure tolerated here to celebrate any sense of justice. Wales' act does not offer the expected consolation, a point the final lines of the film make clear. Fletcher essentially asks Wales if his war is over or not. Wales admits that the war is over, but he does not accept that he survived it: "I guess we all died a little in that damn war." With this line, Wales admits a psychological death. His family's death, and especially his son's death, which not only haunts him most of all, but denies him his sense of continuance, leaves Wales unable to reform or form new connections. His sense of humanity is lost.

This end to the film drastically diverges from Carter's original, where Wales re-captures the traditional, socially acceptable ending. The film presents "the lone hero who must stand apart from the civilization that he protects," whereas at the end of the book Wales is no longer depicted as the lone hero (McGee). Rather, his trauma seems healed by Laura Lee and their new child. A chronic trauma is reduced to an acute one. Wales may never forget his earlier loss, but he experiences some sense of rebirth with his new family, if only through the birth of a new son. Eastwood refuses Carter's original design. The book's happy ending seems almost implausible when compared to the film's ride-away ending when analyzing the hell-bent, death wish, revenge-seeking mentality imbued by both incarnations of Wales and his differing versions of PTSD. But with that, chronic and acute PTSD can offer differing resolutions—or none at all. Carter's Wales is allotted a resolution; Eastwood's is not.

Wales is lost to himself, but Fletcher seems to have reconciled some of his trauma with this scene. He has been traumatized by the war and the slaughter of his men, but also is seemingly torn by hunting Wales. He views the hunt as a necessity to reunite the country, thus utilizing himself as a mechanism of unification, though it invalidates part of what he feels to be true—that Wales is a good person truly wronged. In this exchange with Wales at the close of the film, the viewer sees Fletcher's catharsis. Though he may suffer from the war, he can accept that it has ended and will move forward. The fall-out must consequentially be moved beyond—Fletcher must allow himself that luxury and he asks Wales to likewise gift himself that release. Wales cannot. The acts of war enacted upon a civilian prove more devastating than those experienced in war. The civilian-turned-outlaw is left a devastated creature. He is broken, terrified of forming new bonds for fear of losing them, but also due to survivor's guilt, he is unable to form any new bonds. Wales cannot remain in his society any more than the tragedy enacted upon him can be a part of a "civilized" society.

NOTE

1. For my grandfather, an intimidating federal agent, who happened to run into Eastwood in a bar out west one day in the seventies, and in doing so met one of the few men that he was actually afraid to approach.

WORKS CITED

Bressert, Steve. 2016. "PTSD: National Center for PTSD." *Complex PTSD—PTSD: National Center for PTSD*, National Center for PTSD, 23 Feb., www.ptsd.va.gov/professional/PTSD-overview/complex-ptsd.asp.
Carter, Forrest. 2010. *The Outlaw Josey Wales.* New York: Leisure Books.
"Clint Eastwood." n.d. *IMDb*, IMDb.com, www.imdb.com/name/nm0000142/?ref_=fn_al_nm_1#director.
Gentry, Ric, and Clint Eastwood. 1989. "Clint Eastwood: An Interview." *Film Quarterly* 42:3, 12–23. doi:10.1525/fq.1989.42.3.04a00030.
Gone to Texas. 1986. Directed by Peter Levin, performances by Sam Elliot, Claudia Christian, and Devon Ericson, CBS.
Kim, Lae U., et al. 2016. "Onset, Timing, and Exposure Therapy of Stress Disorders: Mechanistic Insight from a Mathematical Model of Oscillating Neuroendocrine Dynamics." *Biophysical Journal* 110:3. doi:10.1016/j.bpj.2015.11.2545.
Lerner, Gerda. 1969. "The Lady and the Mill Girl: Changes in the Status of Women in the Age of Jackson." *The Intersection of Work and Family Life.* doi:10.1515/9783110968835.32.
Lukas, Karli. 2014. "On Hell's Hero Coming to Breakfast: Clint Eastwood and The Outlaw Josey Wales." *Senses of Cinema*, Cinematheque Annotations on Film, 4 June, sensesofcinema.com/2004/cteq/outlaw_josey_wales/.

McGee, Scott. 2016. "The Outlaw Josey Wales." *Turner Classic Movies*, Turner Classic Movies, www.tcm.com/this-month/article/79824%7C0/The-Outlaw-Josey-Wales.html.

The Outlaw of Josey Wales. 1976. Directed by Clint Eastwood, performances by Clint Eastwood, Sondra Locke, and Chief Dan George, Warner Bros.

Shea, Alison et al. 2005. "Child Maltreatment and HPA Axis Dysregulation: Relationship to Major Depressive Disorder and Post Traumatic Stress Disorder in Females." *Psychoneuroendocrinology* 30:2, 162–178. doi:10.1016/j.psyneuen.2004.07.001.

"Trivia." *IMDb*, IMDb.com, www.imdb.com/title/tt0075029/trivia.

"What Is a Trigger? | Psych Central." 2016. *Psych Central*, University of Alberta, 17 July, psychcentral.com/lib/what-is-a-trigger/.

Welcome to the Ranks of the Disenchanted
Feminism and Pacifist Spectacle
in The Gauntlet

ANDREW GROSSMAN

The advertising poster for *The Gauntlet* (1977), designed by Frank Frazetta, imagines star-auteur Clint Eastwood standing stolidly before a bullet-riddled bus, his torn shirt exposing idealized musculature, his long-haired co-star and real-life love interest Sondra Locke clinging helplessly to his side, her pants tattered and her mouth agape in terror. Behind them, a white government office building emblematic of untold power and corruption rises from a bureaucratic wasteland. Then as now, the mythic image of rugged individualism brutishly conquering both womanhood and modernity could hardly be taken as anything but farce. Indeed, *The Gauntlet*, an action film that treats its violence farcically, marked the first time Eastwood subjected his impossibly virile star image to self-critique. In many ways, *The Gauntlet* is a concession to the post–Nixon, post–Vietnam years of national reflection, when unchecked machismo and tough-on-crime posturing were becoming less morally viable (and less marketable). Rather than perpetuating the rigid, retrograde masculinity of Dirty Harry, Eastwood plays a gullible hero whose consciousness is raised by an enlightened woman—a disillusioned rape victim, no less, who knows that the hero's violent mythologies of law and order are a sham. As such, *The Gauntlet* not only interjects a feminist consciousness into the generic action film, but it also sidesteps Hollywood's post–Vietnam tendency to reclaim the unexamined masculinity of the damaged hero, who finds redemption not through introspection but only through "cathartic" acts of violence (as in *First Blood* [1982] or Eastwood's own *Firefox* [1981]).

Following *The Gauntlet*, Eastwood the auteur would continue to adjust

Eastwood the star to inevitably liberalizing times, as his aging persona coyly confronts its own masculine mythology. In the self-effacing *Bronco Billy* (1980), Eastwood remakes the Western gunfighter into the charlatan of a modern-day sideshow. Once lauded by critics for its realistic, "ethical" scrutiny of film violence, *Unforgiven* (1992) attempts to demystify the outlaw hero, who now acknowledges his own immorality and discards pretensions of nobility. In the largely comic *Heartbreak Ridge* (1986) and the earnest *Million Dollar Baby* (2004), a grizzled Eastwood confronts his persona's own inveterate sexism, wooing an embittered ex-wife in the former and coming to grudgingly respect a female warrior in the latter. Though one of Eastwood's minor efforts, *Blood Work* (2002) grapples tellingly with the encroaching mortality of Eastwood's star persona. Then about '72, Eastwood allows the camera to linger over his formerly invulnerable torso, still fit but now betraying signs of wrinkling decay and chronic disease, as his protagonist struggles to adjust to a heart transplant. Nevertheless, most of Eastwood's self-examinations fall short of fully unmasking the masculine superhero, even when his auteurism attempts to lay bare the heroic conscience. If we accept the final *mea culpa* of *Gran Torino* (2008), whose climax sees the hidebound Eastwood sacrificing himself in a Christ-like pose before a hail of bullets, his auteurist attempts at deconstruction only wind up redeeming (or at least renovating) his overarching mythic stature. His most recent film, *Sully* (2016), goes as far as to suggest this mythic stature may not be a myth at all. In *Sully*, Eastwood dispenses with any sense of irony to deliver a biographical story of a "genuine" individualist, who safely landed an imperiled airliner against all odds. Here, a pilot successfully averts the trauma of yet another horrific airline crash in New York City.

The Gauntlet proves the one exception to this self-sustaining pattern, even if it remains among Eastwood's least admired films. Perhaps because of (and not despite) its oft-cited implausibility, the film can do what Eastwood's Dirty Harry films—and Hollywood genre films overall—do not or cannot do: emasculate and consequentially rehumanize the stoic hero while making a self-reliant, cunning heroine his full partner and equal. If Sondra Locke's spoiled, overly civilized heiress in *Bronco Billy* needs to be liberated from social convention and warmed by Eastwood's charms, her shrewd prostitute in *The Gauntlet* is far more feministic, unshackling Eastwood's dimwitted cop from his own conventionality and blind allegiance to authority. In *The Gauntlet*, Locke's heroine effectively enacts the rare emancipatory role imagined by second-wave feminists such as Joan Mellen. Locke does not merely oppose, belittle, or castrate a sexist patriarch, as the heroines in *The Big Doll House* (1971), *Coffy* (1973), or as so many other exploitation film heroines of the seventies do; instead, she transforms him as he undergoes an irreversible crisis of conscience.

Although the previous year's Dirty Harry outing *The Enforcer* (1976) acknowledged the second-wave feminism then ascendant in American film and television, that film ultimately (and unsurprisingly) defanged any possible feminist consciousness by having Harry's asexual female partner (Tyne Daly) become a martyr, climactically taking bullets meant for Harry. Indeed, the next sequel, *Sudden Impact* (1983), proves the uselessness of *The Enforcer*'s attempted feminism, for now Dirty Harry is even more of an unreformed, one-dimensional "dinosaur" than he was in the seventies. Daly's great sacrifice in the prior film, now long forgotten, has hardly enlightened or humanized Harry, who, according to Hollywood's notion of eternal return, regresses to square one with each sequel. By the end of *The Gauntlet*, however, we feel that a rare transformation has occurred in the consciousness of Eastwood's hero. Locke's feminist heroine draws upon her traumatic experience of rape to disrupt the genre's conservative functions and evolve a male hero, taking him beyond action-genre rules that typically embalm masculine identity. A conventional sequel to *The Gauntlet* would have corrupted the film's singular, pacifistic ending, for the logic of sequels demands a stasis and redundancy that this film's final scenes of consciousness-raising deny. It would have risked doing what the four sequels to *Dirty Harry* (1971) do when they ignore that film's cynical ending by pretending that Harry never experienced the disillusionment that marks the close of Siegel's original film.

Suggesting that disillusioned yet empowering knowledge can follow from the experience of rape, *The Gauntlet* doesn't propose a realistic portrayal of post-traumatic consciousness, nor does it pretend to. Indeed, Locke's character is very much a wisecracking Hollywood fantasy; apart from several contrived, actorly monologues, she evinces none of the spiraling depression, knee-jerk reticence, generalized paranoia, or torturous self-blaming that are characteristic of· rape trauma or post-traumatic stress in general. The film's individualized description of traumatic experience, furthermore, has little in common with much recent psychoanalytic and post-psychoanalytic academic literature on trauma, which emphasizes the instabilities and uncertainties of historicized experience (Cathy Caruth). Yet if there always exists an unbridgeable chasm between lived experience and reflective representation, not even the most nuanced, problematized, or carefully researched theory of trauma can communicate what trauma and its aftereffects actually feel like. Every sensory or linguistic attempt to represent the injustice of trauma will be unsatisfactory for certain victims of personal, cultural, or political abuse, even if victims tend to share similar constellations of post-traumatic symptoms. Nevertheless, one might question *The Gauntlet*'s assertion (or fantasy) that traumatic disillusionment can empower so easily. Raymond Douglas (2016), for instance, begins his autobiographical *On Being Raped* unequivocally, declaring that "[r]ape is knowledge, but not the sort that does you, or anybody else, good. When I was raped, I learned things about myself and the world I live in that it would have been far better never to know. And for most of my adult life, the knowledge has been killing me" (4).

Though Douglas' simple, poignant confession strikes an undeniably truthful chord, it should be clear that the "knowledge" conveyed by Sondra Locke's character acts symbolically, as part of feminism's sociological project of consciousness-raising. Locke's rape survivor embodies a sanguine, quasi–Nietzschean understanding of pain, in which bitter enlightenment scabs over the scars earned in "life's school of war." In reality, the aftermath of trauma is often as irrational and incommunicable as its cause, but for the film's feminism to work, Locke's rape—and the critique of patriarchy her experience ultimately conveys—must be intelligible and didactic, prompting Eastwood's character to discover humane desires lost beneath acculturated layers of cop-hero stoicism. Although the film's second-wave feminism, which seeks to decouple masculinity from violence, might seem démodé, it still remains a relevant approach when dealing with the cultural legacy of ingrained masculine archetypes. The rarity of The Gauntlet's action-movie feminism contrasts starkly with the reactionary trends of the ensuing Reagan years, when the post-traumatic, post–Vietnam hero—the socially marginal "Rambo" archetype—sought retrenchment rather than reform, finding succor only by returning to the traumatic battlefield and enacting fallaciously cathartic slaughters. Though war-weary and world-weary, Hollywood's post–Vietnam, PTSD antihero (also present in Blue Thunder [1983], Missing in Action [1984], and countless others) must be "re-illusioned" through exercises of violence greater than those that originally traumatized him. In Beyond the Pleasure Principle, Freud famously theorized that compulsive repetition is the commonest mark of trauma survivors; to the degree that the stoic, militaristic heroes of 1980s and '90s Hollywood repeatedly regress to violence even after they profess fashionable disillusionment, one might say that the action genre itself betrays the greatest neurosis.

When The Gauntlet was first released, overall critical reaction was resoundingly negative, an opinion that persists in many surveys of Eastwood's work. John H. Foote's (2009) rather unenlightening Clint Eastwood: Evolution of a Filmmaker, for example, characterizes The Gauntlet as "one of the worst films of his career, both as an actor and as a director" (35). Even Sondra Locke (1997) barely mentions the film in her autobiography, merely remarking that the film afforded her a "character … different from how I was then 'typed'" (145). Upon its release, critics were generally skeptical of (or simply dismissed) Eastwood's mildly feministic assertion that Sondra Locke enjoys "a terrific role, not just token window dressing like in so many action films," and that her "part is equal to the male part, if not even more so" (Kapsis and Coblentz 2012, 37). Eastwood even suggested—much to the incredulity of biographer

Richard Schickel—that the film harkens back to Hollywood classics such as Frank Capra's *It Happened One Night* (1934) and John Huston's *The African Queen* (1951), films whose strong-willed, empowered heroines could outwit the likes of Clark Gable and Humphrey Bogart, respectively. If *The Gauntlet's* screenplay obviously lacks the wit of Hollywood's golden age, the film nevertheless portrays the gendered consciousness-raising of a patriarchal hero, much as a freewheeling Katharine Hepburn sexually emancipates an anal-retentive Cary Grant in Howard Hawks' *Bringing Up Baby* (1938). (Hawks' comedy even shares with *The Gauntlet* analogous phallic symbolisms: Locke continually appropriates Eastwood's revolver, just as Hepburn seizes Grant's anthropological "dinosaur bone.") If we further accept that *The Gauntlet*, with its hyperbolic, over-the-top gunplay, is essentially a comedy of violence, the analogy to screwball comedy acquires another level of significance. Though Eastwood's one-time mentor Don Siegel found the film's bullet-riddled finale laughably unrealistic, I'd suggest that it is *anti*-realistic, an intentional self-parody in which violence signifies not gun-wielding rugged individualism but corruption, conformity, and unthinking excess.

Before examining *The Gauntlet* more closely, it's worth revisiting the conservative ethos of the Dirty Harry series, which *The Gauntlet* interrupts chronologically and disrupts thematically. By positing Harry as a misunderstood, anti-authoritarian loner, Don Siegel's original *Dirty Harry* (1971) attempted to hedge its blatant conservatism from the outset, especially as mainstream critics (like Pauline Kael) would predictably characterize Harry as a "fascist" and the film's morality as a simplistic reaction to late '60s leftism and permissiveness. Indeed, the film's noirish cityscape, teeming with sexual deviance unimagined by Siegel's tame *Madigan* (1968), willfully indulged conservative paranoia of the day, particularly fears of a court system that enabled both delinquency and victimhood. The film's prearranged logic has Harry, emasculated by the progressive dictates of post–Miranda civil law, resort to a final act of heroic, terrific vigilantism. In the film's coda, tinged with one of Lalo Schifrin's most plaintive melodies, Harry casts his police badge into the water after executing Andy Robinson's sociopathic murderer. The soundtrack's melancholy suggests that taciturn Harry is not disgusted with his vigilantism, but with a burgeoning liberalism that forces his hand and, according to the logic of the film, renders the very notion of justice an unenforceable ideal.

All of this, of course, is a cynical calculation, and the whole Dirty Harry series contemptuously frames its San Francisco setting as a swamp of sexual perversion, not a harbor for civil liberties. Admittedly, Harry's conservatism places him in a clear minority circa 1971. This was an era awash in the countercultural posturing of *Born Losers* (1967) and *Easy Rider* (1969), the Black Panther Marxism of the emergent Blaxploitation film, and the revisionism of

Soldier Blue (1970) and *Little Big Man* (1970), Westerns that reframed Frederick Turner's frontiersmen as imperialist marauders. Gradually, the Dirty Harry series acknowledged the contentious politics of the 1970s and attempted to invest its hero with political nuance. The first sequel, *Magnum Force* (1973), shrewdly scripted by conservative John Milius, goes to great lengths to defend Harry against his critics and distinguish him from genuine vigilantes, while simultaneously demonizing the "decadence" San Francisco allegedly signifies. Here, Harry is pitted against genuine fascists, vigilante police who execute not lone psychos but organized criminals—mostly in the sex and drug trade—who operate beyond the law's reach. Conveniently, the vigilantes are also coded as homosexual ("everybody thought they're all queer for each other," says Harry's African American partner in *Magnum Force*), implying, in obviously dated fashion, a simplistic equation between legal transgression and sexual deviance.

Villainous homosexual caricatures reappear in *The Enforcer*, in which queer anarchists (not queer cops) kidnap a milquetoast mayor and (for some reason) seek to undermine city government. The film's overriding homophobia is established crudely in the credit sequence, in which the primary villain, his lips quivering wildly, derives a clearly homosexual pleasure from stabbing an armed security guard from behind with a long blade. If this prologue is too subtle, the finale clarifies the film's sexual politics, as impenetrable Harry grunts, "You fucking fruit," before dispatching the same villain with a rocket launcher. Ostensibly, the plot of *The Enforcer* is meant to expose Harry to a mid–seventies feminist consciousness, as he comes to begrudgingly accept the unassuming competence of Tyne Daly's technocratic policewoman, whom he initially believes is the undeserving recipient of the mayor's affirmative action policies. *The Enforcer*'s superficial, arguably specious feminism is ultimately positioned against its homophobia, as the film's climax neutralizes both potential threats to normative masculinity, whether through Harry's escalating phallic symbols (.44 Magnum to rocket launcher) or through narrative mechanics that, as mentioned above, demand Daly's martyrdom and negation. Furthermore, by presenting Daly's policewoman as a stereotypically asexual (i.e., unattractive and short-haired) feminist, the film caricatures the already reductive gender roles then contested in Hollywood genre films. Whereas a Pam Grier or Angie Dickinson could be simultaneously lethal and (hetero-) sexualized, Daly's asexuality renders her neither fully female nor fully male—she is an ersatz man who performatively attempts to equal Harry in occupational competence, but who, as a biologically "inadequate" woman, must ultimately fail and be sacrificed to and for the status quo. In *The Gauntlet*, Sondra Locke ultimately does what Tyne Daly is not allowed to do— become a true feminist heroine, an agent who is not merely the action hero's equal partner but who challenges and remakes his masculinity through her own post-traumatic, disillusioned knowledge.

It is no accident that the relative "liberalism" of *The Gauntlet* immediately follows *The Enforcer*'s spurious feminism and pillaging homosexuals. Directed by Eastwood himself, *The Gauntlet* seems a seriocomic apology for the sincere sexism of the Dirty Harry series, for here legal-patriarchal authority—rather than deviance—is presented as destructive, even sociopathic. Not only is Eastwood here demoted from godlike Dirty Harry to an inept cop with a .38 far less phallic than Harry's trademark .44, but Eastwood's hero kills *no one* throughout the film, allowing Locke to enact the film's most heroic moments. The police, meanwhile, are presented as equally fascistic and ludicrous, a sort of malevolent Keystone Kops ever willing to unleash volleys of bullets to impotent effect. If the Dirty Harry films raised the phallic firearm to the level of over-compensatory status symbol, gunplay in *The Gauntlet* is a farcical charade, extreme in quantity but utterly lacking in efficacy.

In *The Gauntlet*'s opening, Eastwood's "Ben Shockley" enters disheveled and unshaven after a late-night poker game (an unimaginable backstory for Dirty Harry, who presumably has no friends). From the outset, we are meant to see that Shockley is a drunken stooge dependent on his Jack Daniels and illusions of duty, even if Eastwood's limited gamut of emotions tends to embalm all of his characters within the same mold of masculine authority. Nevertheless, he is not a rugged individualist, but like many would-be heroes, a conformist loser with delusions of individualism. When the villainous police chief Blakelock (William Prince) assigns Shockley the task of escorting to court a mysterious witness, Locke's prostitute "Gus Mally," we assume he'll be as unflappably capable as Dirty Harry always is. The film's joke, however, is that Shockley never realizes Blakelock sets him up as a stooge—and in fact wants Mally dead—until the more cunning Mally enlightens him. The righteousness and preternatural knowledge of life and death that superhuman Dirty Harry take for granted must here be *taught* to an inadequate hero, who, under the tutelage of a knowing woman with an ironically masculine name, graduates from savage ignorance to civilization.

From the outset, however, Shockley is clueless, and his first response when escorting Locke from jail is to slap her when she feigns illness. "Terrific … my life's on the line and they send me an on-the-ropes bum," she deadpans, immediately challenging the masculine posturing typical of Eastwood characters. Shockley then slaps, drags, cuffs, and eventually binds and gags the uncooperative Mally—a scene played for tasteless laughs, much like Eastwood's rape of an uptight townswoman in the beginning of *High Plains Drifter* (1973). Despite (or perhaps because of) Shockley's brutish sexism, it's obvious to her that he is a loser who desperately needs the "civilizing" of a woman, especially one with far broader emotional experience than he. (Beneath Dirty Harry's façade there is presumably either nothing to civilize, or, at most, a general state of incurable discontent). "I just do what I'm told," he tells Mally as he drags her away in handcuffs. "Well, so does an imbecile," she replies, beginning the gendered verbal sparring that Eastwood had described as his urban reimagining of *The African Queen*.

Shockley's impotence is emphasized at every turn, especially when plot mechanics force Eastwood to surrender his revolver to Mally as he dodges (rather than assaults) sundry villains. The first action scene has a conspicuous black sedan pull up behind the pair on the first leg of their journey; while Shockley drives, Mally dispatches the villains with three easy shots. Quite remarkably (or unrealistically) for someone unaccustomed to killing, she quickly assumes the role of savior, yet reluctantly and without embracing the fetish of the firearm. The film's second action scene goes much further, not simply transferring lethal power from one gender to another but rendering farcical the firearm's phallocentric and authoritarian significations. Trapped in a ramshackle house and framed by the evil Blakelock, Shockley and Mally must withstand a hail of bullets from dozens of trigger-happy policemen who—out of corruption or rank ignorance—are all too willing to follow Blakelock's orders and become unwitting pawns in his criminal enterprise. While the police open fire for minutes on end and the besieged Shockley clumsily ducks behind a toilet for cover, Eastwood films his hero from the most unflattering angles possible. The police, meanwhile, are depicted as remorseless automatons, ridiculous in their banal brutality and, for all their militant swagger, as impotent and ineffectual as Shockley is when he, too, only "follows orders." As the professionalization of violence appears mindless and decidedly unheroic, we cannot read the scene as anything but a blatant critique of the "fascistic" Dirty Harry ethos of shooting first and asking questions later.

The film's critique of violent masculinity, both oppressive and repressive, comes to the fore when Shockley and Mally, now on the run from corrupt police and Blakelock's goons, kidnap a redneck cop. A misogynous, leering caricature, he suggests to Shockley that he turn Locke in to the police after "getting a taste of her." When the cop asks Mally, "I always wanted to know what it's like being a whore," she, college-educated and acid-tongued, responds with a lengthy monologue: "Actually, I always thought it was like being a cop, being on the take, being corrupt … the only difference between you and me is that at the end of the day I take a long, hot bath and I'm clean as the day I was born. But a cop, especially a flunky like you, when the sheriff whistles, you squat, and what he does to you rots your brain. No amount of water on earth could get you clean again. I know you don't like women like me, we're a bit aggressive, we frighten you … but that's only because you've got filth in your brain, and the only way to ever clean it out is to put a bullet through it. Does your wife know you masturbate?"

With that last line, Mally hits a nerve, and the cop suddenly becomes hysterical, madly driving into oncoming traffic (the impromptu equivalent of "putting a bullet" through his brain) before Shockley restrains him. One gets the impression that Mally, who speaks with a deep-seated calm, has rehearsed this monologue to herself many times in private, or perhaps she repeats wisely what she once confronted tremulously on a psychiatric couch. Regardless, her monologue is clearly the (male) screenwriters' way of conveying post-traumatic knowledge. Though a prostitute and a victim of rape—at the hands of Blakelock, we later learn—the self-possessed Mally is not beholden to systems or institutions prone to corruption, violence, or chauvinism. The redneck, sexist cop, on the other hand, is the one suddenly consumed by suicidal hysteria, so ideologically fragile are his masculine uniform and rigidly gendered worldview. In a sense, Mally subjects the cop to a kind of "reverse talk therapy," casually giving voice to the misogyny and impotence that she (correctly) believes underwrite his false consciousness. By no accident, her monologue links corruption to themes of filth and purification. Mally can purify and recreate herself not because she is a woman per se, but because she exists beyond patriarchally corrupted social institutions, even as she, a prostitute, knowingly exploits the male sexual insecurities those institutions produce. The redneck cop, on the other hand, must "squat" before his boss, a word that suggests not only bootlicking humiliation but the ideological excrement in which his machismo is mired.

Though a bit crude and clearly self-conscious, Mally's monologue cuts to the heart of Hollywood's neurotically narrow constructions of masculinity. Here masculinity is revealed as decidedly unheroic, not an exertion of rugged free will but the symptom of a corrupt bureaucracy, or, more broadly, of a corrupt Hollywood genre. The only pleasure that remains for the subservient, excrementally squatting cop is the hope of surreptitious masturbation—analogous to the disempowered male audiences of genre films, who may have little political power in reality, and thus presumably depend on the standard action film's masturbatory fantasy of wanton gunplay and passive women. One could only wonder how Mally's monologue might vex the cinematic thugs impersonated by Stallone, Schwarzenegger, or any other action hero whose effeminizing orgasm is typically an off-screen secret. In any case, the monologue emphasizes not only the impotence but also the social masochism expected of uniformed (and uninformed) functionaries, and thus avoids an overly reductive equation between misogynous *ressentiment* and sexual impotence alone.

That the film directs Mally's tirade against the redneck cop is admittedly a ruse, for Shockley, though amused by Mally's monologue, is also the implicit target of her critique. Regardless, as Mally continues to school Shockley in the hypocritical, repressive ways of the masculine world, femininity becomes associated with candor and virility with deception, a deliberate inversion of traditional gender tropes. Before he can be fully enlightened, however, their "gendered banter"—now a far cry from *The African Queen*—escalates into sexually loaded invective. "For two cents and a stick of gum, I'd kick the shit out of you," he tells her, infuriated by the fact that she (and not he) has figured out that the corrupt Blakelock has set them up. "Whatever gets you off, Butch," she replies, knowing the macho hero's alleged sexual prowess arises from neurotic insecurity, not self-assurance. Shockley's weak retort attempts to mock her vocation: "And after we were through, where would I leave the $20?" Her sarcastic reply, however, turns the tables on the unthinkingness of Shockley's own profession: "I don't want your money, Shockley, I love you for your *mind*." After they strike each other, the scene comes to its point: "Why do you think you drew this assignment?" she asks. "Because I get the job done!" he, still clueless, replies. "They don't want the job done.... They picked you because you're a drunken bum.... Welcome to the ranks of the disenchanted."

It's not enough to disenchant the hero, however—he must also be shown a viable, affirming goal for which he can strive. A sober, peaceful, and loving partnership with Mally becomes this goal when the pair, still pursued by Blakelock's henchmen, take shelter in a cave. Framed by the cave's "maternal" opening, Mally finally allows herself to be vulnerable, disclosing that Blakelock in fact had raped her, placing his gun inside her vagina as he masturbated himself (as with the redneck cop, public authority is equated with private impotence). When she describes Blakelock's gravelly voice as a sound that might emanate from a tomb, the maternal symbolism of the daylit, open-mouthed cave acquires generative, life-affirming qualities that oppose Blakelock's barrenness and morbidity. Letting down her guard, Mally's agonized affect in the scene contrasts with the confidence of her earlier, "therapeutic" monologue delivered to the redneck cop. However, her didactic intent remains unchanged; now speaking deliberately and confessionally, she obliges Shockley to adopt the uncharacteristic role of empathetic therapist.

After this moment of transformative empathy, however, the film stumbles into an arguably misguided sequence in which Shockley—still partly clueless—reasserts his manhood by threatening a gang of drug-taking, vagrant bikers. Presumably, the film deems it necessary to show true outlawry in the form of a biker gang, lest Shockley, now also a fugitive along with Mally, come across as *too* rebellious. As he menaces the gang with absurd tough-guy dialogue ("Alright you mother-jumpers, this is a bust!"), he seems to parody the legacy of Dirty Harry–ism, especially as the Roger Corman-esque bikers seem more appropriate for the late '60s or early '70s (as opposed to 1977). More problematically, this sequence restages Mally's trauma when the bikers kidnap her and threaten gang rape; replaying her private violation as a public act in which Shockley can now intervene is an obvious concession to Eastwood's star persona, who must act heroically at some point. On the other hand, the bikers also crucify Eastwood (a male equivalent of rape) before can he rescue Mally from the gang, and through this rare moment of humiliation, he more fully understands the bodily violations Mally has long taken for granted.

Seeking refuge in a sleazy motel, Shockley and Mally reveal to each other their private histories—a scene unthinkable for Dirty Harry, whose mythic invulnerability and eternal return can claim no linear parentage or biological explanation. Shockley explains that as a teenager he was in a gang and would have "shot every cop on sight" if possible. He then philosophizes: "As you get a little older, you realize what cops are all about…. They're just doing a job, enforcing the law, raising families." This, certainly, is a bizarre claim for either Shockley or the film to make, for until now the film has condemned the rank-and-file's blind submission to corrupt authority and has hinged upon Shockley's realization that he requires emancipation from (not further allegiance to) illegitimate systems of power. That cops "raise families" and "enforce the law" are typical apologias for the systemic abuses of an increasingly militarized police force, and corrupt officials often justify their actions through an impersonal sense of dutifulness. The film's paradoxical (if also conventional) desire to both critique and apologize for a flawed legal system is temporarily put aside, however, when Mally suddenly calls her mother to tell her that she's met the man she'll marry. In another reversal of gendered and generic expectations, she nonchalantly proposes to him by allowing him to overhear this teasing phone conversation, just as she'd deliberately made him privy to monologues typically suited to the psychiatric couch. Though Shockley is now truly "shocked" to discover that a fallen woman will facilitate his emancipation, his nonplussed reaction soon melts away. Through his facial expression, relaxed for the first time, we see that he imagines a nonviolent, empathetic, and unalienated life previously unknown to the urban action hero.

Throughout the narrative, Eastwood the director has been at pains to render Eastwood the hero passive, victimized, and thus a prime candidate for consciousness-raising. It was Mally who kills their early pursuers, and a lengthy helicopter chase concludes not when Shockley takes the offensive, but when their airborne pursuers accidentally fly into electrical wires (conveniently absolving Shockley of any moral responsibility for their deaths). This passivity, in effect, becomes outright pacifism in the film's finale, in which Shockley dares Blakelock's entire police force to fire upon them as they (slowly) roll into town in an armored bus, intent on (finally) delivering Mally to the courthouse. As the bus absorbs the police's over-the-top barrage without either Mally or Shockley returning a shot, the film enacts a uniquely "defensive" action climax. Indeed, I cannot think of another Hollywood action film in which the hero's position is *entirely* defensive—after all, even Billy Jack thrashed bigots. (Elsewhere, only Buddhistic martial arts films like *A Touch of Zen* (1971) or *Eight Diagram Pole Fighter* (1983) envision martial heroism as a defensive ethic.) When, three decades later, actor-director Eastwood submits himself to a hail of bullets in the climax of *Gran Torino*, it is the apologetic suicide of an old chauvinist past his prime. In *The Gauntlet*, the gesture is passive without being submissive, for as the bus resists the police onslaught all too easily, Eastwood exposes the impotence of alleged power and allows his middle-aged hero a second chance at life. The hero, disenchanted, has been allowed to mature beyond his genre.

Eventually, the trigger-happy, mechanistic army of cops empties its load and tentatively allows the bus to pass. For the first time, the camera pans across the cops' faces rather than fetishizing their fascistic uniforms. Finally revealed as human, they lower their weapons and refuse a raving Blakelock's command to execute the fugitives, presumably demonstrating Shockley's earlier thesis that cops are decent folk just doing their jobs. Obviously, this long-overdue moment of self-reflection is hardly sufficient, and the film—quite against its own intentions—demonstrates instead that the police are so submissive to authoritarian structures that they will question their orders only *after* every absurdly violent possibility has been exhausted. In the final confrontation, it is Mally who again assumes the heroic pose while Shockley remains passive. After Blakelock multiply wounds Shockley, she reluctantly appropriates his fallen gun and dispatches the villain as the army of cops looks on dumbfounded—and perhaps disillusioned. Importantly, the helicopter shot that serves as the film's coda refuses any closure, for it shows Mally and Shockley walking *away* from the courthouse, abandoning the traditional site of justice and moving toward an unknown, extralegal future. Whereas Dirty Harry returns in four sequels even after disgustedly tossing away his police badge in the first film, here there can be no sequel, for Mally, representing the same civilizing, domesticating influence signified by the frontierswomen of John Ford, has cured the Eastwood archetype of his machismo, authoritarianism, and generic sociopathy.

If Shockley has not been entirely freed from aggression per se, he has at least been divested of his ideological blindness. He becomes ruggedly un-individualistic, disappearing into the horizon not as a lone cowboy condemned to the wilderness but alongside a marriageable domestic partner. Yet we cannot realistically imagine what might become of the pair, even if *The Gauntlet* tries to propose character transformations normally anathematic to genre films. While an unusually revisionist *cum* humanistic Western such as Kevin Costner's *Open Range* (2003) can posit the outlaw hero's redemption through belated domestication and marriage, Eastwood's over-riding intertextual persona makes any domestic scenarios difficult to imagine. And just as the thought of Shockley tossing his badge into the river to become a shoe salesman or insurance adjuster seems absurd, so too would the domes-tication implied by the film's coda betray worldly, college-educated Mally, whom we cannot imagine as a cookie-baking housewife. As such, it is prefer-able that their shared future remains unimaginable or ambiguous, lest we witness their revolutionary humanity descend to a more degraded, bourgeois form.

Its ambiguous ending aside, *The Gauntlet* remains a rarity, an action film that emphasizes the transformational role of feminism and parodies the allegedly "cathartic" (but in fact fruitless) effects of violent spectacle. Here, Locke is not the caricatured *femme castracice* she'd become in *Sudden Impact*, nor does the film merely invert the genders, envisioning saintly heroines and iniquitous men—as does the alleged "revisionism" of a gun-slinging Western such as Jonathan Kaplan's *Bad Girls* (1994), which reimagines *The Wild Bunch* (1969) as a redemptive story about subjugated young women rather than out-moded outlaws. Rather, *The Gauntlet* enacts the transformational feminism articulated from the time of Seneca Falls through Joan Mellen's *Big Bad Wolves* (1975), a feminism that seeks not to render women as performatively violent men, but strives to filter from masculinity inherited, unexamined histories of stoicism, sadism, and mindless aggression.

In its attempt to strip the hero of his generic violence, *The Gauntlet* invites comparison with Eastwood's *Unforgiven* (1992), which, though an artistically finer film, proposes a far more conservative thesis. For all its moral hand-wringing about the terrible responsibility that murder entails—a laud-able attempt to rebuke the genocidal Rambo ethos of the 1980s—*Unforgiven* nevertheless emerges as an apologia for generically masculine violence and the cultish worship of rugged individualism. By the film's climax, Eastwood's mercenary killer "William Munny" has accepted the fact of his murderous immorality, and when he admits to having killed women and children in a final speech dramatically punctuated by thunderclaps, the cumulative effect aims for catharsis and absolution. The audience is relieved by Munny's frank, unpretentious admission of guilt and is then given license to enjoy the final massacre as a masculine spectacle uncompromised by nagging morality. We distinguish Eastwood's Munny from Gene Hackman's sadistic sheriff and Richard Harris' cowardly English Bob not simply because he's less despicable than they are, but because only he rejects the mythologizing attentions of Bob's obsequious biographer, Beauchamp. Accepting his moral flaws and spurning literary invention, Munny thus repudiates the final claim of Ford's *The Man Who Shot Liberty Valance* (1962)—that myth, when socially useful, should replace historical fact. Yet realism alone cannot account for Munny's larger-than-life aura, for his flawless gun-slinging and godlike invulnerability are ultimately indistinguishable from Dirty Harry's preternatural gifts.

Though aligned with Munny's motives, the audience cannot really identify ethically with his character—a distance that allows audiences to enjoy the climactic gunfight without feeling complicit in his violence. Rather, audience identification is split among the exploitative Beauchamp, who stands in for a worshipful, myth-hungry audience and who, in the film's coda, must be chastised by Munny, and the secondary character of a headstrong, would-be novice who is ultimately sickened by all of the cold-blooded killing. The film's division of audience identifications is clearly too convenient. We enjoy Munny's violence, but are disconnected from his super-heroism and proud immorality; the young, would-be hero represents our own, long-lost longing for purity and naiveté; and Beauchamp, mythologizing Munny as eagerly as the audience does, is deservedly humiliated by him, much as a mythmaking journalist is chastened by John Wayne's fabled gunfighter in Don Siegel's *The Shootist* (1976). Yet *Unforgiven*, like Siegel's film, also goes to great lengths to amplify (not deflate) the charismatic aura of its gun-slinging hero, thus rendering hypocritical scenes in which Munny rebuffs Beauchamp—whose myths, apparently, are inferior to the myths reproduced by the film itself. Perhaps only a deliberately antiromantic film like Stan Dragoti's Western *Dirty Little Billy* (1972) truly comes close to demythologizing the outlaw hero. Here, Michael J. Pollard's Billy the Kid is neither fearsome nor charismatic; he is merely an ugly, feebleminded farm boy scrounging in a dismal frontier. Dragoti reduces Billy from folk hero to anthropological specimen—a radical gambit alien to an auteur as romantic as Eastwood.

Its shortcomings and spotty reputation notwithstanding, *The Gauntlet* surprisingly makes no concessions to old mythmaking. Rather than mummify its hero's masculinity—*Unforgiven*'s William Munny is a widower set in his solitude—*The Gauntlet* allows its middle-aged hero the off-screen chance to be reborn as a liberal humanist, an opportunity ritually denied to the outlaw hero and the socially marginal, Dirty Harry–esque loner. Rather than self-defensively divide audience identifications among multiple, contradictory characters, *The Gauntlet* forces a male audience expecting typically murderous genre fare into an unusual predicament. A male audience, forced to adopt Shockley's ignorant point of view, would likely see his attempts at bravado as either embarrassing (the biker gang sequence) or as unexpectedly, subversively passive (the armored bus finale). But if Eastwood-as-Shockley can be humanized, a bloodthirsty audience likewise can be delivered from its own trigger-happy culture, traced through the ages from the Turner thesis and the self-made frontiersman to the institutional cop and rogue vigilante. A film in which the gun is wielded psychotically by a villainous police force and heroically only by a reluctant, traumatized woman, *The Gauntlet* perhaps strives to create a new myth, one in which gunplay is remade as bloodless farce and in which personal strength arises from agonizing knowledge, not from the barrel of a gun.

Works Cited

The African Queen. 1952. Directed by John Huston, performances by Humphrey Bogart, Katherine Hepburn, and Robert Morley, Romulus Films.

Bad Girls. 1994. Directed by Jonathan Kaplan, performances by Madeleine Stowe, Mary Stuart Masterson, and Andie MacDowell, Twentieth Century Fox Film Corporation.

The Big Doll House. 1971. Directed by Jack Hill, performances by Roberta Collins, Pam Grier, and Judith Brown, New World Pictures.

Blood Work. 2002. Directed by Clint Eastwood, performances by Clint Eastwood, Jeff Daniels, and Anjelica Huston, Malpaso Productions and Warner Bros.

Blue Thunder. 1983. Directed by John Badham, performances by Roy Scheider, Warren Oates, and Candy Clark, Columbia Pictures Corporation.

Born Losers. 1967. Directed by Tom Laughlin, performances by Tom Laughlin, Elizabeth James, and Jeremy Slate, American International Productions.

Bringing Up Baby. 1938. Directed by Howard Hawks, performances by Katherine Hepburn, Cary Grant, and Charles Ruggles, RKO Radio Pictures.

Bronco Billy. 1980. Directed by Clint Eastwood, performances by Clint Eastwood, Sondra Locke, and Geoffrey Lewis, Warner Bros.

Coffy. 1973. Directed by Jack Hill, performances by Pam Grier, Booker Bradshaw, and Robert DoQui, American International Pictures.

Dirty Harry. 1971. Directed by Don Siegel, performances by Clint Eastwood, Andrew Robinson, and Harry Guardino, Warner Bros.

Dirty Little Billy. 1972. Directed by Stan Dragoti, performances by Michael J. Pollard, Richard Evans, and Lee Purcell, WRG/Dragoti Productions.

Douglas, Raymond. 2016. *On Being Raped.* Boston: Beacon Press.

Easy Rider. 1969. Directed by Dennis Hopper, performances by Peter Fonda, Dennis Hopper, and Jack Nicholson, Pando Company Inc.

Eight Diagram Pole Fighter. 1984. Directed by Chia Liang Liu, performances by Chia-Hui, Sheng Fu, and Lily Li, Shaw Brothers, 1984.

The Enforcer. 1976. Directed by James Fargo, performances by Clint Eastwood, Tyne Daly, and Harry Guardino, Warner Bros.

Firefox. 1982. Directed by Clint Eastwood, performances by Clint Eastwood, Freddie Jones, and David Huffman, Malpaso Company.

First Blood. 1982. Directed by Ted Kotcheff, performances by Sylvester Stallone, Brian Dennehy, and Richard Crenna, Anavais N.V.

Foote, John H. 2009. *Clint Eastwood: Evolution of a Filmmaker.* Westport, CT: Praeger.

Freud, Sigmund. 1922. *the Pleasure Principle.* Trans. C. J. M. Hubback. London: International Psycho-Analytical; Bartleby.com, 2010, www.bartleby.com/276/, accessed December 14, 2016.

The Gauntlet. 1977. Directed by Clint Eastwood, performances by Clint Eastwood, Sondra Locke, and Pat Hingle, Warner Bros. and The Malpaso Company.

Gran Torino. 2008. Directed by Clint Eastwood, performances by Clint Eastwood, Bee Vang, and Christopher Carley, Matten Productions.

Heartbreak Ridge. 1986. Directed by Clint Eastwood, performances by Clint Eastwood, Marsha Mason, and Everett McGill, Jay Weston Productions.

High Plains Drifter. 1973. Directed by Clint Eastwood, performances by Clint Eastwood, Verna Bloom, and Marianna Hill, Universal Pictures.

It Happened One Night. 1934. Directed by Frank Capra, performances by Clark Gable, Claudette Colbert, and Walter Connolly, Columbia Pictures Corporation.

Kapsis, Robert A., and Coblentz, Kathie, eds. 2012. *Clint Eastwood: Interviews.* Jackson: University Press of Mississippi.

Little Big Man. 1970. Directed by Arthur Penn, performances by Dustin Hoffman, Faye Dunaway, and Chief Dan George, Cinema Center Films..

Locke, Sondra. 1997. *The Good, the Bad, & the Very Ugly*. New York: William Morrow.

Madigan. 1968. Directed by Don Diegel, performances by Richard Widmark, Henry Fonda, and Inger Stevens, Universal Pictures.

Magnum Force. 1973. Directed by Ted Post, performances by Clint Eastwood, Hal Holbrook, and Mitchell Ryan, Warner Bros.

The Man Who Shot Liberty Valance. 1962. Directed by John Ford, performances by John Wayne, James Stewart, and Vera Miles, Paramount Pictures.

Mellen, Joan. 1978. *Big Bad Wolves: Masculinity in the American Film*. New York: Pantheon Books.

Million Dollar Baby. 2004. Directed by Clint Eastwood, performances by Hillary Swank, Clint Eastwood, and Morgan Freeman, Warner Bros.

Missing in Action. 1984. Directed by Joseph Zito, performances by Chuck Norris, M. Emmet Walsh, and David Tress, Cannon Group.

Open Range. 2003. Directed by Kevin Costner, performances by Kevin Costner, Robert Duvall, and Diego Luna, Touchstone Pictures.

Schickel, Richard. 1997. *Clint Eastwood: A Biography*. New York: Vintage.

The Shootist. 1976. Directed by Don Siegel, performances by John Wayne, Lauren Bacall, and Ron Howard, Paramount Pictures, 1976.

Soldier Blue. 1970. Directed by Ralph Nelson, performances by Candice Bergen, Peter Strauss, and Donald Pleasence, Embassy Pictures.

Sudden Impact. 1983. Directed by Clint Eastwood, performances by Clint Eastwood, Sondra Locke, and Pat Hingle, Warner Bros.

Sully. 2016. Directed by Clint Eastwood, performances by Tom Hanks, Aaron Eckhart, and Laura Linney, Flashlight Films.

A Touch of Zen. 1971. Directed by King Hu, performances by Feng Hsu, Chun Shih, and Ying Bai, International Film Company.

Turner, Frederick Jackson. 1972. *The Turner Thesis: Concerning the Role of the Frontier in American History*. Ed. George Rogers Taylor. Lexington, MA: D.C. Heath and Co., 3rd edition.

Unforgiven. 1992. Directed by Clint Eastwood, performances by Clint Eastwood, Gene Hackman, and Morgan Freeman, Warner Bros.

The Wild Bunch. 1969. Directed by Sam Peckinpah, performances by William Holden, Ernest Borgnine, and Robert Ryan, Warner Bros.

Eastwood's Depiction of Violence and PTSD in Private Citizens

ALISON S. WALLACE

Director Clint Eastwood's definition of trauma varies from film to film, but he remains consistent in his tendency to place seemingly ordinary characters in extraordinarily violent situations. *Unforgiven* (1992), *Midnight in the Garden of Good and Evil* (1997), and *Changeling* (2008) examine the theme of violence and how the average person responds to traumatic events. These particular films take place in time periods that span over 100 years, are set in three separate regions of the United States and explore both intentional and unintentional violence and trauma. Eastwood even looks at different social classes within these films, exploring the extremely poor to the outrageously wealthy and how these characters react to both theoretical and real violence. A consistent measure throughout the films is that the characters themselves are unaware of how they will deal with trauma, and they are usually surprised at their own reactions after killing another person or experiencing the loss of a loved one. Ultimately, with these films Eastwood suggests that one's reaction to violence is unpredictable, but often post-traumatic stress disorder (PTSD) affects even the most apathetic protagonists. He consistently shows the difference between a character's attitude before trauma and his or her attitude post trauma. The various situations presented in these three films support contemporary studies regarding PTSD, showing that civilians are just as susceptible to PTSD as are combat-hardened veterans. Eastwood's ability to exhibit a before and an after account of his protagonists helps the audience understand what an indelible impression trauma can have on the average person.

Eastwood's drama *Unforgiven* focuses on several different aspects of

PTSD, most remarkably concentrating on the vast difference between one's attitude toward violence before and after killing another human being. Eastwood acknowledges that he purposefully explored aspects of violence in *Unforgiven* that he failed to look at in his previous Westerns. In his 1992 interview with *Cahiers du Cinéma*, Eastwood explains: "[T]he film deals with violence and its consequences a lot more than those   I've done before. In the past, there were a lot of people killed gratuitously in my pictures, and what I liked about this story was that people aren't killed, and acts of violence aren't perpetrated, without there being certain consequences. That's a problem I thought was important to talk about today, it takes on proportions it didn't have in the past, even if it's always been present through the ages." With this strategy in mind, *Unforgiven* becomes a film about the metamorphosis a person goes through from ignorant civilian to hardened, guilt-ridden killer. In order to do this, Eastwood presents two very distinct kinds of characters—those who have murdered in the past and those who have not killed yet, but look at killing with an aloof apathy. With the characters William Munny (Clint Eastwood), Ned Logan (Morgan Freeman), and Little Bill (Gene Hackman) we see the effects of PTSD and the difficulties that accompany it. In contrast, Eastwood provides the Schofield Kid (Jaimz Woolvett), W.W. Beauchamp (Saul Rubinek), and Strawberry Alice (Frances Fisher). These three characters talk about violence in a jovial and bragging way, or simply with casual disregard. In particular, the Schofield Kid's presence in *Unforgiven* is essential to illustrate the juxtaposition between a person untouched by killing and one who has experienced killing another person.

The Schofield Kid's development is complicated and chaotic. He spends the majority of the film acting in an immature manner, bragging about the five men he supposedly killed in the past, and behaving anxious and hyper. It is important for Eastwood to create this long history of insensitivity with the Kid to make it all more powerful when the Kid experiences PTSD later.

When Will and Ned catch up to the Kid on their way to Wyoming the Schofield Kid fires at them indiscriminately. Unable to see clearly, the Kid is unable to identify Will and Ned. Rather than approach the two men until he can see them, he erratically fires on them, very nearly shooting his two partners. This is the first incident that indicates the Kid's ignorance regarding the value of human life. Granted, he does not know if the two men are friend or foe, but assuming foe and shooting to kill simply illustrates the Kid's indifference toward life. The Kid keeps up this bravado until the moment he has to actually kill one of the wanted cowboys. Eastwood includes the Schofield Kid within the film because he most likely behaves how Will and Ned did when they were the Kid's age, and before their PTSD developed. It's as if Eastwood is simultaneously showing the audience the same person before and after a trauma. The Schofield Kid could be labeled "Young Will" or "Will from 20 years ago." This allows the audience to understand the difference between the average person before and after violent trauma; having them act side-by-side makes for an easily understandable comparison, which effectively shows the distinct difference between men's experiences.

The Kid expresses his naïve perspective when he discusses going after the two cowboys without Will. He tells Ned, "I'll ride up close and shoot 'em." Ned's experience shows a stark contrast when he solemnly asks in return, "Just like that, huh?" This conversation takes place while the Kid maintains he has killed five men in the past. He has not developed as a character, even though this scene is more than half way through the film. Will and Ned do not brag about their pasts, they feel weary and depressed over their killings; this is to be expected because they have felt the heavy reality of their actions. The Kid cannot fathom the profundity of killing until the act is committed in reality, not only in theory. Insisting to Ned that he is dangerous, he says, "I told you I'm a damn killer! I done it before. I'm more of a killer than he[Will] is anyhow." However, the Schofield Kid's bravado ends when he finally kills his first man. His hyper-confident, loud mouth, and bragging ways unravel. With the shootout between Quick Mike (David Mucci), Eastwood demonstrates the easy descent from cocky young man out to make a fortune to penitent and depressed killer. The Schofield Kid points his revolver only a few feet away from Quick Mike, who sits defenseless in an outhouse. After an achingly long pause the Kid finally shoots Quick Mike three times, hand and body shaking uncontrollably, his face frozen in shock.

This is where Eastwood adds many facets to the character of the Schofield Kid; the Kid's lack of development to this point is moot because his character changes during the time it takes to fire his pistol. Eastwood adds dimension and several different aspects to the Kid's personality that did not exist mere moments before, while illustrating how a man may go from his baseline normal attitude toward killing to the attitude he has after killing. This is essential in Eastwood's presentation of PTSD because the audience is not introduced to the Schofield Kid as a middle-aged man with a past, like Will and Ned, but as a young man with no experience; we get to see the experience, the actual event that causes the PTSD, and then the aftermath. It is an honest and unglamorized depiction of how the average civilian could react to the brutal reality of killing another person. Eastwood could have easily made the Kid look like a hero; the Kid's hands could have been steady and he could simply look pensive after the shootout, but Eastwood chooses to show the gritty, ugly nature of killing another human being. At this point the audience feels more connected to the Kid because they too only think of killing in a theoretical fashion and also only hear second-hand accounts of what happened years before. The audience now becomes uncomfortable with the brutal reality of killing. This scene places the Kid and the audience at the epicenter of murder, without flash or glory or reward. Thus, the Kid's PTSD comes as no surprise after Quick Mike's death.

While the Kid and Will talk after the shootout, the Kid chugs on his bottle of whiskey, holds himself, and rattles on endlessly. "I killed the hell out of him, didn't I?!" he asks Will. It is clear that the Schofield Kid is attempting to remain in control of his emotions and not be affected by what just happened to him, but he quickly goes into decline and begins to cry. He continues, "It don't seem real. He'll never breathe again. Now he's dead ... and the other one too. All on account of pulling a trigger." His mention of the situation not seeming real is imperative to understand an average person's susceptibility to PTSD. The Schofield Kid talks about killing so casually throughout the film that when he experiences the reality of murder he is ill-prepared, not expecting to feel so much guilt and anguish, even though he justifies the killing because Quick Mike attacked a defenseless and innocent woman. According to Emily J. Ozer and Daniel S. Weiss, in their article "Who Develops Posttraumatic Stress Disorder?," "Diagnosis of PTSD requires exposure to a traumatic event that causes feelings of extreme fear, horror, or helplessness. Traumatic events are defined as experiences that involve death, serious injury or threat of death" (169). It is important to note that according to this definition traumatic events need only involve death, thus the Kid's murder of another can cause PTSD, even though he is technically not the victim. This indicates that the experience of premeditatedly taking a life is a trauma in itself.

While the Schofield Kid's character has developed a great deal from his murder of Quick Mike, Will remains unaffected. Though the two men react differently, this actually enhances the accuracy of Eastwood's depiction of PTSD within the film because individual response to drama varies dramatically from person to person (Ozer 169). Will Munny has killed before and does not experience the shock the Kid goes through. While the audience is never aware of everything Will has done in his past, we do find out small details about his violent past through his brief conversations with Ned and his hallucinations, which also indicate the presence of PTSD.

While traveling to Big Whiskey Will falls ill with a fever and subsequently lets his guard down and begins to openly reflect about his past. He tells Ned he recently saw Eagle Hendershot, "I saw him, Ned. His head was all broke open. I could see inside of it." Ned assures Will that Hendershot is dead, killed by Will many years ago. These kind of hallucinations are common among some PTSD sufferers. In the *Journal of Traumatic Stress*, John A. Kostek et al. writes that re-experiencing symptoms (intrusive memories, flashbacks) are often triggered by situations or stimuli that reflect aspects of the traumatic event or events (717). The authors go on to say that some subjects experience intrusive memories or flashbacks if they are prone to "generalization," meaning "overly general memories of traumatic events would then be vulnerable to being triggered by a wide range of stimuli that otherwise would not provoke recall" (717). Will experiences his flashback with Eagle Hendershot prior to killing either of the two cowboys, so it is likely he is susceptible to generalization; he has placed himself in a situation that he knows will most likely involve violence and death, so he has PTSD-related visions before killing the cowboys. By including Will's symptoms of PTSD, Eastwood suggests that if Kid were to continue on this path of killing his future psyche may be somewhat like Will's. While the Kid is excited by the anticipation of killing his first man, Will is weary and his mind reminds him of past horrors. In the future the Kid could easily be haunted by his many murders, if he were to continue as Will.

There is victory in the story not because the two wanted cowboys are finally gunned down, but because the Kid chooses to turn away from this life that looks so appealing to him before the shootout. After handing his rifle to Will, the Kid says, "I ain't like you, Will." Will's past acts as a cautionary tale. Rather than the same sad history repeating itself the Kid decides to recognize that his previous notions about killing were inaccurate, though he only learns this after a trauma and experiencing PTSD. However, the Schofield Kid is not the only character under the delusion that killing is a mysterious and exciting adventure. W.W. Beauchamp, English Bob's biographer, is much like the Kid in this respect, but rather than seeking direct experience he prefers to write about others' exploits, and in this way he experiences violence in a safe and theoretical way. In fact, Beauchamp's presence mirrors that of the audience- both are present to live vicariously through the fantasy that accompanies story-telling.

W.W. Beauchamp is a character who is similar to the Schofield Kid in that he fantasizes about shootouts and relishes the excitement that comes from vicious stories, but is left traumatized when he actually experiences violence. His first brush with genuine violence ends with him urinating in his trousers. Little Bill and his deputies point their guns at both English Bob and Beauchamp, and while this may be fairly normal for the tough residents of Big Whiskey, Wyoming, it is not common for the professional writer. Beauchamp's attitude visibly changes from his snickering and pompous facial expressions on the train to Big Whiskey, to the frightened, sweating, and urinating wreck that he is when a gun is pointed at him. This is yet another instance that Eastwood shows theoretical violence and actual violence are wholly dissimilar. The reality of a loaded gun being pointed at Beauchamp causes him to unravel. Because Beauchamp symbolizes the audience, the audience can assume that if real violence were to occur to them it would not be entertaining, but horrifying.

After English Bob finds himself in jail after Little Bill beats him for not turning in his firearms, W.W. Beauchamp transfers loyalties and begins to voraciously document Little Bill's stories. However, as Eastwood tends to do in this film, reality comes crashing in to what seems a perfectly pleasant scenario. Little Bill, who is similar in age to Will and Ned, and who also has a violent past, states, "It ain't so easy to shoot a man anyhow, you know?" Beauchamp nods his head, but does not fully understand. To demonstrate, Little Bill hands a revolver and the keys to the cell to Beauchamp and says that if he can shoot Little Bill, then he and English Bob are free to go. Beauchamp is unable to shoot Little Bill. All of the writing and his avid appetite for gruesome stories of gun slingers does not prepare him for the reality of shooting a person. So, unlike the Schofield Kid who goes through with killing a man and ends up regretting it, Beauchamp recognizes that he is incapable of committing the act at all. Eastwood does not end with this predictable outcome, however. He has Beauchamp suggest Little Bill give the gun to English Bob and recommends the same bargain be struck. Beauchamp only knows of English Bob's alleged past, and while he witnessed Bob's shooting skills on the train, firing at pheasants, the somber reality of killing a person is much different. The audience also knows English Bob has killed in the past, and Eastwood sets up the audience to think that Little Bill will soon be shot and killed, but even English Bob is unable to go through with the crime. This may be because at point blank range he does not have the fortitude to commit murder, or it may be because he does not believe himself to be fast enough against Little Bill, but either way violence between the two known killers does not occur and English Bob leaves town on a train in the morning.

Holding back violence in this scene is essential to the overall outlook Eastwood takes toward violence in this film. The two men are older and have killed in the past. With their collective knowledge they decide not to shoot each other; if these two were young cowboys the outcome would most likely have been death for one or both of the men. With neither man shooting Eastwood expresses how experience with killing affords the men the clarity that killing is not an easy thing to do, and should be avoided if possible. In fact, the night Quick Mike assaults a prostitute, the old and experienced Little Bill chooses not to whip or hang the culprits, but instead fines them as punishment. The person who demands their death is Strawberry Alice. As Beauchamp easily suggests English Bob have the opportunity to shoot Little Bill, Strawberry Alice effortlessly demands justice in the form of death to her friend's attackers.

Delilah Fitzgerald (Anna Levine) is the disfigured prostitute this story centers around, but she generally speaks very little throughout. However, her fellow prostitute, Strawberry Alice, is outraged and rails against Little Bill for not at least whipping the two assailants. She suggests the ladies pool their savings and offer a reward for the cowboys' deaths. While Alice is nearby when Delilah is attacked, she does not actually experience the violence or pain for herself, nor does she plan on killing the cowboys herself. This disconnection from violence suggests that she demands the cowboys' murder easily because she thinks about violence in a theoretical way, much like the Schofield Kid and W.W. Beauchamp. Delilah never demands the cowboys' deaths, or any kind of physical punishment. This may be due to the fact that she is in shock after her trauma, but ultimately she is the one person who should logically want revenge, yet does not. By developing her character in this fashion Eastwood suggests that if someone experiences violent trauma they are less likely to desire more violence in order to quench their desire for revenge or justice; those who look for violent justice are those who remain unaffected by direct trauma and who do not have to inflict the justice themselves.

Strawberry Alice feels like she is defending her friend and demanding what is, in her view, ethically right. She justifies paying to have two men killed because they are guilty of disfiguring her friend. In this sense she is much like the Schofield Kid, who has no issue pursuing the cowboys because "they had it coming." However, Alice is blinded by her desire for violent justice. When Quick Mike's accomplice gifts Delilah his best pony and offers his apologies, again Delilah says nothing, but Alice runs into the street and screams at the young man. The audience never knows if Delilah appreciates the gesture because Alice quickly denies any attempt at forgiveness. Alice does not lack empathy, as she clearly supports Delilah, but she is unable to view the culprits as anything other than evil. Though she never picks up a weapon to dole out her own form of justice, the audience wonders if she would have reacted like the Schofield Kid and somewhat regretted her demands for justice in the form of death. However, Alice remains disconnected from the cowboys' deaths, and thus does not go through a transformation as does the Schofield Kid. Ultimately, Eastwood shows it is easy to demand violent justice while maintaining a theoretical view toward violence, but it is a very different thing to execute in reality. He also suggests that supporting violence does not result in PTSD; in *Unforgiven* one must experience the trauma for themselves to suffer from PTSD.

While in *Unforgiven* violence is often equated to justice, in *Midnight in the Garden of Good and Evil*, violence is almost always referenced as a source of entertainment or gossip. *Midnight* is a world away from 19th-century Big Whiskey, Wyoming. In the modern day affluent sections of Savannah, Georgia privileged characters look as if they exclusively throw parties and gossip. The only aspect both films have in common is the carefree attitude toward violence many characters hold, with the primary difference being that the characters in *Midnight* actually embrace and desire the excitement that comes with violence. PTSD is not as prevalent or transparent in *Midnight*, but it is present. In fact, PTSD does not make an impression on the main character, Jim Williams (Kevin Spacey), until the last few minutes of the film. However, what is significant about this film is that almost all of the characters and the screen time are devoted to a glorified view of violence. There are more jokes and light-hearted banter regarding murder and suicide than there are moments of gravity. Much of this is attributed to the quirky and eccentric nature of those who live in Savannah. However, as Eastwood does in *Unforgiven*, after all of the witticisms about death and killing end and the main character is left with the unfortunate truth that he committed murder, the crushing reality of killing results in PTSD.

Approximately 20 minutes into the film, at Jim Williams' annual Christmas party, which draws the richest and most respected members of Savannah society, we meet Serena Dawes (Dorothy Loudon). After Harry shows everyone "the latest addition" to his arsenal, Dawes comments that she knows the caliber of the weapon because it is the very same that her husband used to "blow his brains out." Rather than be disturbed or upset by such a comment, another lady states that her husband also killed himself with the same weapon, exclaiming what a coincidence it was, almost as if she is surprised by something as banal as wearing the same dress as the other woman. It is quickly clear to the audience that this group of people is deluded. Rather than eliciting any kind of sympathy or even silence to the knowledge that both ladies' husbands killed themselves, the people gathered laugh hysterically. Dawes then pulls a small hand gun from her cleavage and waves it around, happily claiming that she will shoot a man some day; she points it at several different men near her and says it could be any of them. This scene quickly establishes the community we are dealing with. These people look at violence as a form of entertainment, as a reason to gossip. While *Unforgiven*'s two antagonists commit an egregious crime and arguably invite some form of retribution, *Midnight* lacks any sort of justice through violence, making this film more disturbing. *Midnight* sees violence as a form of entertainment and a source for juicy gossip.

Several other instances convey the apathetic nature of this community even after Billy Hanson's (Jude Law) murder. For instance, Joe Odom (Paul Hipp) hands out canapés and cocktails on the street outside of Williams' house while Hanson still lies dead inside. The crowd parties through the night, waiting for any gruesome detail they can snag from the recent tragedy. The next day we meet The Lady Chablis (Chablis Deveau), who is more upset that she has not received condolence flowers regarding Billy's death than Billy's death itself. In most respects *Midnight* seems like it is going to be a dark comedy more than a murder mystery, nor does it seem like it will provide commentary about violence or PTSD. However, much like the over-paint

Williams shows Kelso at the beginning of the film, there is the obvious and clear picture we see, and there is the picture underneath that we cannot see, but that is the truth.

While speaking with Serena Dawes, John Kelso (John Cusack) discovers that most people do not have an issue with the act of Billy's murder itself, but with the fact that Jim Williams is now out of the closet as a homosexual man, and that murder was an "unseemly way" of announcing his sexuality. Dawes also reveals that the community is upset because they did not all get to have sex with Billy Hanson prior to his death. So, rather than be upset that a man in his early twenties was gunned down in alleged cold blood, they are upset that they were not able to have sex with him first, and that Williams' sexuality is no longer discreet. This conversation happens mid-way through the film. At this point the audience is not particularly concerned with the murder, much like the cast of characters. The pain Billy Hanson went through or the sadness that his family may feel is irrelevant to the story. Even though trauma affects everyone differently and PTSD is not necessarily a guaranteed affliction after experiencing trauma, it appears the cast of characters are sociopaths because there is such a lack of remorse for Billy's murder. This lack of empathy for human life signals a lack of PTSD amongst the characters, until the last few minutes of the film.

Having been acquitted of Billy's murder, Jim Williams returns home and begins planning his next Christmas party, carefully ignoring the fact that he confessed to Kelso that he killed Billy, not in self-defense, but in cold blood. As Kelso says good-bye to Jim it seems that the story is finished. The audience is led to believe that this is a story of gratuitous violence met with an indifferent reserve. However, Eastwood cleverly makes his biggest impact within these last few moments of a film that is nearly two and a half hours long. Jim Williams grabs at his chest while he looks to be in distress, and falls to the ground in the very office where he killed his lover. While lying on the carpet he sees Billy's body lying on the ground next to him. Billy raises his head and smiles at Jim. Jim simply looks in awe at his deceased lover who seems to have appeared out of nowhere and quietly dies. Though this ending seems ironic, having fought for his freedom in court only to die soon after his acquittal, the conclusion is far more complicated and telling.

Jim's vision of Billy, and his painful heart attack, both indicate that he is suffering from PTSD. In Allan Young's *The Harmony of Illusions* he speaks about case studies conducted at the National Center for the Treatment of War-Related PTSD. Though he focuses primarily on Vietnam veterans one individual in his study exhibits similar symptoms to Jim Williams.' "Flip" suffers from physical pain due to his trauma suffered in Vietnam. As one clinician in the study observes, "Flip's pains are an inventory of the deaths that he carries with him." For instance, one of Flip's friends was shot in the mouth, and consequently Flip always touches that spot on his mouth and complains of the pain there. He also claims to have chronic shoulder pain and his friend was also shot in the shoulder. Though this case study specifically has to do with war-related PTSD, it is important to note that trauma can result in a form of PTSD that produces physical pain. Jim Williams' guilt could be weighing on him so heavily that he suffers pain through a heart attack. His vision of Billy is also a common symptom of PTSD. Viewing people, particularly those involved in the trauma, who are not actually there is commonly reported among PTSD sufferers (Sladjana).

Kelso allows Jim one last opportunity to confess all that happened the night of Billy's death, to assuage his guilt, but Jim refuses. So, while Billy was shot in the chest and died lying on the carpet, so Jim dies of pains in his chest while lying on the same carpet. His heart attack allows us to understand what has been weighing heavily on his conscience. Through his confident bravado and witty banter, we think Jim is devoid of empathy, but because he has visions of his ex-lover who was killed during a traumatic event we see that he is unmistakably affected by his past. Also, Jim's vision of Billy is of when Billy lay dead on the floor immediately after he was shot, so rather than see him healthy and happy he sees him within the violent context of their last moments together. Much like soldiers who are often described as having visions of severe incidents that occur during combat, Jim has a vision of the violent murder he committed and even feels pain in the same place that his victim/lover was shot in.

This short, but intense, instance of PTSD is essential to the story line because the vast majority of *Midnight* expands upon the idea that these citizens of Savannah are wealthy, heartless, and apathetic, and possibly sociopathic in some respects. However, Jim's heart failing and seeing visions of his ex-lover mean that although he remains quirky and eccentric after Billy's death, he is in fact emotionally affected by the death. We do not see Jim shoot Billy, like we see the Schofield Kid kill Quick Mike, but due to Jim's nonchalant attitude throughout the film it's easy to believe that perhaps Jim did not have the same emotional turmoil while pulling the trigger that the Schofield Kid clearly had. However, what is clear is that though these two characters react differently after killing another person, it does not necessarily mean that one is not as emotionally affected by it than the other. In fact, both are haunted by their situations.

Changeling is similar to *Midnight* in that there is a feeling of subtle and repressed trauma throughout, while lacking the dark comedy that makes *Midnight* bizarrely entertaining. Los Angeles in 1928 does not seem inherently violent, but we soon learn from John Malkovich's character, Reverend Gustav Briegleb, that the police in Los Angeles have run amok and create heinous crimes in order to control the city. The police department's reputation is tat-

tered, so having a happy ending story for the press is of the utmost importance. Unfortunately, Christine Collins (Angelina Jolie) falls victim to the
police department's agenda. In fact, Collins suffers several traumas throughout the film. Not only is her son kidnapped, but the police return her "son"
months later in order to receive a positive headline in the press. The boy in
question is clearly not her son, so she now must live the trauma of believing
her son to be recovered, realizing that he is not her son, and then being bul-
lied by the police into accepting this boy. A trauma that is arguably as egregious as losing her child occurs when the police finally section her to the
psychopathic hospital against her will. Collins experiences trauma after
trauma without any sign of redemption until the Reverend comes to her aid
and garners public support. What is particularly interesting about Collins is
that she does not seem to suffer from PTSD. She remains calm in the face of
adversity, even when she is locked into a psychiatric ward. The audience can
safely assume that she goes through mental torture over her lost child, but
Eastwood does not explore this aspect of the story.

However, Eastwood carefully provides other characters who go through
multiple traumas throughout the film. Rather than have the main character,
Christine Collins, go through PTSD on screen, he chooses to include two
others stories, one from a boy who was kidnapped and held against his will,
as well as the boy who assisted the serial killer in obtaining his victims. It is
imperative to note the multiple traumas and how each character reacts to
and deals with their individual ordeals, and consequently how PTSD affects
each. While Collins remains poised and distraught, Sanford Clark has visions
of the past, and David Clay goes into hiding only to return to Los Angeles
after he has years of recovery. Also, unlike Eastwood's other films, *Changeling*
discusses trauma in young adults, who may have more difficulty processing
violent action against them.

Sanford Clark (Eddie Alderson) has the unfortunate position of being
the serial killer's nephew and assistant. He has little choice in the matter and
ultimately helps kidnap and bury approximately 20 children. After being
arrested for illegally living in the United States he is told he will be deported
back to Canada; however, he makes sure to confess to the police all of the
deviant activities that went on at the ranch. While waiting in a hallway at the
police station a young man innocently taps a ruler against his leg, but this
seemingly harmless act causes Sanford to experience a gruesome flashback.
The ruler reminds him of Gordon Northcott (Jason Butler Harner) wielding
an axe on one of his victims, blood splattering up at him, creating a horrific
moment. This scene provides insight into Sanford's mental state. We know
that he was not murdered by his uncle, but questions arise concerning what
other atrocities happened to Sanford. It is never clear if he was molested or
physically beaten or violated in anyway, but he did help lure the boys into

his uncle's truck, as well as help his uncle dispose of the bodies. These two traumas cause guilt so great that he would rather confess and risk going to jail than simply be sent home without incident to Canada. While Sanford's situation is disgusting and horrifying, it is important to include some details concerning his trauma because we see that though he is a young man with no familial support, he is able to survive an ordeal that we assume is impossible to deal with mentally. Eastwood shows that even after experiencing repeated acts of violence this young man has survived physically, but is scarred emotionally. Indeed, he suffers from PTSD, but he is alive and seeks to confess all that happened. This show of strength is what is missing from *Midnight* and *Unforgiven*; Eastwood shows that even someone who has PTSD can overcome and survive, particularly if they seek help.

To support this theme, another young victim eventually seeks help from the police in order to be reunited with his family. David Clay (Asher Axe) admits that he escaped from the ranch, with the help of Christine Collins' son Walter, and spent years away from home on his own in general fear. While it initially seems strange that a victim would rather remain alone and homeless than go back to their parents, this can also be explained by PTSD. This young man escapes from his oppressor, but he continues to run and even tells people that he is an orphan. He was simply "scared." It does not seem logical to an impartial observer, but the traumatic event causes this young man to retreat not only mentally, but physically. By not going home he stays in a state of denial. According to the Rape, Abuse & Incest National Network this is also very common in rape victims who are uncomfortable going to the police and/or identifying their attacker. In "Mental Health Disorders in Adolescents" Mark and Myrna Goldstein and Eric Hazen cite "social withdrawal and isolation" as a major sign of an adolescent having difficulty recovering from a traumatic event. By avoiding the reality of his trauma, David Clay is able to start a new life. Eventually, however, he misses his parents and has recovered enough mentally to seek them out.

At the beginning of *Changeling* Christine Collins tells Walter, "You never start a fight, but you always finish it." While Christine suffers severe depression and hopelessness during her ordeal, she remains strong and takes the police and doctors to court. She even continues to call police stations in major cities and asks if they have seen her son years after his disappearance. David Clay responds to his trauma in an opposite fashion, running away and trying to start a different life. Though David Clay's experience with PTSD is different than Christine Collins' and Sanford Clark's, it is no less real and painful. The investigating officer even asks David, "Why come forward now?" It simply does not make sense for him to not have come back directly after escaping, but psychologically David has to recuperate before returning home. Eastwood's presentation of several different forms of PTSD and how three people react to their traumas is essential in showing the complicated affliction that is PTSD.

In many ways *Changeling*'s two young male characters add a breadth of dialogue concerning PTSD because Eastwood's other films do not focus on so many varying symptoms of PTSD, nor do they involve adolescents. *Changeling* allows the audience to observe how innocent, young victims may react to severe violent trauma. While they are not the main characters, their symptoms are more clearly defined than Collins,' i.e., Sanford's vision of the axe. By including two victims of similar age who experienced essentially the same scenario, Eastwood is able to explain that PTSD affects everyone differently, even those who go through the same trauma.

While *Changeling* is disturbing and uncomfortable to watch, it actually has a happy ending for the severely damaged victims. Collins maintains hope for Walter's eventual return, Sanford goes home to his family in Canada after confessing, thus assuaging some guilt, and David finally returns home to his loving parents. Much like the Schofield Kid in *Unforgiven*, the triumph in *Changeling* is the ability for an average person to face severe trauma, suffer from PTSD, and yet continue on with life.

PTSD is most commonly applied to combat veterans, but *Unforgiven*, *Midnight in the Garden of Good and Evil*, and *Changeling* expertly explore the effects of violent trauma on the average civilian. Their stories allow audiences to enter discussions about PTSD in a population that might otherwise be ignored. Eastwood very clearly establishes that PTSD can affect the average citizen as easily as it does a soldier. Young, old, male, and female all face trauma, both physical and emotional. Eastwood's films can help each of these groups gain insight into their situations, in part, because Eastwood's characters continue to feel pain and to suffer rather than simply get better. The pain and suffering are part of the recovery. In this sense Eastwood's films almost serve as a public service, providing those who have experienced trauma a new group of individuals who can share in their trauma, and the rest of society a chance to see this issue in unexpected places.

WORKS CITED

Changeling. 2008. Directed by Clint Eastwood, performances by Angelina Jolie and John Malkovich, Imagine Entertainment, Malpaso Productions, and Relativity Media.
"The Criminal Justice System: Statistics." n.d. RAINN, www.rainn.org/statistics/criminal-justice-system. Accessed 25 August 2016.
Hazen, Eric P., et al. 2010. "Reactions to Trauma." *Mental Health Disorders in Adolescents*. New Brunswick: Rutgers University Press.
Kostek, John A., et al. 2014. "Acquired Equivalence in U.S. Veterans With Symptoms of Posttraumatic Stress: Reexperiencing Symptoms Are Associated With Greater Generalization." *Journal of Traumatic Stress* 27: 717–720. JSTOR. Accessed 24 August 2016.
Midnight in the Garden of Good and Evil. Directed by Clint Eastwood, performances by Kevin Spacey, John Cusack, and Jude Law, Malpaso Productions and Silver Pictures, 1997.
Ozer, Emily J., and Daniel S. Weiss. 2004. "Who Develops Posttraumatic Stress Disorder?"

Current Directions in Psychological Science 13.4: 169–172. *JSTOR.* Accessed 22 August 2016.

Sladjana, Ivezic. 1999. "Psychotic Symptoms in Post-Traumatic Stress Disorder." *Military Medicine* 164, no. 1, 73–75.

Unforgiven. Directed by Clint Eastwood, performances by Clint Eastwood, Morgan Freeman, and Gene Hackman, Malpaso Productions, 1992.

"What face do you put with your enemy?"

Identifying Trauma in In the Line of Fire *and* Absolute Power

MÁRIA I. CIPRIANI

> Do you realize the skill in breaking the security of a security company? I don't know how those guys do it.—Luther Whitney, *Absolute Power*

The brain is the human's most complex security system. When a person experiences a life-threatening event, the brain initially attempts to protect the entire organism by triggering the increase in adrenaline that is part of the fight-or-flight response; after the event, the brain attempts to reregulate the person's physical and emotional state (van der Kolk). When these forms of protection work, the human subjects are able to leave traumatic events in their past. When they do not, human subjects remain stuck in their traumatic event even after that event has passed. These subjects struggle to shake-off their experience. They begin to exhibit traumatic reactions in the form of flashbacks, dissociation, and depersonalization (Levine 16). Each reaction leaves the body holding onto the trauma. In the case of dissociation, for instance, the consciousness will hold onto the trauma to such an extent that one becomes disconnected from an awareness of moving one's body (American Psychological Association, 2013, 291). In the case of depersonalization, the consciousness will detach from its host's mind, body or sense of self. A subject experiencing depersonalization may not connect an image in the mirror with the self, for example (*ibid.*).

These responses can arise after a variety of experiences, rather than those that might most commonly be associated with these reactions. Trauma itself can be experienced after exposure to actual or threatened death, after serious injury or sexual violence to oneself, after the firsthand witnessing of that experience, or even after learning that a close family member or friend experienced a traumatic event (American Psychological Association, 2013, 271). The firsthand witnessing or experiencing of an assassination or other public murder would certainly constitute a traumatic event. Crucifixion, for example, is one of the oldest and most widely publicized forms of trauma depicted on a regular basis. Christ on a cross, accompanied by two thieves, a familiar scene in Christianity, serves as one of the most widely recognized and disseminated depictions of this event. It is not, of course, the only one.

Clint Eastwood's film *Absolute Power* (1997) is premised on a traumatic event: the helpless witnessing by a thief, Luther Whitney (Eastwood), of a violent sexual encounter and murder. A close reading of the filmic text demonstrates Eastwood's penchant for depicting trauma, and a clinical eye can see signs of post-traumatic stress disorder (PTSD) evidenced by several characters. Given the narrative and the actions of those characters, *Absolute Power* is rife with traumatic events and trauma reactions. While the plot's timeline (approximately one week) is too short to allow any characters the possibility of a PTSD diagnosis due to those events (a PTSD diagnosis requires four weeks post-trauma for the diagnosis, prior to that, the diagnosis is acute stress), a careful viewing of the film reveals that, although Luther, the main character, does not display signs of PTSD, several other characters in the film are symptomatic, including Secret Service Agents Burton (Scott Glenn) and Collin (Dennis Haysbert).

When considering the trauma reactions of several characters in *Absolute Power*, and Eastwood's directorial decisions to portray PTSD, several elements of the film bring to mind *In the Line of Fire* (1993), the last film in which Eastwood acted but did not direct at least until *Trouble with the Curve* (2012). Like *Absolute Power*, *In the Line of Fire* depicts the reactions of Secret Service agents to a series of work-related traumatic situations. The difference between these two stories is in their story time and the questions they ask. *In the Line of Fire* occurs across decades. It reaches back to Secret Service Agent Frank Horrigan's (Eastwood) failed attempt to stop the assassination of President John F. Kennedy. Other traumas emerge during the film, most especially after Frank loses his partner, D'Andrea (Dylan McDermott), but all traumas extend back to Frank's experience "standing over a dead president," as Frank's antagonist, Mitch Leary (John Malkovich), makes explicit at one point in the film. *Absolute Power* takes place in a week, as above mentioned. This difference in time encourages different questions to be raised, and Eastwood allows those questions to be asked explicitly in both films. The question of *Absolute Power* is "When you're alone at night, and your rage takes over … what face do you put with your enemy?" The question in *In the Line of Fire* is "What do you see when you're in the dark and the demons come?"

Both questions assume intrusion symptoms, negative alterations in cognition, and marked alterations in arousal that fulfill current diagnostic criteria for PTSD. Both questions depict the midnight ruminations of a person plagued by insomnia, re-living a traumatic event, either through flashbacks, nightmares, or repetitive thoughts, while re-living the feelings of helplessness, rage, and/or fear that accompany the experience or witnessing of a traumatic event. One has to wonder if Eastwood's experience with *In the Line of Fire* impacted his decision to direct *Absolute Power*? Maybe the later film allowed Eastwood to address questions as a director that could only be raised in a film in which his one role was that of actor? Either way, the two films read alongside one another prompt a comprehensive review of trauma in the audience. *In the Line of Fire* and *Absolute Power* offer a complex presentation of trauma that can address not only ways in which trauma can arise in everyday experiences, but some of the possibilities for healing, too.

In the Line of Fire

"What do you see when you're in the dark and the demons come?" The question is asked twice in *In the Line of Fire*. The first time, it is intended to provoke a PTSD reaction: would-be presidential assassin "Booth" Leary (John Malkovich) knows that Secret Service Agent Frank Horrigan (Eastwood) has suffered after being part of President John F. Kennedy's protective detail on the day of Kennedy's assassination. Leary asks Frank the question, then proceeds to answer it in terms designed to evoke a PTSD response: "Late at night when the demons come, do you see the rifle coming out of that window, or do you see Kennedy's head being blown apart?... If you had [reacted], that could have been your head being blown apart...."

According to the fifth edition of the *Diagnostic and Statistical Manual of Mental Disorders* (DSM-5), Criterion A, an event is traumatic when it involves "exposure to actual or threatened death, serious injury or sexual violence in one or more of the following ways: directly experiencing the traumatic event, witnessing in person the event as it occurred to others, learning that the traumatic event(s) occurred to a close family member or friend [... and ...] experiencing repeated or extreme exposure to adverse details of the traumatic event(s)" (271). According to this definition, all the Secret Service agents, the First Lady, and the others in the motorcade on November 22, 1963, were traumatized by Kennedy's assassination. In retrospect, whether any or all of these individuals suffered PTSD (a diagnosis not introduced until 1980) could only be determined according to the symptoms they exhibited one month after the event (DSM-5, 272). Some form of "abnormal" behavior in the immediate days turns out to be normal. PTSD occurs when these behaviors continue longer than a month. This distinction makes the backstory of *In the Line of Fire* particularly important. These details fully classify Frank as a sufferer of PTSD symptoms even ten years after the assassination. His fellow agents on the detail reportedly suffered so much that they left the Service.

Leary attempts to use Frank's trauma to obtain psychological advantage. Leary knows that Frank's phone has been tapped and their conversations are being heard and traced. Thus, when Leary catalogues the difficult aspects of Frank's life a decade after the assassination—Frank's wife left him, taking their daughter, and Frank became an alcoholic, admitting in an interview that he was "not easy to live with"—Leary is attempting to humiliate Frank in front of his fellow agents. Leary is also describing someone with the symptoms of PTSD, a person who has become withdrawn, possibly depressed or violent, and an alcoholic (often addiction is an attempt to numb psychological pain and stop ruminations or flashbacks). Later, when Frank turns the tables and asks Leary (whose name he has recently discovered) the same question, Leary turns it back on Frank, again attempting to retraumatize Frank with his answer: "I see you, Frank, standing over the grave of another dead president."

Although we never see Frank Horrigan with President Kennedy, the things people say about Frank's relationship with Kennedy indicate that he and Kennedy were close. Frank's supervisor, Secret Service Director Sam Campagna (John Mahoney), states in an aside to Frank, that Agent Watts (Gary Cole) was "nowhere near as arrogant as you were when you had Kennedy's ear." Prior to that "Booth"/Leary says, "you were JFK's favorite agent, the best and the brightest," a statement that sounds like a quotation from a magazine article but bears more weight when confirmed by Frank's supervisor. Another piece of information about Frank's personal connection and loyalty to Kennedy comes after Frank disrespects the current president's chief of staff. Fellow Agent Lilly Raines (Rene Russo) tells Frank that he must protect the president's dignity as well as his life, reminding him that he did this for Kennedy: "What about the time Kennedy's girlfriend was caught in the White House, and you said she was with you?... You were suspended a month without pay...." That connection indicates Frank's personal investment in not "losing" another president, as does his response: "I was different.... Everything would be different right now too if I had been half as paranoid as I am today."

This last recriminatory statement gives insight into the demons that visit Frank in the dark. These are the demons of a man whose connection with the president he protected and lost was personal as well as professional, and this makes Kennedy's assassination doubly traumatic for Frank. The personal connection drives Frank to make sure he does everything in his power to prevent another presidential assassination: knowing that he might have been able to save another president and did nothing would risk a retraumatization from which Frank might not recover, according to the trauma work of Judith Herman, Bessel van der Kolk, and others.

At several points in *In the Line of Fire* Leary tells Frank how similar they are, and Frank resists, because Frank sees Leary as a murderous sociopath, not something with which Frank self-identifies. However, we witness Frank's sociopathy, disguised as professionalism. When Frank and his partner Al are working undercover gathering evidence against a counterfeiter, their target challenges Frank to put a gun to Al's head and pull the trigger—Frank does. The gun is unloaded, but Al does not know that, and we are unsure whether Frank knows it or not. Al is again threatened by the counterfeiters when they put a plastic bag over his head to suffocate him, and Frank again reacts coolly, asking for his gun back and shooting two of the men who are going to kill Al before pulling the bag off his partner's head and arresting the third man. Al's terrified responses in this scene are what one would expect in a life-or-death situation; Frank's are not. Although Frank's level-headed actions save them, the lack of affect that we see during this scene infers that Frank's professionalism requires a lack of affective reaction which is consistent with sociopathy. A similar lack of emotional response, despite the very different situation, occurs when Leary—described by his former boss as "more like a predator"—randomly shoots two hunters by a duck pond.

In contrast to Frank, Al is traumatized by a sequence of events with counterfeiters which fulfills DSM-5 Criterion A listed above. Three weeks later, Al reports to Frank that because of that day, he has nightmares, flashbacks, and impairment so severe that he is resigning from the Service. Each successive threat to his life, such as having a gun to his head when they are investigating Leary, retraumatizes Al. With each trauma, Al has a more difficult time recovering. The chances are high that, if he had survived to the end of the film, Al would have been suffering with diagnosable PTSD as, three weeks after the first threat to his life, his acute stress is not abating. Instead, he is experiencing ongoing trauma reactions, and he continues to encounter life-threatening situations which retraumatize him.

Trauma reactions such as dissociation, amnesia, and other PTSD symptoms are survival mechanisms, coping methods to keep the mind secure when it cannot process a terrible event, and Frank's lack of affect is likewise a survival technique. When a person faces death, that person is literally frightened out of his or her mind. Many who work with trauma and PTSD use the metaphor of being frozen (e.g., Herman, Levine, van der Kolk) to describe their patients who suffer from the aftereffects of traumatic events. In *In the*

Line of Fire, Frank is frozen, as indicated by his lack of emotional response. Al is not. When Al tearfully tells Frank that the last encounter with death "just clinched it," Frank looks askance as he says, "The service has counseling for that."

The way Frank delivers this response makes it seem that he has been trained to say this but has never experienced counseling himself. However, Al's tearful admission models for Frank an appropriate affective reaction, and the exchange between the agents preludes a series of stressful and traumatic events which occurs within a short period of time. These events create the perfect opportunity for Frank to unfreeze: First, Leary reveals the depth of his sociopathy: "Do you know how many times I've watched you go in and out of that apartment? You are alive because I have allowed you to live. SO YOU SHOW ME SOME GODDAM RESPECT." Second, while chasing Leary, Frank almost falls to his death, but Leary saves him, taunts Frank to shoot him as he is saving Frank, and third, after pulling Frank to safety, Leary immediately kills Al, Frank's partner and friend. Three traumatic events in quick succession will trigger an anxiety reaction. Following these events, Frank receives another taunting phone call from Leary which further heightens Frank's anxiety, as Leary questions whether Frank really did all he could do to save Kennedy and whether he has "the guts to take the bullet," echoing the private obsessive thoughts Frank has been harboring for 30 years. On the advance team for the current president, Frank is able to sublimate some of his anxiety from this series of traumas into his work; at the back of his mind, as he states, is the thought that he, and the rest of the agents, including Lilly (another person he cares about), could be killed in the crossfire of Leary's attempt to shoot the president. When Lilly tells Frank he has been pulled from the detail, he can no longer use his job as a way to avoid the impact of his recent traumatic experiences, and it appears that all his defenses have been breached.

Frank's monologue following Lilly's news that he must leave the team is an excellent portrayal of someone becoming unfrozen after three decades of PTSD. Healing begins, according to psychiatrist Judith Herman, "[o]ut of the frozen fragments of imagery and sensation, [when] patient and therapist slowly reassemble an organized, detailed, verbal account, oriented in time and historical context…. The recitation of facts without the accompanying emotions is a sterile exercise. As Breuer and Freud noted a century ago, 'recollection without affect almost invariably produces no result'" (177). Up to this point, Frank engages in the sterile exercise of reciting facts, about Kennedy's assassination, about his personal tragedies, and about his current series of traumatic experiences. With Al's death, he softens, but then he sublimates his anxiety by being overly authoritarian with the advance team and physically violent with a bellhop. When Lilly reminds Frank he is not fighting

Leary alone, she speaks to the PTSD criterion, which states that the sufferer feels alienated from others (DSM-5 Criterion D.6, 272). Lilly invites Frank to emerge from the alienated state to which he has become habituated. When Frank stands with Lilly, describing the day of the Kennedy shooting, he is finally recalling the incident with appropriate affective emotion, telling the story to someone he trusts. This is not the recitation of facts we have seen from Frank in previous scenes.

Frank also tells Lilly what Leary has said to push him to the edge of his coping mechanisms: "Leary questioned whether I had the guts to take that fatal bullet." As Frank lets his defenses—his security—fall away, Lilly wisely remains silent. He starts the monologue, giving an organized, verbal account, and the audience and Lilly see emotion that Frank likely has not ever allowed himself to display. He recalls the details of his experience, and he articulates all the second-guessing he has done in the three decades since Kennedy's assassination. Lilly's simple act, taking his hand at the end—no words—allows him to express sorrow and regret, and gives space for his tears, without offering a salve or trivializing what he has said. This is a scene in which a character who has been suffering from PTSD begins the healing process. Although Frank experiences several more life-and-death events before the film's conclusion, this scene provides the hope that he will continue the healing process, and it gives credibility to the implication that he and Lilly can have a healthy relationship.

From a clinical perspective, *In the Line of Fire* ends on an optimistic note. Frank and Lilly leave, literally closing the door on the posthumous message Leary has left on Frank's answering machine, saying the two of them—Leary and Frank—are destined to be alone. "What do you see when you're alone in the dark and the demons come" implies a solitariness from which no healing can occur, and it echoes a statement in *Absolute Power* that Luther Whitney makes to Walter Sullivan, with a very different effect: "When you're alone at night and the rage takes over … what face do you put with the enemy?"

Absolute Power

The first face we see in *Absolute Power* is frozen. The film opens with a hand raised in horror, leading to the frozen, wide-eyed stare of the monk, in a painting. The camera follows his gaze; the monk appears to be looking at a crucifixion. As already noted, crucifixions are traumatic, both for the crucified and those who witness it. In this case, the trauma imagery is redoubled: the painting is "St. Francis Receiving the Stigmata" by Domenikos Theotokopoulos ("El Greco"). The monk, St. Francis, is literally re-living the crucifixion and receiving the wounds of that trauma. Metaphorically, this is a depiction of the flashback and re-experiencing symptoms of PTSD: the crucified image is reflected in the monk's eye, and his wounds are fresh as he re-experiences the trauma.

Luther Whitney (Eastwood) is in a museum, copying the crucifixion scene. The serenity of the museum directly contrasts with both the scene Luther is copying and his activities later that night when he breaks into a highly-secured mansion, witnesses a murder, and becomes a marked man. Luther is obviously an experienced thief, and initially the robbery seems routine, despite a momentary adrenaline rush when he is waiting for his mini-computer to break the mansion's security code.

While in a fourth floor master bedroom vault, Luther is interrupted by the entry of a drunken man and a woman, Christy Sullivan, whose house Luther is robbing. He hides in the vault, which features a full-length two-way mirror, essentially trapping himself. The two-way mirror enables Luther to witness the activities that occur in the room.

While the suspense of the break-in and near-discovery cause momentary anxiety, they do not constitute traumatic events. The two prerequisites of psychological trauma, according to DSM-IV-TR, are "[first (A1), a] direct personal experience of an event that involves actual or threatened death or serious injury, or other threat to one's physical integrity; or witnessing an event that involves death, injury, or a threat to the physical integrity of another person; or learning about an unexpected or violent death, serious harm, or threat of death or injury experienced by a family member or other close associate.... The second prerequisite (A2) require[s] that the survivor must have experienced 'intense fear, helplessness, or horror'" (American Psychological Association, 2000, 463, 467). While DSM-5 has eliminated "intense fear, helplessness, or horror" as criteria, these descriptors are pertinent when watching the immediate reaction of Luther to the attempted rape and subsequent murder that he witnesses. This film sequence cuts between the scene Luther is witnessing and a close-up of his face which registers his affective reactions to that scene. Luther's fear of being discovered, his helplessness to do anything to assist the rape victim, and his shock and horror at watching her being shot, all serve to reinforce that Luther is experiencing a series of traumatic events.

Thus, initially being trapped in the vault to hide from the unexpected interruption does not qualify as a trauma, but once in the vault, Luther experiences a series of traumatic events that fulfill prerequisites A1 and A2 outlined by the DSM-IV-TR above: the sex becomes violent, the beginning of a rape, but Christy fights back, and Luther, watching helplessly, sees her stab her assailant once. Then she is on top of him, arms raised, holding a letter opener, poised to stab him again. The audience, from the would-be rapist's point of view, looks up at Christy, who has the upper hand in the altercation as shots ring out, and she falls, lifeless eyes wide open. A close-up of Luther's face shows his horror at the scene and then shock and surprise as two gunmen run into the room. The man's bodyguards, who, apparently, have been waiting outside the bedroom door, have killed Christy.

Both the attempted rape and the murder, which Luther watches with horrified helplessness, fulfill the DSM's initial criteria for trauma. Luther is still hiding in the vault when the man's assistant appears. She tells him she will "take care of everything," threatening one of the shooters, who wants to call the police, and telling both to cover up the murder, remove all fingerprints, and make it appear that Christy interrupted a robbery in progress. The shooters, who are also witnesses to a traumatic event, remain in the trauma environment for two hours, cleaning up the murder scene. Prolonged exposure to a traumatic event inhibits the mind's reregulating functions (van der Kolk), including the fight-or-flight response, which the shooters must stifle to complete their clean-up.

When, finally, the group leaves, they neglect to bring the plastic bag containing the letter opener which Christy used to stab the man. It has his and her blood and fingerprints on it. At their car, the assistant notices the letter opener is missing. They look up to see a curtain move in the fourth-floor window where they have left Christy's body. Luther, at the window, has picked up the bag containing the letter opener, and from the moment that the two gunmen and the assistant realize that someone has seen them, Luther experiences another series of traumatic events as he runs, literally, for his life: he must exit the fourth-floor bedroom window with his loot-filled backpack as the gunmen run up to the room to kill him; then he must continue running as he is being chased by the men, get to his car, remove the backpack, get in, and make his getaway. This chase scene alternates between the gunmen's point of view and the audience's third person point of view. From a trauma perspective, one can see that Luther is not the only one running for his life: the gunmen are also running for their lives—Luther's presence and possession of the evidence means that they can be accused of murder.

This chase scene must be contrasted with the shooters' original, self-exonerating statements immediately after the shooting. Both state, almost robotically, "No choice in the matter," which is odd, until we realize, two scenes later, that the gunmen are Secret Service agents, their boss is president of the United States, and, therefore, Luther is a marked man. In the initial scene, the two agents, Bill Burton (Scott Glenn) and Tim Collin (Dennis Haysbert) demonstrate signs of a dissociative subtype of PTSD, according to DSM-5. Dissociation is a direct psychological defense against overwhelming traumatic experiences. The robotic responses of Burton and Collin likely signal the onset of acute stress and can be read as dissociation, or detachment, from the horror they just witnessed, according to Pierre Janet, one of the earliest researchers of dissociation as a trauma response (van der Hart and Horst 8).

As discussed in detail below, the characters with the most discernable PTSD symptoms are the two Secret Service agents, although their symptoms cannot be traced to the shooting of Christy Sullivan because of the one-week time frame encompassed by the plot. The president, Alan Richmond (Gene Hackman), and his assistant, who turns out to be his chief of staff, Gloria Russell (Judy Davis), have been traumatized, though the chief of staff to a lesser extent, not having witnessed the death first-hand as the president, the agents, and Luther have. PTSD due to this shooting death will not be diagnosable for one month. Acute stress, the initial reaction to a trauma, is evident in the short-tempered, extreme reactions of the chief of staff and disconnected, self-serving responses of the president.

In contrast, Luther's playful banter with investigating homicide detective Seth Frank (Ed Harris) and Luther's relationships with his associates do not make him seem like someone with PTSD, even though Seth reports Luther is a decorated war veteran. The detective indicates that Luther was in combat and saw wartime death and experienced fear for his life that would precipitate a PTSD diagnosis. However, Luther, as Eastwood plays him, does not appear to be someone currently evidencing PTSD symptoms. In contrast to Luther's estranged daughter Kate (Laura Linney), whose demeanor is no-nonsense, unsmiling, and somewhat humorless, Luther is friendly, relaxed, and easygoing. In his several encounters with other people—an artist while sketching in the museum, his friend Red at the bar, Valerie the forger, and Detective Frank—Luther appears to make good personal connections. Kate implies that Luther also had a good relationship with his ex-wife, although she could not live with him. Kate says, "My mother loved him, all right?—Even after she left him—even when she was dying, she always talked about him…." Luther is careful, to the point of being wary, but he is not disconnected from people, least of all Kate—despite her claim of a lack connection with him.

Kate, a prosecutor, is a prime candidate for a PTSD diagnosis. In their first encounter in the film, Kate reminds Luther of the fact that when she was a child, he was never around because he was in prison: "you know what it's like being the only kid in show and tell who got to talk about visiting day?" According to psychiatrist and trauma expert Bessel van der Kolk, children who have been separated from one or both parents for a significant amount of time are traumatized by that separation (van der Kolk). From the photographs in Kate's apartment, she appears to be a workaholic, a loner, and someone who does not sustain lasting relationships. She reminds Luther, "We don't see each other anyway—we haven't seen each other since Mom died and that's a year…. You were never around for me. Fine. But I have no plans to be around for you." Kate also makes abundantly clear at several other points in the film that she does not have any connection with Luther. She tells Seth, "I'm simply not involved with my father, so this may not be a waste of time for you, but it sure is for me." Again, in another scene, she tells Seth, "I don't know the man—he was in jail when I was a kid, when he got out my mother and I went off to live by ourselves. We don't make contact...."

Although Kate's photographs and actions imply that she does not make contact with many people, William Goldman's screenplay does not describe Kate as a traumatized person. As directed by Eastwood, however, actor Laura Linney plays Kate as someone who clearly distances herself. During the first scene between Kate and Seth, Goldman's script reads, "Seth and Kate realize something: In a different world, under different circumstances, they'd probably be starting an affair" (74.186). Under Eastwood's direction, however, Kate keeps Seth at a distance just as she keeps Luther at a distance. There is no hint that Kate is attracted to Seth in their first encounter, and Seth's manner is purely professional with Kate. Moving away from Goldman's script, Eastwood portrays Kate as someone who has symptoms of ongoing trauma, including a negative world-view, alienation from others, and a constricted affect (DSM-5 Criteria D and E, 271–72). Part of this is the absence, in the first scene with Seth in Kate's office, of any hint of her contemplating an affair with him, a departure from Goldman's script. Even when Seth is flirting with her after he fails to capture Luther, Kate is unwilling to engage, relenting with a laugh only after Seth repeats, "I live alone" several times.

Once Seth leaves the apartment, Kate's first words to Luther are self-recriminating, and her affect is constricted. She says, "I betrayed you twice, Luther. You should know that." Kate's immediate concern is for Luther; she is not enamored of Seth, and when she realizes that Luther is in the apartment, Seth's momentary flirtation is forgotten. Kate cannot open her heart to anyone until she resolves her issues with Luther. The film tempts viewers to see Kate's hobby, running, as a visual indication of this first step, too. Kate's running could certainly count as a direct reference to the "flight" of the fight-or-flight reaction to trauma. In addition to the major trauma in the backstory—her father's absence due to incarceration—within the action of the film, Kate experiences three attempts on her life (the two snipers aiming for Luther almost shoot Kate, she is in a car that is pushed off a cliff by Secret Service agents, and an agent attempts to kill her in the hospital). Whether Kate will experience the flashbacks, interrupted sleep, and other symptoms of PTSD cannot be determined within the timeline of the film. However, in the character of Kate, the film depicts an adult's aftermath of childhood trauma due to an absent parent; Kate evidences PTSD symptoms in her adult life. Kate's alienation from others fulfills DSM-5 criteria for PTSD (272). She lives alone. She runs alone—many people run in pairs or groups to support each other and for the camaraderie. She is seated alone when Seth comes to question her at her law office, and she seems to have no significant relationships, other than with her mother before the latter died. Photographs of Kate in her apartment depict her by herself or with her mother. The image of Luther has been cut from the one photograph in which he was originally included, metaphorically and literally completing the mother-child dyad that Kate blames Luther for having created by his absence. This, too, is consistent with PTSD symptoms which, according to DSM-5, include persistent, distorted blame of self or others and persistent negative beliefs about the world (272). That Kate holds these beliefs is indicated by her words: "We don't see each other … he doesn't care about me…." In addition, in her most telling statement of her negative beliefs, she tells Luther: "It's dangerous outside."

As Eastwood portrays him, Luther is very much grounded, focused, and not dissociated, although Goldman's script indicates that "Luther always seems to glide" (88.246), which could be a somatic indication of dissociation. Additional symptoms of PTSD, according to DSM-5, include hypervigilance, exaggerated startle response, and problems with concentration (272). Luther displays none of these characteristics, even when he is in the Sullivan mansion, waiting for his computer to detect the security combination (which it does with only two seconds to spare), and later, during the rape and murder of Christy Sullivan. In fact, Luther's affective responses are appropriate for that situation, and he recovers quickly enough to run for his life, indicating that he neither dissociates nor derealizes, which is to say that he neither disconnects from his reality emotionally, as in the case of the former reaction, or in terms of his perception of his really being in this moment, in the latter; instead, Frank focuses on what he needs to do to survive.

Luther and Walter Sullivan (E.G. Marshall) are very much alike in this way. Walter is traumatized by the murder of his wife, but, like Luther, he is a survivor, not a victim. Walter takes the matter of avenging his wife's death into his own hands. First he hires a gunman to kill the suspected killer, Luther. Then, when he discovers the true identity of his wife's killer, he goes to the White House and personally stabs the man. Walter demonstrates an appropriate affect upon facing the traumatic event of his wife's murder. His eye-for-an-eye philosophy leads him to kill her murderer, but he makes clear that he does not take the action lightly. In fact, in the encounter with Luther acting as his chauffer near the end of *Absolute Power*, Walter's responses to the information about Christy's murder and the inevitable actions Walter must take clearly weigh on him. However, he takes the actions he deems necessary and proper, according to his world view. Walter's emotional responses to Luther in the limousine, as well as his parting words, "I really did love her, you know," are the words of a man who is heartbroken, but not dissociated: Walter, like Luther, is in full command of his mental state, grounded, and focused on the task at hand.

In contrast, the two Secret Service agents who actually kill Christy, Burton and Collin, reveal two ends of the spectrum of possible PTSD reactions. Both appear to be activated by the killing—though viewers cannot be sure whether they are, in fact, activated, or whether they are acting as usual. As noted above, the robotic, "No choice in the matter" about the shooting can be seen as dissociative. The statement's implied verb, "had," has no active subject, raising the question, who had no choice in the matter? "I" takes responsibility (*I* had no choice in the matter); "he" indicates a type of depersonalization, someone else, that other guy, shot her—and since only one bullet hit Christy, one could infer that each shooter believed that the other fired the lethal bullet.

As the story unfolds, however, it becomes clear that Agent Burton likely fired above Christy's head, a warning shot, while Agent Collin's aim is deadly. Agent Collin speaks ten times in the film. In addition to a couple of expletives, his lines, "I got him," "Then I kill him," and "Mercy," are interspersed with actions that show an agent with a deadly accurate aim and a murderous bloodlust. Collin evidences sociopathic enjoyment for the job of killing. He wants to be the one to assassinate Luther at the restaurant, and he pushes Kate's car over the cliff. Collin also impersonates a doctor to administer a lethal injection to Kate in the hospital. He would be the agent more likely to shoot to kill Christy.

Agent Burton also says, "No choice in the matter" when he sees that Christy is dead, but Burton wants to call the police, an action he later reports regretting not having taken. In contrast to Collin's sociopathy and his ability to run fast and shoot accurately, Burton is slower, more deliberate, more articulate, and he is enraged. He openly challenges Chief of Staff Russell on several occasions, at one point telling her, "Miss Russell, I should have called the police that night, but I was weak. You convinced me to stay silent. I regret that. Know this: every time I see your face, I want to rip your throat out." While this is said with no affect and no change of tone, Burton is clearly enraged. He is not speaking in metaphor, and Russell, obviously taken aback, initially responds with silence. Had Burton yelled or cursed, the rage might have been dissipated. The fact that he speaks clearly and quietly discloses his underlying emotions which frighten the usually prolix Russell into silence. While Burton does not exhibit the bloodlust of Collin, both men appear to be suffering from PTSD due to unknown prior traumas. Burton has been wounded "a few times," a good indication that he has experienced trauma.

As discussed above, both men react to the shooting of Christy Sullivan with no affective reaction. In addition, although not much background is given on Collin, his willingness to kill demonstrates either sociopathy (unlikely from the rigorous background checking required to become a Secret Service agent) or the recklessness and physical aggression toward people that fulfill DSM-5 Criterion E for PTSD (272). This, again, would be due to other traumas experienced prior to, but reactivated by, the killing of Christy Sullivan.

While the same clear arousal symptoms are not in evidence on the part of Burton, Eastwood as director provides two signs of Burton's probable PTSD. First, there is a shot of him, sitting alone at night in his apartment with a half-empty bottle of whiskey: this would fulfill DSM-5 Criterion E, self-destructive behavior and sleep disturbance (272). Second, and more telling, is Burton's suicide. Suicide has long been seen as a consequence of PTSD (see, e.g., Legaretta, et al., Davis, et al., Bakalar, et al.), a final PTSD symptom which admits no reparation. Burton's suicide, coupled with his remorse over the killing of Christy, his stated regret about not calling the authorities, and his compilation of evidence against the president before his death are all consistent with the man whose low-voiced rage at Russell culminates in his death by his own hand. Taken together, these aspects of Burton's character indicate a person who is suffering from PTSD.

Comparing the agents in *In the Line of Fire* to those in *Absolute Power*, *In the Line of Fire* agents Leary and Frank Horrigan have both witnessed traumatic events during their tenure at the CIA and Secret Service, respectively. Leary, a CIA assassin who was unable to readjust to civilian life, is a sociopath, like Secret Service Agent Collin in *Absolute Power*. Although one could argue that Frank displays moments of sociopathy, too, Frank is more like Burton in *Absolute Power*. Both agents have suffered with alcoholism, both have killed in the line of duty, and both have struggled, second-guessing actions taken on the job.

The difference between the president Burton protects and the one Frank protected might well be a determining factor in the different outcomes for the two agents. Frank's relationship with Kennedy was an entirely different experience than Burton's with Richmond. Frank was Kennedy's favorite agent. Richmond barely acknowledges Burton and taunts him about being wounded even after Burton puts himself at risk by covering up the President's indiscretions. Frank is affected—both professionally and personally—by Kennedy's assassination. The likelihood is that Burton would not have felt this way if he had lost Richmond as Frank lost Kennedy. This is because the relationship between Burton and Richmond lacks the same personal connection as the one Frank had with Kennedy, a relationship inferred by the reports of Frank's co-workers and Frank's own description of the assassination. Levine, Herman, van der Kolk and others have documented the aspects of relationship that heighten or ameliorate a traumatic experience. Comparing Agent Bill Burton to Agent Frank Horrigan, the outcome of Burton's PTSD is suicide; Horrigan's is a request to be reassigned to Presidential protection decades after the trauma.

The motivating factors that drive one agent to suicide and another to the possibility of recovery from PTSD are many, including the agent's background from childhood to adulthood, other relationships, and life experience. None of these things can be determined in the case of Bill Burton and Frank Horrigan; however, a comparison of the presidents to whom the agents are assigned provides some insight. Bill Burton successfully protects Alan Richmond, a philandering egotist (evidenced in part by the way he looks at himself in the two-way mirror before the murder and the way he uses Walter Sullivan to political advantage after the murder) who is willing to rape his benefactor's wife, in his benefactor's house, with the assumption of his personal bodyguards' silence. The interactions between Richmond and Burton are few; most of the orders and demands from the president come through the chief of staff. For the most part, Richmond does not seem to acknowledge Burton's presence, except when sneeringly asking whether Burton has ever been wounded, obviously expecting a reply in the negative. Burton's response, "Yes, sir. A few times," is not what the president wants to hear, and it is the first direct conversation we witness between the president and his bodyguard. The second interaction between Richmond and Burton comes in the same scene: Richmond apologizes, saying the incident was "a blip on the screen" and will not happen again. Subsequent to that perfunctory apology, Burton and Collin return to being part of the presidential background, seemingly non-entities to him.

Richmond expects continuing loyalty, protection (of his reputation as well as his life), and silence from Burton and Collin, who already have killed for him, broken the law by covering up the murder for him, and put their jobs and freedom on the line for him, even though he does not have a personal relationship with either. The demands are purely professional, expected without gratitude. This suits Collin, who derives pleasure from the license to kill. It has the opposite effect on Burton. The reality of Burton's life is captured in the image of Burton alone in his apartment and later by Burton dead at his desk.

Walter Sullivan, on the other hand, although traumatized by the murder of his wife, does not seem to suffer from PTSD. Luther provides new information about Christy's murderer during their limousine ride—about Richmond, Walter's protégé, the man to whom he "gave the presidency" who has betrayed him twice (an echo of Kate's statement to Luther after their truncated meeting in the plaza). The information shocks Walter, but it does not retraumatize him. Richmond has betrayed the man who trusted him and spent time building him up to be the most powerful man in the world, a man who Richmond publicly says is "like a father," though not actually his father. Conversely, in Kate's case, Luther, Kate's actual father, expected, or at least suspected, the betrayal in the plaza. Luther replays Kate's message because it is unique, a suggestion to a cautious man that something is amiss.

Although neither Walter nor Luther seem to suffer from the effects of PTSD, in the limousine, Luther asks Walter a question which is significant within the context of PTSD as it addresses many DSM-5 PTSD criteria, including intrusion symptoms, negative alteration in cognition, and marked alterations in arousal (272): "When you're alone at night, and your rage takes over, and you want to revenge her, what face do you put with your enemy?" This question could not be formulated by someone who is in the throes of PTSD because the symptoms do not allow for the type of focused, grounded introspection necessary to ask it. It might, however, come from a person who has experienced and recovered from PTSD. A skilled psychotherapist might ask this question of someone suffering with PTSD during the healing process. In the stress of a situation like the one in which Walter finds himself with Luther, a person with PTSD could not benefit from the question, much less give a coherent, useful response. Even in a calm moment, a person suffering with untreated PTSD, like Burton, would see his own face as the face of the enemy; conversely Collin would likely respond by seeing every enemy, real or imagined, that he ever faced. Walter reacts, first with appropriate affect, stating, "This is too terrible." Then calmly, knowing that Richmond is the enemy, Walter takes measured action.

In *Absolute Power*, a story premised on multiple traumas, the horrified, frozen eyes at the beginning become peacefully sleeping eyes at the end. Although the two Secret Service agents who suffer untreated PTSD do not survive, Luther and Kate "are going to be all right." Kate, likely suffering from PTSD, will be able to have a relationship with her father, and this opens the possibility for her to have a relationship with Seth, implying a healing. *In the Line of Fire* much more directly presents PTSD and its healing in Secret Service Agent Frank Horrigan, the character whose frozen affect melts to present the possibility of recovery, which, in turn, opens the possibility of Frank's relationship with Lilly.

* * *

In both his acting in *In the Line of Fire* and his directorial decisions in *Absolute Power*, Clint Eastwood offers his audience a reliable depiction of trauma and its effects, the possibility of recovery, and a measure by which healing can be gauged. *In the Line of Fire* explores the aftermath of PTSD symptoms 30 years removed from the triggering event. *Absolute Power* also depicts PTSD symptoms created by past events; however *Absolute Power* presents a more nuanced, multifaceted exploration of trauma while demonstrating the importance of meaningful relationships to help heal from the symptoms of PTSD.

WORKS CITED

Absolute Power. 1997. Directed by Clint Eastwood, performances by Clint Eastwood, Gene Hackman, and Ed Harris, Castle Rock Entertainment.

American Psychological Association. 2000. *Diagnostic and Statistical Manual of Mental Disorders. 4th ed. Revised.* Washington, D.C.: American Psychological Association.

American Psychological Association. 2013. Diagnostic and Statistical Manual of Mental Disorders. 5th ed. Washington, D.C.: American Psychological Association.

Bakalar, Jennifer L., et al. 2016. "Generalizability of Evidence-Based PTSD Psychotherapies to Suicidal Individuals: A Review of the Veterans Administration and Department of Defense Clinical Practice Guidelines." *Military Psychology.*

Davis, Margaret T., Tracy K. Witte, and Frank W. Weathers. 2014. "Posttraumatic Stress Disorder and Suicidal Ideation: The Role of Specific Symptoms Within the Framework of the Interpersonal-Psychological Theory of Suicide." *Psychological Trauma: Theory, Research, Practice, And Policy* 6.6: 610–618.

Goldman, William. 1996. *Absolute Power.* May. Unspecified Draft Script. Ret. 7/20/2016 from www. screenplaydb.com/film/scripts/absolutepower199605/. PDF file.

Herman, Judith. 1992. *Trauma and Recovery.* New York: Basic Books.

In the Line of Fire. 1993. Directed by Wolfgang Pederson, performances by Clint Eastwood, John Malkovich, and Rene Russo. Castle Rock/Columbia Pictures.

Legarreta, Margaret, et al. 2015. "DSM–5 Posttraumatic Stress Disorder Symptoms Associated with Suicide Behaviors in Veterans." *Psychological Trauma: Theory, Research, Practice, And Policy* 7.3: 277–285.

Levine, Peter. 1997. *Waking the Tiger.* Berkeley: North Atlantic Books.

Price, Stuart. 2005. "American Mentality? Trauma, Imperialism and the Authentic Veteran in Mainstream Hollywood Narrative." *Journal of Media Practice* 6:2: pp. 83–91.

van der Hart, Onno, and Rutger Horst. 1989. "The Dissociation Theory of Pierre Janet." *Journal of Traumatic Stress* 2:44.

van der Kolk, Bessel. 2016. *Intensive Trauma Treatment Course.* Lecture 1.2. Pesi, Inc.

Mourning and Melancholia
in *Blood Work*
and *Vanessa in the Garden*

FERNANDO GABRIEL PAGNONI BERNS
and CANELA AILÉN RODRIGUEZ FONTAO

Sigmund Freud (2006) describes mourning as a positive process that brings a sense of resolution to suffering. Melancholia, on the other hand, does the exact opposite: it refuses proper closure. From Freud's view, closure can only occur when subjects gain some distance from their loss. Freud argues that those suffering melancholia cannot find this distance. They remain trapped in a compulsive re-enactment of their trauma as they search for the beloved, lost object (19). Subjects leave melancholia when they let go of this object and begin to discover a new self. Despite their differences, both mourning and melancholia can live within the present-day descriptions of post-traumatic stress disorder (PTSD). Mourning might seem the least unnatural fit of the two if only because mourning involves a natural process of healing. Those in mourning will grieve, but their grief will subside. The difference, then, between those who might be typically identified as PTSD suffers and Freud's mourners is that the latter have come to terms with the psychological impact of a traumatic event through their mourning (Palmer 604).

Those who remain attached to their loss fail to negotiate their mourning. They suffer from melancholia. Emma Hutchison (2016) describes melancholia as a "state of 'complicated' or 'frozen' grief" (231). Subjects are unable to finish their process of grief and, thereby, never experience "genuine healing" (*ibid.*). In melancholia, the patient is caught in a fixed state of perpetual grief. The wound remains open. Elizabeth Krause, Ruth DeRosa, and Susan Roth (2002) claim that men often experience the debilitating effects Hutchison describes,

84

and they do so for socially constructed reasons. Many male survivors of trauma experience the powerlessness and vulnerability of post-trauma "as a loss of their right to manhood" (Krause, DeRosa and Roth, 361). Such men feel weak, vulnerable, and emasculated. They are overwhelmed by a "loss of power, control, identity, selfhood, confidence, and independence" (362). Stripped of these "essential" qualities, these men struggle to exert self-assertion, aggression, competitiveness, strength and bravado, all character-istics socially associated with masculinity. The traumatized man, then, as the traumatized woman, cannot enact these traits. They struggle to see themselves as "manly." Brenda Boyle (2013) emphatically argues that men with disabilities such as PTSD are left to "negotiate or reformulate the standards of hegemonic masculinity" (113). Their wounded masculinity becomes a catalyst for the same kind of process Freud described in his discussions of mourning and melancholia.

The present essay reads two Clint Eastwood's films—*Blood Work* (2002) and *Vanessa in the Garden* (1985)—from the perspective of melancholia and mourning, at least as these two states exist within contemporary forms of PTSD as they arise from a wounded masculinity. Both films focus on male characters in the midst of trauma, and, more importantly, in the midst of a need to renegotiate the qualities of traditional masculinity. These negotiations are worthy of attention on their own. Masculinity is often taken as a recurrent trope in Clint Eastwood's oeuvre. Abby Graves (2016) considers Eastwood's characters and the actor/director's persona as an icon served as an image "of what true American masculinity means" (132). Drucilla Cornell (2009) offers a similar if not more nuanced description of masculinity in Eastwood's films. For Cornell, the typical male in an Eastwood film exists as the image of "remorseless masculinity," the phallic power par excellence (2). In his famous Westerns, the director privileges the paradigm of hypermasculinity, and East-wood revisits this paradigm with regularity. From Cornell's view, Eastwood molds his career around these reconsiderations of masculinity. John Foote (2009) agrees, offering, "Eastwood has quietly advanced a revisionist notion of masculinity" (138). This engagement with artistic representations of mas-culinities has been accelerated in the new millennium due to a crisis of mas-culinity that featured heavily in popular and critical forums in the 1990s and 2000s. As Donna Peberdy (2011) notes, this crisis creates a context where "definitions of maleness were contested, renegotiated, or simply made visible" (5). It seems logical to expect a director so preoccupied with masculinities and its artistic depictions to venture into contemporary trends of placing manhood under the microscope. The potential surprise is the extent to which Eastwood relies on trauma to force this negotiation.

Those who know the bulk of Eastwood's films might not be as surprised as those who come to the famed director for particular films. Eastwood's first film, in fact, the horror-thriller *Play Misty for Me* (1971), marks the actor and director's commitment to serious studies about the loss of masculinity as a traumatic event. Eastwood puts the central character of *Misty*, Dave (Clint Eastwood), through a transformation, one that moves the hero from "tomcat to loyal heroic boyfriend" through a "rape" (Carlson 39). Neither Eastwood's renegotiation of masculinity, nor his use of trauma to spark that reconsideration, are as sharp in *Misty* as they will be in later films. The two films that comprise the focus of this essay illustrate this point. In *Blood Work*, Eastwood has hard-working detective, Terry McCaleb (Clint Eastwood), suffer a massive heart attack that forces him into an early retirement. Terry receives a new heart. It appears that a healthy recovery is imminent, but the story shifts focus when a woman, Graciella (Wanda De Jesus), pays Terry a visit in the hospital. Graciella explains to Terry that her sister, Terry's donor, was murdered. She asks the famed detective to help her identify her sister's killer. One could argue that this request is little more than a plot point, one that provides space for Terry's story to explore the most common responses fond in posttransplant populations, which includes PTSD and other adjustment disorders. Statistics show, after all that between 13 percent and 16 percent of people with heart transplants meet criteria for PTSD (see Fogel and Greenberg, 2015, 1446, and Friedman, 2011, 541). Eastwood has his main character face these anxieties, but he makes it clear that the heart transplant is not the only reason for his suffering. Terry's need to renegotiate his own masculinity provides another.

One can make sense of Terry's renegotiation by looking only his story, but the extent to which he evolves clarifies most fully when his story is set against the story of Byron Sullivan (Harvey Keitel) as it is presented in *Vanessa in the Garden*—an episode for the TV series *Amazing Stories* directed almost two full decades before *Blood Work*. While *Blood Work* allows its hero to move through its grief in such a way that it can be set within the boundaries of mourning, *Vanessa* leaves its hero within the limits of melancholia. Byron's wife dies in a carriage wreck. The grief-stricken husband finds that he is capable of materially (and supernaturally) bringing his lost wife back to life through his art. This ability is a negative effect, though, in that it keeps Byron in his grief. Byron's ability leaves him unable to relinquish his love for his wife. His love for his wife, if not his very being, is preserved and re-absorbed within his ego and plays on indefinitely in an internalized (and essentially narcissistic) romance (Bates 145). In other words, Byron is unable to move from melancholia to mourning. Taken together, then, *Vanessa in the Garden* demonstrates the threat of grief as it relates to melancholia, while *Blood Work* establishes the more positive possibility of moving past grief and into mourning. In this way, the two films together demonstrate Eastwood's clear command of both *melancholia* and *mourning*, and his willingness to locate both negotiations in an engagement with traditional masculinity and PTSD. They also serve as examples of PTSD and living beyond PTSD. This essay will turn to a fuller look at each film, but only after a more thorough account of the critical terms being applied to these films is provided.

There is good reason to link discussions of trauma, PTSD, mourning and melancholia. One finds a precedent for such linkage in Sigmund Freud, who "grappled extensively with the concept of PTSD (i.e., traumatic neurosis) from 1895 to 1920" (Wilson 4). Freud attempted to help his patients uncover repressed aspects of their trauma by examining their subconscious (Krippner, Pitchford and Davies 105). The goal was to identify both causes and solutions about why some people fixate on their trauma and others do not. Freud's analysis might be taken as an early etiology of trauma, anxieties and PTSD. Freud's famous essay "Mourning and Melancholy," in fact, worked to shed a "light on the nature of melancholia by comparing it with the *normal* affect of mourning" (Freud 267, emphasis mine). In these lines, Freud establishes the central difference between mourning, as a normal response to loss, and melancholia, as a form of mental illness. For Freud, the latter worked as a kind of hysteria. More presently, scholars might refer to Freud's view of melancholia as a type of PTSD.

In truth, Freud's account of melancholia and mourning might both relate to contemporary views of PTSD if only because both states arise at the loss of something beloved. Mourning reacts to a loss of a loved person, or at least to the loss of "*some abstraction*," which can take the place of a person (*ibid.*). It is interesting to note that Freud points to the fact that mourning is not entirely produced by the loss of a person, but some abstraction. Some likely substitutes include things like country, liberty, an ideal, and so on (*ibid.*). This allowance creates space for the loss of socially constructed realities, things like masculinity, to serve as triggers for trauma. The loss of a human being or some abstraction can go one of two directions, toward mourning or melancholia. The difference between the two states lies in the pathological condition melancholia tolerates.

Freud views mourning as the more natural of the two. Mourners do not require medical treatment to see their response fade. Freud even claims that people can conduct a normal life even if under the stress of grief when they are "merely" mourning. At some point, the suffering person will be able to resume his or her normal life. Those who enter melancholia, on the other hand, experience a "profoundly painful depression, a loss of interest in the outside world, the loss of the ability to love, the inhibition of any kind of performance," and a general sense of depression of the Self (*ibid.*). Freud quickly recognizes that the same traits can be found in mourning, with the important exception of the absence in mourning of the disturbance of the self-regard, understood as self-hatred and feelings of unworthiness. In mourning, the beloved object (a material thing, such as a person, or an abstraction, such as the loss of the sense of nationhood in an immigrant) does not exist anymore. All libido previously attached to that object must be withdrawn from it. At first, the task seems to be too demanding, and the person experiences attachment to the lost object, and the person refuses to let go. However, eventually, the subject finds acceptance and begins to resume his or her common life. The loss is accepted. The ego is preserved. The subject breaks from the lost object (Freud 268). But grievers do not simply detach libido from the lost object. According to Freud, they reinvest the freed libido in a new object, and, in so doing they accept consolation in the form of a substitute for what has been lost. The work of mourning comes to a decisive closure.

The melancholic state, in turn, displays something that is lacking in mourning. The melancholic exhibits a libido that completely identifies with the lost object. So, the loss of an object can equate to the loss of the self. Stated another way, object-loss is a kind of ego-loss. The ego is diminished on a grand scale. The patient reproaches himself, vilifies himself to the point that he begins to feel unworthy. The subject might even develop a feeling of rage or anger toward the object that has been lost. Those who go through this second loss suffer melancholia. They cannot properly continue their daily life. They have, given an earlier surrender to some object, lost their ego and their sense of Self with the loss of a loved one or ideal (Freud 270). Persons in this state become trapped in the very kind of narcissistic cycle audiences see in Eastwood's *Vanessa in the Garden*. One additional explanation is in order, though, before the trauma in that film can be properly represented.

The majority of early studies dedicated to the most obvious problems that develop following traumatic exposure have focused on physical aspects and experiences (rape, war, amputation, etc.). The danger is that exclusive emphasis on physicality may result in other forms of post-traumatic distress not being adequately addressed. For example, Litz and Maguen (2007) claim, "survivors of disasters and other large-scale traumatic events may be mourning the death of a close friend or relative, on top of experiencing anxiety symptoms associated with the immediate trauma" (315). In other words, the traumatic experience of loss can be understood in terms of mourning. Of course, not every process of mourning necessarily involves PTSD. Researchers often ask whether people who experienced stressful events—things like a divorce, the loss of economic incomes, serious surgical intervention or the natural death of a loved one—would also develop PTSD. Some have found that "few people developed PTSD unless they had experienced an extremely stressful life event" (Friedman, Keane and Resick 5). Thus, what connects mourning and PTSD is not just the presence of trauma, but some *persistence and intensity* of that trauma. If a trauma continues for too long, it will result in melancholia. The trauma will remain unresolved.

This insight challenges scholars to reconsider what constitutes trauma and what does not. The American Psychiatric Association defines trauma as "recognizable stressor that would evoke significant symptoms of distress in almost anyone" (American Psychiatric Association 238). One would not be surprised to see the death and the disappearance of a beloved human being or an abstract idea as sources of anxieties and distress in most people. With regard to the stressor itself, academics note that the stressor may be an overwhelming traumatic experience involving serious threat to the security or physical integrity of the individual or of a loved one, or an unusually sudden and threatening change in the social position and/or network of the individual (Joseph, Williams and Yule 16). This essay contends that the sudden loss of some sense of manhood could be read as a form of trauma. In other words, a loss of masculinity could be as traumatic as any other loss, and *Vanessa in the Garden* and *Blood Work* show this, and they show the two ways in which this trauma can go. The former film settles in melancholia; the latter moves through mourning. This difference is most interesting given that the stressor in both films is the loss of something beloved, health in the former, and a wife in the latter, and that both films place their characters in a crisis of masculinity. Set in this light, these two films show Eastwood's evolving thoughts in masculinity, trauma, and, how to move through PTSD.

Vanessa in the Garden is episode 12 of the first season of the series, *Amazing Stories*, produced by Steven Spielberg. It can be argued that the story was commissioned to Eastwood rather than something that was a kind of "love-project." However, it is certain that the episode, even given its brevity, tackles some issues strongly linked with ideas spread throughout Clint Eastwood's career. Masculinity and PTSD are two such ideas. The episode frames its story around the trauma that arises when the main character, Byron, loses his wife. Interestingly, the film refuses a sense of closure for the suffering man, which leaves this character in the midst of melancholia when the episode ends. One can point to a number of reasons for this ending. For one thing, *Vanessa in the Garden* is one of the rare films in which Eastwood adopts a historical frame rather than contemporaneity. The temporal setting could be interpreted as late 19th or early 20th century, a perfect historical frame for melancholia since it is the time in which Freud wrote his essay on melancholia and established with rigor its theoretical formulation. The turn-of-the-century setting foregrounds modernity, a historical time inextricably linked to the sense of melancholia. Dan Blazer (2005) contends, "the engine of modernity disrupts the sense of place and time for people," and expects closed, well-formed gender identities (142). These issues work as sources of anxieties rather than securities. Jean-Francois Lyotard (1984) further claims that the modernist aesthetics constitute a discourse of melancholy: it fails to successfully mourn the metanarratives of emancipation so dear to modernism

(81). The crisis of modernity and its goal of social progress mark an inexorable trauma in the social fabric, the betterment promised by social progress refuses to come while melancholia slips within the general frame of mind (Moglen, 2007, xiv). Eastwood's choice to set *Vanessa in the Garden* in this context raises each of the political questions mentioned in these authors, if only for the critic aware of them. That said, the story itself seems most especially given to the struggles these authors describe, and the emergence of depression as a primary disorder (Mahendra 14).

Byron's existence as an impressionistic painter would also locate *Vanessa* in the above concerns. Impressionism reproduces reality to that which can be seen by the senses. The interpretation of forms shifts from mimetic depictions of reality to "impressions" of it. Impressionism still involves mimesis, but it does so through convincing illusions. In this way, Byron's artistic technique, doomed to disappear with the emergence of photography, materially "fixated" things through the painter's subjectivity. The recurring subject of Byron's painting, Vanessa in the garden, fixated to canvas, also suggests a trapped character. Eastwood's choice of shots even emphasizes this aspect of impressionism. Most of the episode is filmed through general shots to increase the pictorial sensation of throwing open a "window to the world" (Mirzoeff 101). In this way, the cinematography serves as a kind of entanglement in time, which further serves the idea that this episode works as a demonstration of melancholia.

The episode begins with the idea of "fixity" as permanence of a more durable presence and/or the presence of an absence "or corpse" (Marin 253). Byron and his wife, Vanessa (Sondra Locke), are in the garden of the house they share. She models for him as he paints her. Vanessa complains of an itch even while she acknowledges that she cannot move or she will ruin her pose, without disrupting her sense of "fixity." Byron dismisses his wife's physical senses. He urges his model "not to think of it." Even this small detail suggests some hints of power plays and repression within the marriage. Byron suggests that his wife think on "something else" to forget her itch. She quickly, and rather dryly, retorts, "What shall I think then? You tell me." This brief exchange of words points to some unresolved issues related to the status of the wife within the marriage. She is asking her husband to think for her, which is somewhat ironic given his later inability to stop thinking of her. This early exchange, though, hints that Byron's thoughts of his wife are really thoughts of himself. She cannot move because it will disrupt her pose for him. Her pose will become his legacy. Vanessa has, in this way, become her husband in a most unhealthy way.

The narrative seemingly defuses the depths the couple has fallen by returning to a more jovial time in the couple's relationship. The story moves to the couple's honeymoon from just one year earlier. This memory certainly establishes some sense of deep love between the two. The hints of power play fall below the surface. The script even tries to place Vanessa in a more prominent position than she held in the earlier scene. Byron and his agent (Lloyd Bridges) mention that the painter's productivity has greatly increased since he has married Vanessa. The wife's influence over her husband is clearly registered. Byron makes explicit this point: "None of this good fortune could ever have happened without you. If there is any merit in my work it is because of you." The statement is delivered in such a way that Vanessa's authority begins to cast shadows upon Byron's manliness. The husband seems to develop most properly only under the wife's influence. His only response is his ability to possess his muse of sorts through his paintings.

Immediately after establishing Vanessa's power upon Byron's work, the script has Vanessa die, and, partly, by Byron's hand after he fails to calm the horses pulling his horse drawn carriage. Byron suffers an unmistakable amount of survivor's guilt. He is unable to battle his pain. Unable to endure "her gaze," Byron burns all of the paintings he has of his wife. The act shows the extent to which Byron is unable to shift his sense of self, his libido, onto another object. His life falls into misery and self-destruction as a result. He struggles to continue his life. His sense of melancholia becomes a kind of PTSD. His loss emasculates him. His only source of "power," his artistic abilities, is missing. Byron can no longer paint. Vanessa takes that ability "with her." Byron's lack of strength to get to work metamorphosizes his impotence as a man. Now that the woman who was the real impulse behind his success is no more, he has been emasculated. Living among his paintings becomes a source of stress. He attempts to alleviate his grief by burning to ashes all his work and drowning himself in alcohol. But rather than an overcoming of the past, these actions only reveal the extent to which he is not engaging his sense of trauma and loss. There is no new object on which he can direct his libido. Byron's doctor recognizes this and determines that the only solution is for the once famed painter to spend time in a sanitarium. His masculinity has been completely stripped from him. The painter suffers a kind of feminization, since the Freudian notion of melancholia renders itself as a characteristically female condition (Pehkoranta 264).

In "Mourning and Melancholy," Freud casts the kinds of reproaches Byron exhibits as a means to mask the reality of a lost relationship between patient and object. This idea pushes for a more nuanced reading of Eastwood's *Vanessa in the Garden*, one that considers Byron as a sufferer of melancholia even when the film ends. The artist remains trapped in a relationship with his deceased wife. The uncanny solution offered by the tale is that Byron can acquire a new power that hyper-masculinizes him even if that means that the painter remains trapped in the past, unable to transcend his loss. Byron starts to paint his wife in different situations and attitudes. Soon enough, after the painting is done, she appears, albeit briefly, to fulfill the dictates of the painting. If Vanessa is painted in the garden, she appears there, as she appears playing piano if Byron paints her doing so. She does whatever he wants her to do and the dynamics of the power play are forever changed.

This magical solution creates two problems. First, Vanessa looks slightly "zombified" in her uncanny apparitions. She does not smile and her gaze seems out of focus. She looks more like a prisoner than a woman coming back for love. It is clear that the being returning is not the woman in the early scenes. She is a being possessed. Second, the story never truly explains the uncanny events nor Byron's new abilities to bring his wife from the dead. Thus, it can be inferred that all of Vanessa's apparitions are, in fact, only mental manifestations, hallucinations of a mind under heavy trauma and stress. This interpretation is reinforced by the fact that no one else ever sees or hears Vanessa. She is invisible to everyone but Byron. This detail might most appropriately be billed as some satisfaction of the expectation for hallucinatory experience anchored in trauma found in extreme cases of PTSD (Wilson 21).

This uncanny ability "man-ups" Byron's previously downplayed masculinity. The story ends with him presenting his paintings in Paris, gaining critical acclaim and economic success. He is depicted wearing rich clothes. The phantasmatical Vanessa stands at his side. The wife will now stay with him forever. If Vanessa—when living—could be read as a menace to masculinity, the real substance of Byron's art, now she has been objectified, turned into a slave of Byron's imagination, a mimetic but still subjective mental "impression." It is of little importance if Vanessa is a ghost or a mental projection enhanced by trauma. The end is the same: Byron has become something of a popular sensation. The painter has regained his status as an artist even if he has wholly objectified his wife not only for himself, but for all of those who see her in his paintings as well. In this way, Byron is left to re-experience his trauma over and over again. He cannot move beyond it. He is hyper-masculinized and left to suffer in his melancholia. The two conditions seem to inform one another, in fact. Byron is trapped in his past unable to redirect his identity in a new way. As such, there is no clear sense of closure. All of his success depends on a re-creation of the past, rather than on the beginning of a new life.

Set in this context, *Blood Work* works as a kind of correction to Byron's error. A self-reflexive elegy to the past as such, the film is one of Eastwood's first steps into a recurring interest in the politics of ageing, a topic that will reappear in films like *Million Dollar Baby* (2004) or *Gran Torino* (2008). *Blood Work* differs from these other films in a fundamental way by reflecting on a series of deaths rather than just a physical death. *Blood Work* takes an interest in the death of its characters, the death of a body's ability to function, the death of a certain form of masculinity, of a star persona, and of the trauma that all this death can prompt. One might expect so many deaths to over-whelm the narrative, but none of these deaths remain dead. Eastwood allows them to gain a new life, which is to say to move from melancholia to mourn-ing and recovery. The boundaries each death marks are crossed only after Terry makes a conscious choice to let go of the past and to evolve into a new person. In this way, the film can ultimately be about dealing with pain and continuing to live the best life possible. And here, living the best possible life comes through one's ability to negotiate not only one's demise, but decaying forms of masculinity as well. Eastwood uses the heart transplant as a way to move through both degenerations. After a period of mourning the forms of traditional masculinity, Terry ultimately accepts the limitations of his body and the possibilities of a world that is not androcentric. In this way, Terry becomes a site for Eastwood to reflect on the changes of the body and of a society, and allows these reflections to result in recovery from what might cause an open wound if not addressed properly.

As mentioned earlier, Freud states in "Mourning and Melancholy" that mourning is a mental state that accompanies more than just the loss of a human being. Following this central idea, *Blood Work* can be shown to build its narrative on two senses of loss: the loss of the body vis-à-vis the heart transplant (deeply linked with the symbols of life) and the loss of identity vis-à-vis a shift in persona, specifically as it relates to masculinity. The film's opening plays on both aspects. The first shots enthrone Terry as the alpha male. The senior detective arrives at a crime scene. All of the other male cops admit that any success they achieve will be given to Terry: "whatever hap-pens," one man says, "it'll be his face on the front page." The narrative estab-lishes Terry's status as "The Man," at least within the homicide department. The next shot shows Eastwood climbing out of his car and taking off his glasses while the camera pans across his face. The shot establishes him as the person that everyone is discussing. In this way, Eastwood (the director) uses his camera to underline the hypermasculinity of Eastwood (the actor). This opening is important in the story *Blood Work* tells because it reveals the extent to which Terry's masculinity gets tested when the detective undergoes a period of severe stress due to his health problems.

Nothing underlies the hyper masculinity that marks Terry at the begin-ning more than the film than the fact that the killer is murdering innocents to grab the detective's attention. All the murders take place because someone is obsessed with Terry. Even the journalists waiting outside the crime scene recognize this fact. They note the way the murderer has turned the detective into a TV star. The other cops express a similar sentiment, referring to the messages sketched in blood upon the walls of the crime scene as "love notes" made by the killer to Terry. Of course, Terry's inability to solve these crimes undermines some of what the opening shots try to establish. Terry remains in the news so to speak only as long as the killer remains on the loose. In this way, the detective's ineffectiveness becomes the reason he is exalted as he is.

Eastwood—the director—slowly expounds on this crack in Terry's celebrity-status and suggests the extent to which this crack will become a kind of emasculation. Terry observes the killer hiding near a crime scene. He chases the wanted man through the streets, only to collapse from a heart attack before he can catch him. This physical failure marks the end of Terry's hypermasculinity and the beginning of his period of grief and trauma. In this sense, it is interesting to contrast the first scenes with those that appear later. The first scene after the heart attack shows Terry during a medical checkup. He exhibits a clearly compromised (hegemonic) masculinity. He acts fragile and thus, emasculated. The term emasculation refers to a symbolic act of castration, the removal of the phallus symbolizing the denial of the fixity of the qualities of traditional masculinity. Those who cannot exhibit the traditional notions of manhood (things like the already mentioned characteristics of aggressiveness or competitiveness) cannot be billed manly. Moreover, the "emasculated" man often finds himself placed under the label of feminine, queer, or deviant, some term that means to suggest he is "less-than-a-man."

The transplant emasculates Terry, turns him into a vulnerable man, a man dependent on medical check-ups. Eastwood's costuming emphasizes this point. Terry lies in a bed, scantly covered by a paper robe, his body attached to serum, his voice crackling when speaking. He is now the opposite of the hypermasculine figure of the early scenes. Still, his previous persona has been undermined by more than just his new status as a man recuperating from a serious heart stroke. His new life implies a new involvement with women and the feminine world. If in the previous scene he was depicted as the "Man" among a world of men, from now on, he will engage mostly with women. His personal doctor is a woman, Dr. Bonnie Fox (Angelica Houston). A woman occupies his former place in the police department. And it is a woman that brings him out of retirement. The most important woman in the story, though, might be the woman who gave Terry his heart, Graciella's sister, Gloria (Maria Quiban). This last detail is particularly important as it means that the once hyper-masculine man now literally has a female organ inside body. A return to his previous status is now completely impossible.

At the same time, the homicides appeared to have stopped the moment Terry stopped working the crimes. Terry's fame and star persona begin to fade as a result. His physical status does not help on this point either. Terry's frailty and delicate state push aside any possibility of strong displays of hyper-virility if understood as aggressiveness and proclivity to violence. Eastwood marks Terry in this way through his performance of that character as well.

Terry routinely touches his chest, which can only remind audiences that he is a man recovering from traumatic surgical intervention. The script replaces the macho man of the previous scene with a new man now chatting with his female doctor about diarrhea and fixated on his wound. At least initially, the traumatic experience has emasculated Terry, which results in an unmistakable mourning of his previous active life and (hegemonic) masculinity. His need to become a new man becomes a new source of anxiety and stress.

Surprisingly, Terry appears to deal with each of these setbacks quite well. One could attribute this early success to some meaningful period of mourning that allows him to give closure to events that might have otherwise derailed his life. Unlike most of the cinematic retired detectives, Terry is not obsessed with his earlier suspect. There are neither walls covered in newspaper reports nor files staked in Terry's house. He is living a happily retired life, thanks in part to his capacity to put things behind him. This sense of a new life continues even after Graciella visits McCaleb to ask that he find Gloria's murderer. Terry initially rejects her request, which on the surface would seem to further underscore how comfortable he has become in his new life. He is no longer interested in solving crimes. A series of signs of PTSD push the audience to search for another explanation, though. To begin with, the script inserts anxiety-ridden nightmares that have Terry get shot in the chest. The pain in the dreams parallels his constant gesture of rubbing his chest, which signals that his recuperation is not complete and reveals that otherwise unresolved issues related to PTSD remain under the surface. Further, the nightmare is filmed on black-and-white reversal or black-and-white negative, thus highlighting its quality and function of a "reverse" of the purely exterior. Terry also expresses to his doctor the feeling that he does not deserve his heart while little children are on the brink of death because there are no donors. Dr. Fox dismisses these worries as "B.S.," but Eastwood ensures that his audiences do not miss these representations or dismiss them too quickly. These details align Terry with those who suffer from survivor's guilt (Sadock 259). Terry's initial refusal to grant Graciella's request, at least when set against these other aspects indicate the extent to which Terry is paralyzed by his new status immediately after the heart transplant. His eventual decision to help Graciella distinguishes him from Byron in *Vanessa in the Garden*. It also gives Terry the chance to erase his feelings as an undeserving recipient of his transplant if he can capture this donor's killer.

It is extremely important to note the extent to which Terry refuses to return to his hyper-masculine persona even if he does return to investigative work. Graciella's presence ensures that he cannot continue in his lone-wolf role, but this is just one of the ways Terry refuses his earlier identity. The fact that a woman provides Terry his heart, and a *Latina* woman at that, quite literally frustrates his "all-man" body. As a Western heterosexual white man,

Terry belongs to the fictions of the Universal subject depicted as the measurement of all things considered as "normal." The placement of a Latino, female organ in his body frustrates his status as the Universal hegemony. It turns Terry into a "symptom," to use Slavoj Žižek's (1999) words for it, an outsider from the Universal fiction (224).

Terry's inability to fight further distances the character from the fiction he occupied earlier in the story. He is quite clearly no longer the famed detective. The script makes this point as explicitly as it can by having Terry be woefully over matched in the one fight in the film that occurs after his transplant. The detective faces his towering enemy, Mikhail Bolotov (Igor Jijikine), but he cannot connect any punches. In a matter of mere seconds, Terry's adversary has thrown him on the couch, and reduced him to a series of defensive postures. Terry can do nothing more than raise his arms to protect his body from the blows of his enemy. His face conveys a clear sense of fear. The detective that previously used his hands to hit criminals or climb fences now uses his hands as protection of his fragile body. The revelation that the killer, Jasper "Buddy" Noone (Jeff Daniels), that earlier tempted Terry with "love-notes" was a male further alters how the audience sees the detective. If nothing else, the killer's obsession with Terry places the once proud detective in a queer frame. Running parallel with his emasculation, he has been turned into an object of desire for other men.

The most interesting prompt for Terry's reassessment occurs when the script surrounds Terry with women—Latin and Afro-American women, to be exact. Somewhat surprisingly, Terry seems unbothered by this shift. He accepts this world of dominant women, rather than being trapped in some stage of traditional politics of manhood. His willingness to accept the care of his female doctor is but one example of this acceptance. The ease with which Terry makes this shift marks his passage from a man of action to a man in retirement. It also marks a clear point of distinction between melancholia and mourning. Terry mourns his lose of virility and his ongoing dependence on medicines for a time, but he also battles through these shifts and comes to accept these new realities. This is especially the case after he catches the killer and resolves his doubts about his worthiness as a transplanted man.

Blood Work's script would seem to return to where it started when it reveals that Gloria was killed so that Terry could have her heart. The killer knows Terry needs a heart and he sacrifices Gloria to deliver it. This detail tempts the audience to organize the story around Terry. One could contend that everything happens in this story because of him. But an over insistence on this point misses the importance of Terry's response to this fact. Terry does not allow the story to revolve around him as much as he learns to operate within other people's world, and a feminine world on top of that. In this way,

Eastwood refuses to settle his story by simply settling Terry's tale. The sense of hypermasculinity that marks the beginning of *Blood Work*, and the whole of *Vanessa in the Garden*, must be left in the past. Some passage to a new, non-hegemonic masculinity must be paved. This passage will travel the same course that marks the end of PTSD, an end that occurs when melancholia gives way to mourning. In Terry's case, this shift occurs when matters of hypermasculinity are set aside so that a new kind of masculinity can emerge, one that fits comfortably alongside feminism. The realms of feminine and masculine can coexist in the diegesis of *Blood Work*. This synchronicity emerges as earlier traumas are overcome and some new sense of self begins to emerge. In *Blood Work*, this new self emerges most explicitly when Terry defines himself as "Mexican" because of his heart. His sense of unworthiness has been erased. The only item casting shadows in his recuperation and the only signpost of PTSD and anxiety has been resolved. Thus, the film can end with Terry returning to his retirement, now in the company of Graciella as his girlfriend and Gloria's son as part of his family. The Terry in the final image no longer needs to rub his chest. He has earned his heart by making the shift Byron was unable to make.

WORKS CITED

American Psychiatric Association. 1980. *Diagnostic and Statistical Manual of Mental Disorders*, 3rd ed. Washington, D.C.: American Psychiatric Association.

Bates, Catherine. 2007. *Masculinity, Gender and Identity in the English Renaissance Lyric*. Cambridge: Cambridge University Press.

Blazer, Dan. 2005. *The Age of Melancholy: Major Depression and Its Social Origins*. London: Routledge.

Blood Work. 2002. Directed by Clint Eastwood, performances by Clint Eastwood, Jeff Daniels, and Anjelica Huston, Malpaso Productions and Warner Bros.

Boyle, Brenda. 2009. *Masculinity in Vietnam War Narratives: A Critical Study of Fiction, Films and Nonfiction Writings*. Jefferson, NC: McFarland.

_____. 2013. "Phantom Pains: Disability, Masculinity and the Normal in Vietnam War Representations." In *Disability and/in Prose*, edited by Brenda Jo Brueggemann and Marian E. Lupo. London: Routledge, 83–97.

Carlson, Michael. 2002. *Clint Eastwood*. Harpenden: Pocket Essentials.

Cornell, Drucilla. 2009. *Clint Eastwood and Issues of American Masculinity*. New York: Fordham University Press.

Davis, Oliver. 2015. "Eastwood Reading Beauvoir Reading Eastwood: Ageing and Combative Self-Assertion in *Grand Torino* and *Old Age*." In *Existentialism and Contemporary Cinema: A Beauvoirian Perspective*, edited by Jean-Pierre Boulé and Ursula Tidd. New York: Berghahn Books. 135–148.

Fogel, Barry, and Donna B. Greenberg, eds. 2015. *Psychiatric Care of the Medical Patient*. New York: Oxford University Press.

Foote, John. 2009. *Clint Eastwood: Evolution of a Filmmaker*. Westport, CT: Praeger.

Ford, Julian, et al. 2015. *Posttraumatic Stress Disorder: Scientific and Professional Dimensions*. Amsterdam: Academic Press.

Freud, Sigmund. 2006. "Mourning and Melancholia." In *The Penguin Freud Reader*, edited by Adam Phillips. New York: Penguin Books. 267–280.

Friedman, Howard, ed. 2011. *The Oxford Handbook of Health Psychology*. Oxford: Oxford University Press.

Friedman, Matthew, Terence M. Keane, and Patricia A. Resick. 2007. "PTSD: Twenty-Five Years of Progress and Challenges." In *Handbook of PTSD*, edited by Matthew J. Friedman, Terence M. Keane, and Patricia A. Resick. New York: The Guilford Press. 3–18.
Gran Torino. 2008. Directed by Clint Eastwood, performances by Clint Eastwood, Bee Vang, and Christopher Carley, Matten Productions.
Graves, Abby. 2016. "There's a New Sheriff in Town: Hegemonic Masculinity in the Zombie Apocalypse." In *The Walking Dead Live! Essays on the Television Show*, edited by Philip L. Simpson and Marcus Mallard. Lanham, MD: Rowman & Littlefield. 131–154.
Hutchison, Emma. 2016. *Affective Communities in World Politics: Collective Emotions After Trauma*. Cambridge: Cambridge University Press.
Joseph, Stephen, Ruth Williams and William Yule. 1997. *Understanding Post-traumatic Stress: A Psychosocial Perspective on PTSD and Treatment*. Hoboken: John Wiley & Sons.
Krause, Elizabeth, Ruth DeRosa, and Susan Roth. 2002. "Gender, Trauma Themes, and PTSD: Narratives of Male and Female Survivors." In *Gender and PTSD*, edited by Rachel Kimerling, Paige Ouimette, Jessica Wolfe. New York: The Guilford Press. 349–381.
Krippner, Stanley, Daniel Pitchford and Jeannine Davies. 2012. *Post-Traumatic Stress Disorder*. Westport, CT: Greenwood.
Litz, Brett, and Shira Maguen. 2007. "Early Intervention for Trauma." In *Handbook of PTSD*, edited by Matthew J. Friedman, Terence M. Keane and Patricia A. Resick. The Guilford Press. 306–329.
Lyotard, Jean-Francois. 1984. *The Postmodern Condition: A Report on Knowledge*, trans. Geoff Bennington and Brian Massumi. Minneapolis: University of Minnesota Press.
Mahendra, B. 1987. *Depression: The Disorder and Its Associations*. Lancaster: MTP Press.
Marin, Louis. 2001. *On Representation*. Stanford: Stanford University Press.
Million Dollar Baby. 2004. Directed by Clint Eastwood, performances by Hillary Swank, Clint Eastwood, and Morgan Freeman, Warner Bros.
Mirzoeff, Nicholas. 2003. *Una Introducción a la Cultura Visual*. Barcelona: Paidos.
Moglen, Seth. 2007. *Mourning Modernity: Literary Modernism and the Injuries of American Capitalism*. Stanford: Stanford University Press.
O'Brien, Ruth. 2002. *Crippled Justice: The History of Modern Disability Policy in the Workplace*. Chicago: University of Chicago Press.
Palmer, Ian. 2005. "Survivors and Shooters." In *Ballistic Trauma: A Practical Guide*, edited by Peter Mahoney et al. London: Springer. 599–605.
Peberdy, Donna. 2011. *Masculinity and Film Performance: Male Angst in Contemporary American Cinema*. Basingstoke: Palgrave Macmillan.
Pehkoranta, Ann. 2014. "Surviving the Loss. Abjection and Hypochondria in Maxine Hong Kingston's *The Woman Warrior* and Fae Myenne Ng's *Bone*." In *On the Legacy of Maxine Hong Kingston*, edited by Sämi Ludwig and Nicoleta Alexoae-Zagni. Zurich: Lit Verlag. 263–276.
Play Misty for Me. 1971. Directed by Clint Eastwood, performances by Clint Eastwood, Jessica Walter, and Donna Mills, Universal Pictures.
Sadock, Benjamin, and Virginia Sadock. 2008. *Kaplan & Sadock's Concise Textbook of Clinical Psychiatry*. Philadelphia: Wolters Kluwer.
Smith, Paul. 1993. *Clint Eastwood: A Cultural Production*. Minneapolis: University of Minnesota Press.
Vanessa in the Garden. 1985. Directed by Clint Eastwood, performances by Harvey Keitel, Sondra Locke, and Beau Bridges, Universal Studios.
Wilson, John. 2004. "PTSD and Complex PTSD: Symptoms, Syndromes, and Diagnoses." In *Assessing Psychological Trauma and PTSD*, edited by John Wilson and Terence Keane. New York: The Guilford Press. 7–44.
Wilson, John, Matthew Friedman and Jacob Lindy. 2001. "Treatments Goals for PTSD." In *Treating Psychological Trauma and PTSD*, edited by John P. Wilson, Matthew J. Friedman and Jacob D. Lindy. New York: The Guilford Press. 3–27.
Žižek, Slavoj. 1999. *The Ticklish Subject: The Absent Centre of Political Ontology*. London: Verso.

The Trauma of Cyclical Violence in *Mystic River*

CHARLES R. HAMILTON

With *Mystic River* (2003) Clint Eastwood introduces viewers to the unfamiliar environment of a South Boston community dealing with the traumatic stress of past and present violence. This film takes audiences into the context of a socio-cultural environment of victimization, and puts them on the streets of a small, self-contained, closed community within South Boston. This community takes care of their own, they do not talk to police, and the traumatic repercussions of their self-contained violence are held and perpetuated within their boundaries.

The first encounter with violence in *Mystic River* takes place within the first few minutes of the film, as viewers are placed into that neighborhood 25 years earlier, and into the lives of Jimmy (Jason Kelly), Sean (Connor Paolo), and Dave (Cameron Bowen), three 11-year-old boys playing street hockey. After losing their ball down a sewer drain, ending their game, they decide to write their names in some fresh concrete on a nearby sidewalk. As they begin to scrape their names, two pedophiles, posing as cops, pull up in what looks like an un-marked police car, lecture the boys for destroying public property, and take Dave away, supposedly to talk to his mother. Viewers are left with the scene of Dave staring helplessly out the back window of the pedophiles' car as they drive away. We find out years later, Jimmy, now an adult, still feels a certain amount of guilt and regret about the past, wondering if there was anything he could have done to help Dave.

Dave's boyhood ends there. He is held by them and molested for four days. After Dave escapes and is reunited with his mother, he is taken to his room upstairs, and looking out of his window to the street below, sees Jimmy and Sean staring up at him and gives them a small wave. All the while background voices of some of the adults on the street are heard referring to Dave

99

now as "damaged goods," a label he never outgrows. The separation and distance between Dave and his two friends exaggerate the separation and distance from the rest of the community he experiences from that moment on. Although he does escape, he is robbed of his innocence and never recovers from the trauma of the violence he has suffered, and neither does the community.

Years later Dave (Tim Robbins) is still experiencing that distance from the rest of the community. Dave's kidnapping and molestation was not his fault, but he is now different. The entire community has been affected by the violence he has suffered, and, rather than comforting him and helping him with the support he needs to begin the healing process, he is rejected, ignored, and still looked upon as "damaged goods," someone to stay away from. Those two words (damaged goods) are emphasized by the visual isolation and separation apparent through the choice of camera angles and the apparent distance from Dave's window to the boys on the street, another example of Eastwood's cinematic style and technique that portray his central theme concerning the traumatic consequences of violence, even on those not normally considered victims.

Eastwood's introduction to this neighborhood, through an establishing shot from above, looks over it and shows it in relation to, and isolated from, the city of Boston by the Mystic River. He then moves to camera angles from the height and perspective of Dave, Sean, and Jimmy, at 11 years of age, putting viewers in the position of the boys, allowing them to see things as the boys saw them. These camera angles create perspectives that enhance the feeling of conflict between child and adult (the boys and the adult pedophiles), visualizing how adults use size as a method of intimidation. Eastwood also chooses close-ups of the faces of Jimmy and Sean as Dave is taken away, the look on Jimmy's face seeming to question the truth in the events that just took place.

Martin Scorsese talks about Eastwood's use of violence in the film during his interview for A&E's *Clint Eastwood* biography. He sees Eastwood as conducting a much deeper exploration of that violence than has been done previously by showing, in *Mystic River*, "how violence ultimately affects not only the victims of violence, the loved ones around them, and how it's literally the un-doing of the very social fabric of the world, of society, and how violence destroys everyone around them." Eastwood takes a very personal view of that violence by showing it through the trauma that affects the individual. This method avoids the use of a Harry Callahan character, who enters the scene to remove the effects of violence with more violence, and also does away with the idea of redemption through violence. Using a variety of situations that center on each major character's personal involvement reveals the complexity created by looking at how individuals deal with violence, rather than having a Harry Callahan deal with violence on the community level. This personal view presents a more intimate look at repercussive of violence and its traumatic effects on each individual.

Mystic River is a very dark film, emotionally, and Eastwood's cinematographic techniques emphasize that darkness by creating, early on, a darkness of mood and tone. Location and weather play important roles in the film of adding to the grim reality of the context, and holding the cold, gray mood until the end. In the case of *Mystic River*, the high angle locating shot of the neighborhood from across the Mystic, over the Tobin Bridge toward the city of Boston, shows the community as actually disconnected, encircled and isolated by the river. The familiar mythology connected with a river has a long association with literature, usually representing a new or different experience, a source of freedom or escape, or symbol of a cleansing effect provided by the constantly changing water that flows along its banks. But in *Mystic River* that mythological symbolism serves a different purpose. The isolation of the river serves to restrict the community to a never-ending cycle of repercussive violence, victimization, and the resulting trauma.

Eastwood prefers to shoot on location, and the weather, luckily in this case, is a major advantage in helping create and maintain the tone and mood of the film. There is no sunshine in this film; the overcast conditions help to set a tone of overall gloom and despair that carries throughout. Shooting on a sound stage where all aspects of the lighting and weather can be controlled or produced might be a much safer and more predictable place to film a scene, but Eastwood, judging by his past films, rules out that method for obvious reasons: (1) he likes to present high-angle views and panoramas that give the audience a lay-of-the-land establishing shot and (2) he sometimes uses the space between the camera position and what is happening at a focal point in the distance to tell part of the story, or set a mood or tone. Cinematographer Tom Stern worked with the existing conditions, and manipulated interior lighting, to either hold or create Eastwood's idea of evil lurking within the darkness. Even when the lighting was not dark or high contrast, there was a sense of coldness that existed within the people of the community that went beyond the simple aspect of cold weather. They offered a cold acknowledgment toward each other as they passed, but none offered the warmth of friendship.

Mystic River is the story of a series of inter-related events and associations—past, present, and future—that continue to reveal themselves, connected by the common thread of violence, victimization, and trauma. The three boys in the opening scene are victims of violence, and they are still connected, even if in different ways, to that event. Eastwood ensures that audiences see how these men have grown into reflections of who they were then. Just prior to the abduction of Dave, the conversation between the boys foreshadows the events and lives of the three viewers are now witnessing. Jimmy (Sean Penn), now the criminal, wanted the boys to steal a car and go joy-riding, but Sean (Kevin Bacon), now the policeman, refused, worried about the consequences, and Dave, still the victim (the most vulnerable in the eyes of his abductors), just went along with the others, agreeing to be part of whatever they did. They are all still connected, but their connection now depends on a new series of violent acts that for them, in this community, are an everyday reality.

As the main story unfolds, some of the underlying stories begin to emerge that give answers to the questions of who, what, when, where, why, and how, that are generated by each new scene, all revolving around, or derived from, the effects of violence and victimization within the entire community. Maynard, Kearney, and Guimond (2011) suggest: "The reason for the revenge, the motive for the murder, the injury that produced the injustice— virtually all of them begin in the past and influence the future" (22).

The recent violence begins with "Silent" Ray (Spencer Clark) and his friend accidentally wounding, and then purposely killing, Katy Markum (Emmy Rossum) with a gun used in a holdup years earlier by Silent Ray's father, "Just" Ray, and Jimmy Markum. Viewers are beginning to see that the violence is cyclical and will never end within this community. Following Katy Markum's death, her father Jimmy recounts his time in prison after taking the rap for the liquor store holdup with "Just" Ray, and his guilt for not being there at the death of his first wife, as he contemplates his daughter's death and his vengeful hunt for her killer. Sean Devine, now working as a state police detective, and assigned to this case, immerses himself daily in violence as a part of his job, constantly getting phone calls from his estranged wife, who only listens and never speaks. Dave Boyle fights his trauma and his inner demons and ends up killing and disposing of a pedophile as an attempt at redemption for the misguided guilt he feels from his past. Dave's wife, Celeste (Marcia Gay Harden), does not believe Dave's story of beating the pedophile to death and shares her suspicions about his involvement in Katy's murder with Jimmy. The Savage brothers laugh and joke about the crimes they have and will commit as part of the reality of their daily routine. Jimmy kills Dave and decides to re-enter a life of crime. Eastwood's central theme of the repercussions of violence is being complexly and successfully played out. He shows the inner and outer conflicts of the individuals and the community as repercussive violence and how the victims deal with the trauma of violence, or simply take it in stride as part of their everyday cycle of life in the neighborhood.

Societal and cultural factors in the film reflect the time period and area in which it is produced, and the intimacy with the context created by the shooting style of Eastwood put viewers inside that social environment.

Included within this environment is the river, shown from high above at the beginning and ending of the film, and in darkness as the burial site for Dave, surrounding and holding close the events contained within the neighborhood. Dennis Rothermel calls the Mystic River "the film's center of gravity," suggesting it "absorbs the past, without forgiving and without healing. Old feuds, forgotten retributions, horrible misdeeds, sins, miscreant evil, all stripped of their generic agency, linger in its depths" (218). The river also seems to at times hold the community hostage, hiding their secrets, while creating a separate world apart from the rest of the city. It is also the resting place for evil. Jimmy threw the gun he used to kill Dave into the river, as he had done with the gun he used to kill "Just" Ray years earlier, contributing once more to the cycle of violence.

As viewers again see violence used within this Eastwood film, questions about its use arise. Does it make a statement of any kind, and, if so, is the statement made to any specific audience, or group, or to an entire population? If there is a statement made, no matter how blatant or how subtle, is that statement influenced by the author's (Lehane's) perceived theme within the text, by society's reaction to that theme within the text or social/cultural environment, or solely by Eastwood's personal concerns woven into the film? Housel's statement that "Film adaptation is a vehicle for life experiences" (xi) is directly connected to the influence of the filmmaker and the writer, especially when adapted from contemporary novels such as Dennis Lehane's *Mystic River* (2001), and on the effects of violence in this small community within the city limits of Boston. The focus of Eastwood's *Mystic River* is, again, based on a central theme concerning repercussive violence and its effects on those who come in contact with it. His audience has expanded to include not only his previous working class fan base, but also society as a whole, as he attempts to project his new central theme into this film, which he has done previously in *Unforgiven* (1992) and *A Perfect World* (1993).

These elements are not new to Eastwood, who has voiced his feelings about the repercussive effects of violence since the 1970s and the beginning of his series of *Dirty Harry* (1971) films, especially as they apply to the social concerns of a specific group in society within a specific time period. He used the Harry Callahan character in *Dirty Harry* as the spokesman who voiced his anger with the justice system's failure to control violence then. In A&E's 2005 *Biography: Clint Eastwood*, Eastwood discusses his concerns with what he saw as the lack of justice for the victims of violent crime, which carried over into those early "Harry" films: "There weren't too many movies at that time that were concerned about the victims of violent crime. They were more interested in the perpetrator. So, it was about a guy that was obsessed about the victim, and that, to me, made it appealing" (Eastwood). Other filmmakers followed suit with *Straw Dogs* (1971), *Get Carter* (1971), *Billy Jack* (1971), and

Death Wish, (1974). But in *Mystic River*, although his main emphasis is still with the victim, his larger concern is with the depiction of the effects of violence, how the trauma associated with it touches all involved, and with his ability to effectively project this message through film.

Eastwood's concentration on the repercussive trauma of violence has proven to be controversial, as referenced by critics who cannot quite see it as anything more than an entertainment tactic used by other films of the time period. Saturating the viewing public with screen violence during the 1990s, the films *Goodfellas* (1990), *Cape Fear* (1991), *Falling Down* (1993), and *Pulp Fiction* (1994) provided new incentives for higher levels of violence to feed the desires of audiences and keep them coming back for more. Each has influenced the judgment of critics and fostered a cynicism that can cloud objectivity. Even Eastwood's *Unforgiven* (1992) was seen by some scholarly and journalistic critics (and some audiences) as extreme violence for the sake of violence. In addition to the films mentioned, the public is constantly reminded of the reality of violence in society by daily reports of robberies, stabbings, rapes, beatings, and murders, common on daily news media sources. Reactions to these instances of violence fuel what Javier, Herron, and Primavera (1998) refer to as society's socio-cultural preoccupation with violence. In *Mystic River*, the violence portrayed moves away from Eastwood's view of the 1970s policeman out for vengeance ("Dirty" Harry), and into the back story of a violent act—a community suffering with the tragic grief of the recent death of one of their own, the death of innocence from years past, and the reality of dealing with the repercussive trauma of violence on a daily basis.

The violence in *Mystic River* seems to proliferate with each new incident, and with no end in sight. Apparent is the sense that there is no attempt to change or counteract the effects of the violence the community lives with. It becomes a reality that is accepted as commonplace in their everyday lives. Dave never recovers from the trauma of his past kidnapping and molestation, and ends up blurring the lines between good and evil by using deadly violence against the child molester he finds with a young boy, then justifying murder because the person he kills is a child molester. He first sees justice and redemption through violence, trying to quiet his own demons by killing a surrogate for the person who robbed him of his childhood, but, in reality his act of violence makes him a victim all over again.

Sean has pushed his wife away, himself a victim of the violence he is exposed to daily in his job as a policeman. Jimmy is driven back to a life of violence and crime, using murder as retribution for the murder of his daughter. As all the relationships and connections to violence are revealed, viewers begin to see the complexity and multi-layers of this story within the layers of the community where it takes place. This is when Eastwood's concept that no one in the neighborhood is un-touched by the trauma of violence is realized.

Deborah Allison (2003), in discussing Eastwood's central theme, cites some other "defining features" of his work—the "theme of the triumphant underdog," his "obsession with characters that fight to achieve," and "his need to be a voice for the victims of violence," as present in this and other of his films. Whether Eastwood wanted to make a political statement during the 1970s, or not, his *Dirty Harry* role of policeman as vigilante, and self-declared role of spokesman for the victim, and his working-class fan base, framed him as a conservative who believed that the rights of the victimized had been pushed aside. As evidenced in *Mystic River*, the method he now uses to implement his central theme is much more complex than the early cop movies that blatantly established his image. The complexity of *Mystic River* is in the exposure of its layers of violence, the effects on the people involved, and how they deal with these effects. The point of view is no longer that of the policeman-vigilante, but now of the victims living with the trauma of their victimization. Eastwood is not only using *Mystic River* to show that violence affects each victim in a different way, but that those effects never seem to release their victims from their post-traumatic stress.

To Rand Cooper (2003) the film is an act of atonement for Eastwood. Cooper discusses Eastwood's method of the portrayal of repercussive violence, which, in *Mystic River*, "complicates the idea of violence with which it is associated" (26). The attention is now on the recipients of the violence, the layers of their suffering, and "far from romancing the silence of the avenger, *Mystic River* is haunted by the silence of the victim," and the indifference of the community which are important parts of the central theme Eastwood emphasizes. When Stella Papamichael (2003) asked him how and why the novel *Mystic River* was chosen, he followed with a statement about his fascination with "the stealing of innocence," calling it "the most heinous crime." There is no mention of retribution, revenge, or vengeance by Eastwood, only sadness that the trauma caused by the violence continually haunts the victim. In an interview with Emma Brockes of *The Guardian*, *Mystic River* author Dennis Lehane makes an almost identical statement, but "Lehane isn't too keen on examining his obsessions, lest they evaporate under scrutiny," writes Brockes. "But," says Lehane, "I'll always be fascinated with the loss of innocence or corruption of the soul at a young age."

Eastwood also explains his choice of *Mystic River* to Michael Parkinson (2003): "I just wanted to tell a story about people, about conflicts, and about people overcoming obstacles in their lives. This story did it for me." But the people in this story never actually overcome their conflicts. The instances of murder, death, and guilt, far from being overcome, seem to be absorbed into their daily lives, relegated to unimportance by their indifference.

What does Eastwood accomplish with *Mystic River*? Carloss James Chamberlin (2004) discusses what he refers to as the horror aspects of the film, and suggests that many of the aspects mirror the aspects of a horror film, and presents the idea that "*Mystic River*'s style plays on these same horror archetypes." To Chamberlin, "its 'realism' belongs to the nightmare. The atmosphere is deliberately grim. We don't feel the sun until the end of the movie."

The aspect of horror seems to be a good fit, especially with Dave as the example. His horror is derived from the loss of his boyhood innocence, and is the focus of the first few minutes of the film. Now, years later, it is still the focus of the police, the focus of his wife, the focus of Jimmy, and lastly, the overall focus of the community. Dave tells Jimmy (falsely) that he killed Jimmy's daughter Katy because when he saw her in the bar he had: "a dream of youth—I don't remember having one. You'd know what I mean if you'd got in that car instead of me." Jimmy follows, just before he kills Dave, with "This part you do alone." This one act releases Dave from the trauma of living with his loss of boyhood innocence, then and now, and rids Jimmy of the sense of guilt he has shouldered since not trying to do something to save Dave from the pedophiles. As the killing of "Just" Ray Harrises had removed his guilt for taking the blame for an earlier crime they both took part in, and causing him to be in prison when his wife died, it is his killing of Dave, with daughter Katy no longer there to act as his conscience, that re-kindles Jimmy's life of crime. The violence has been carried forward, from child to adult and back to child.

Chamberlin's reasoning for *Mystic River* as a horror film comes not from individual events and acts of violence, but from Eastwood's use of repetition of those events. As his use of repetition becomes apparent, it is obvious that it is not coincidence. Multiple recurring views of the sidewalk with Dave's name half finished, Dave (as an adult) getting into the back seat of a black car a second time and looking out the back window as it drives away (the same as when he was 11), the two Ray Harris' and two wild shots from the same gun, and the continual depictions of symbols of the cross create a feeling of horror that develops from the sense that there is some underlying evil within the community that just will not go away, revealing a cycle of violence that has become a constant in their daily lives.

Eastwood's stylistic technique, through lighting, camera point of view, and pacing of dialogue, emphasizes the horror of these acts, and their place in the cycle of violence. His artificial lighting techniques purposely kept the mood cold and distant, complementing the cold tones of the overcast weather. In making the final print of the film he de-saturated the color, emphasizing even more the cold mood created by the existing weather, while foreshad-owing the coldness of the film's central theme. Beginning with the long shot of Boston from a position high above, he shows the isolation of the community by the Mystic River and grounds the location for the audience. Eastwood's choice of camera angles and positions maintain the feeling of closeness and interconnectedness between the main characters. He continually uses medium and extreme close-ups, emphasizing individuals instead of groups, which isolates characters and their conflicts from the community. Especially significant is an overhead shot of Jimmy Markham as he charges into a dark abyss of police officers in an attempt to see his daughter's twisted body hidden beneath the leaves. He seems to be awash in a sea of dark blue as he is hoisted, writhing, above their shoulders, the colors blending with the weather, further emphasizing the dark mood. The dialogue is not rushed and is allowed to play out slowly in short deliberate comments, providing the time to absorb what is being said and allowing enough time for the tension within the scenes to fully develop.

Eastwood attempts to steer attention toward his interest in the far-reaching effects of violence in many of the interviews he has done in the years since *Unforgiven* (1992) and *A Perfect World* (1993), but emphasizes that it is not a topic the studios have always been eager to support. He tells Charlie Rose that, although Warner Bros. did agree to back the film, they only backed it at the minimum rate. He admits having competition from other films the studio was backing at the time (*Lord of the Rings, Harry Potter,* and *Matrix Reloaded*) made it difficult for studio executives to become excited over his pitch for *Mystic River*. But Eastwood did receive the backing he needed, and, to the surprise of studio executives, won two Oscars and 60 other awards out of 68 nominations.

Dennis Lehane discusses his inspiration for the idea of the opening scene in an interview with Linda Richards for *January Magazine*, noting that it developed from a similar event that happened to Lehane and his best friend, also age 11, on their way home from school. They were having a fight in the street in their neighborhood when a car with two detectives came by and stopped the fight. The moment they drove away the boys started fighting again. The detectives came back a few minutes later and they were upset because the boys had not stopped fighting, so they put them in the car and took them back to their parents. The part that really struck home for Lehane, and inspired the fictional tragic circumstances for Dave, happened after the two plain-clothes policemen dropped Lehane off at home. His mother was so shaken up by his getting into a car with two men, and not asking to see a badge, that he remembered the incident years later. Eastwood comments that he changed the fighting to street hockey in order to add more sympathy for the boys and more innocence to the situation (Papamichael).

Lehane comes from a working-class neighborhood in Boston and most of his other novels deal with the type of class struggles he grew up with, allowing the background information concerning the socio-cultural environment of a typical South Boston Irish Catholic neighborhood to set the tone in the novel, and also become a focal point for Eastwood in this film. Working class struggles have been a constant interest for Eastwood in many of his other films: *Honkytonk Man* (1982), *A Perfect World* (1993), and *Million Dollar Baby* (2004). He is constantly advancing his purposes and trying to ensure that his ideas about the traumatic repercussions of violence are seen, not only through his choice of works, but also through his choice of authors, texts, screenwriters, and actors.

Brian Helgeland, writer of the screenplay for *Mystic River* (2003) (and Eastwood's *Blood Work*, 2002), just happens to have grown up near the area where *Mystic River* is set, and, in an interview with Holden Pike, provides some insight into the amount of control Eastwood had during the screenplay-writing stage of production for *Mystic River*: Helgeland said that after he had written and delivered the screenplay, Eastwood re-read the book, then read the scenes in the screenplay to see how they fell in the script, and that he would either be happy or he would say, "I don't think we need this." Usually he would say, "I like this line in the book, if you could find a way to work that into the scene," showing his involvement in the script, and ensuring that his ideas were emphasized. Eastwood's main concern is that the effects of the violence on the individual are featured (Pike).

Eastwood highlights the ways violence can victimize those it touches in a very straightforward way through his depiction of Dave, as an adult, who wanders the streets of the neighborhood, his large frame pitifully hunched over, holding his son's hand as if to keep him safe, constantly reminded of what happened to him when he was 11 by everything and everyone he sees, and with what appears to be the same look on his face, as he had when he rode away with the pedophiles 25 years earlier, staring helplessly out of the back window. More than just an expression, Robbins gives his character, Dave, an overall un-changing look of sadness, and the stoop-shouldered posture of a beaten man who can find no happiness in his life, and one who does not like to make eye contact. He and the neighborhood have never forgotten what happened to him, and even give the impression that he is somehow to blame. Dave, like Jimmy, attempts to receive redemption through violence by brutally killing a pedophile who he finds in a car with a young boy, later admitting it solved none of his emotional problems. But, as people do in this neighborhood, he goes on with his life as if nothing has happened. When he is questioned by Jimmy, who then stabs and shoots him, his body floating away in the Mystic, it is as if the ending of his life has finally brought him peace and release from the trauma he has carried for 25 years. Dave's death seems to have done more for the redemption of Dave than for Jimmy.

While Eastwood uses Dave as his most explicit examination of how violence victimizes people, he offers the same realization in his portrayal of Jimmy, former young thug of the neighborhood, who seems only to harbor guilt for taking the rap for his partner in crime, and being in prison when his first wife died. Although his previous life of violence and crime are past, he easily slips back into that life with the death of his daughter Katy. He is intent on vigilante justice and revenge for her death, to the extent that he conducts his own investigation, which results in his killing Dave, but does not provide redemption. His coldness and adaptation to his violent act are reinforced by the support of his wife, who reminds him to be strong, and that killing Dave was only a mistake. Jimmy's remorse easily vanishes with the sense that he will soon be the leader of the community and crime boss he once was.

The choice of actors who can show "what is in their heads" is essential in Eastwood's films, and the actors in *Mystic River* are well chosen. Viewers can imagine what is in Jimmy's head as he sits in the back room of his corner grocery store, ambivalent to everything around him. He seems bored with the ordinary life of an owner of a small neighborhood bodega. But, his face lights up when his daughter Katy enters the scene. When he visits the scene of his daughter's murder, the tortured expression of a mad man, the excruciating pain of a father experiencing the death of a child, is obvious in Jimmy's expression as he surges against a sea of policemen who block him from seeing his daughter's body.

The morning after killing Dave, sitting drunk on the stoop of his house, Jimmy encounters Sean, who tells him they have arrested the person who killed his daughter. Jimmy's realization that his killing of Dave was wrong is apparent in his facial expression and through his body language, but not because it was murder. Jimmy is upset because Dave was his friend, but more because he is the wrong man. He is driven to tears upon hearing the news, and, with a tortured look on his face, jumps up from the step he is sitting on and begins to wander aimlessly down the center of the street sobbing. Jimmy still believes in redemption through vigilante violence, and his wife Annabeth (Laura Linney) later consoles him, as Roger Ebert suggests, playing the part of a modern-day Lady Macbeth, quietly convincing him he did nothing wrong, as he stands looking out of their bedroom window, shirt off, the soft glow of the outside light encircling his body, shoulder to waist tattoo of a cross on his back—he has just gotten his own form of sexual absolution from his wife.

Sean appears to be the same person he was as an 11-year-old. He was the kid who would not break the law and steal a car with Jimmy for a little joy-riding, and now he is a cop with the blank, emotionless expression of a person whose daily contact with violence in his job has made him impervious to the tragedies and trauma of the world. Even when he gets one of his estranged wife's phone calls, he does not respond emotionally, just asks her to talk to him as she silently listens to his voice. Throughout the film, he and his partner Whitey (Laurence Fishburne) employ the generic facial facade of emotionless concern, an expression used often in police dramas, and by Eastwood himself in his Harry Callahan and Western characters. Sean only breaks the facade at the end of the film, during a parade, as he stands re-united with his wife and newborn baby girl, smiling, looking across the street at Jimmy and pointing his finger like a gun, signaling to Jimmy that he knows Jimmy killed Dave. Jimmy, also smiling as if things are now back to normal, responds with a shrug of his shoulders that shows his ambivalence to Sean and his accusation. Eastwood has chosen actors who can speak volumes without dialogue, solving the problem screenwriter Brian Helgeland mentioned earlier of having to figure out how to show all the "richness of the characters' internal worlds" and "get it on screen."

In the location of the neighborhood of *Mystic River* there was no need for more than the overall view of the establishing shot at the beginning of the film to place viewers within that environment. Eastwood's current practice has been to put the viewer in close proximity with the character, to look into their eyes, see them sweat, feel their hatred or their fear. He sometimes accomplishes this by moving in with a hand-held camera, invading their personal space, to place the audience into the scene, adding to the realism by giving the audience the point of view of one of the characters. But, it was the high angle spiraling shot of Jimmy Marcum from directly overhead as he was held back and hoisted into the air by a sea of policemen that set the emotional context and the mood and tone for the rest of the film. This shot is an integral element of the Eastwood cinematic style. He reads the script, watches the actors rehearse, decides how the scene would normally be shot, and then seems to surprise his audience with an unexpected camera movement, angle, or position that adds emphasis or gives the viewer a different perspective, and one that continually gets his audience involved with the scene.

In the production of *Mystic River,* Eastwood's collaboration with the author and screenwriter, the technical expertise used by a trusted crew (most of whom he has worked with for a long period and who know what he expects) to physically produce the film, and the "back-story" behind the novel, work to emphasize the central theme of the repercussions of violence he wants to present. Linda Hutcheon (2006) says adapters "must have their own personal reasons for deciding first to do an adaptation and then choosing which adapted work and what medium to do it in" (92). She believes one reason for choosing a certain text is "an adaptation can obviously be used to engage in a larger social or cultural critique," such as Eastwood's "violence begets violence" theory. "It can even be used to avoid it" (94). Eastwood has stated that he is concerned with crimes involving children and their loss of innocence, and with the effects of violence. *Mystic River* fits his criteria and is a venue that allows him to emphasize his ideas through applying them to the effects of personal incidents within the story.

Eastwood's filmmaking style, included in the collaboration, is an important element in the telling of the story. His history as a director has been to let the scene, the actors, and the shooting environment lead him in choosing the camera angles, lighting, and cinematic techniques necessary to emphasize his theme. Eastwood has not been known to use storyboarding or overly scripted shooting directions to pre-visualize each scene or camera angle, as do many other directors. Because he works with a crew that, in many cases, has been with him for many years, he relies on collaborating with them for their technical expertise, combined with their knowledge of how he works and what he wants, using the input from all involved.

Adding support for Eastwood's process and cinematic style, theorist Robert Ray (2000) notes the ability of film to produce signifiers that use the mixed forms of language and image to convey meaning. This applies to the repetition of symbols mentioned earlier in *Mystic River*, which takes place, and was released, during the sexual molestation scandal surrounding the Catholic Church, especially the Archdiocese of Boston, and connects the violence in the film and the loss of innocence with the reality of the scandal. Ray cites the images from an earlier-referenced scene in the film *Casablanca* (1942), in which Rick Blaine is introduced, as an example of signifiers that achieved their understood meaning through their use in a variety of other movies, publications, and advertising of the era. "[Blaine] Bogart, seated in a white dinner jacket, smoking a cigarette, playing with a chess set placed next to a half-empty champagne glass, the image (a sophisticated, jaded, clever man, simultaneously proud and melancholy) derived from the objects (tuxedo, champagne glass, and chess set)" (Ray 40), constructed meaning for the audiences of that era without the need of dialogue.

Eastwood uses elements within scenes that audiences should be aware of because of their socio-cultural environment. The symbol of the cross is featured on a ring worn on the finger of one of the pedophiles who kidnaps Dave, and in a tattoo, that covers the back of Jimmy Markum. Featured in these ways it becomes a sign of evil and makes a statement about religion in a heavily Irish Catholic community in close proximity to the Boston archdiocese, at the time caught up in a church scandal involving pedophile priests. In the scene of Jimmy standing shirtless at the window of his upstairs bedroom, the cross tattoo covering his back while getting a sort of absolution from his wife for the killing of Dave, all connect directly with Dave's loss of innocence. Repetitive shots of the storm sewer where many baseballs and street hockey pucks were lost, the concrete sidewalk with Sean and Jimmy's names and the unfinished DA that represents Dave are elements

Eastwood uses to remind the audience of the reasons why this story is important.

In *Mystic River* Eastwood presents situations of death and retribution, or redemptive violence, easily understood on the surface, and a staple of the Western genre. Theologian Walter Wink discusses how society rationalizes what he calls the "myth of redemptive violence," and why its ease of acceptance is justified: "Any form of order is preferable to chaos, according to this myth. Ours is neither a perfect nor perfectible world; it is theatre of perpetual conflict in which the prize goes to the strong." Reaching further down, below that surface, is the symbolic death of Dave at 11 years old—the death of his innocence and his childhood—something from which he never recovers. There is the accidental wounding but intentional murder of Katy Marcum—affecting her family, Dave, her boyfriend and his family, and the entire community. Then, there is the symbolic death of Jimmy Marcum, after re-building his life following a violent past, the death of his daughter, his search for her killer, and his killing of Dave, sending him spiraling back into a life of crime, while using violence to temporarily bring order from chaos.

Young people are used as the main characters in many of Eastwood's films, and, in many cases, are the victims of violence. Will Munny's children become victims of his violent past and present in *Unforgiven* (1992). Phillip and his association with Butch is the center of attention in *A Perfect World* (1993). Dave, Sean, and Jimmy, as young boys, and then as adults, begin as and remain the victims of violence in *Mystic River*. Maggie Fitzgerald and her connection to boxing trainer Frankie Dunn in *Million Dollar Baby* (2004). Walt Kowalski's kids, grandchildren, and the Hmong teenagers next door are featured in *Gran Torino* (2008). Eastwood seems to feel they are more vulnerable, and crimes against them more heinous; therefore, his use of them carries more impact.

Mystic River is another instance of Eastwood's use of personal style and cinematic technique to illustrate the central theme of repercussive violence and the trauma it causes, while gently revealing other sub-themes residing just below the surface. Although viewers know his central theme is there, it is the story beneath the surface that furnishes support for the narrative. Rothermel concludes that Eastwood shows "the maturity and grace of a filmmaker who has acquired the art of telling a complex story ... without distracting from the story told" (239).

Eastwood has learned the use and importance of creating visions of reality in his films that enhance the plausibility of the narrative. He has also learned that reality does not always satisfy audience expectations, but that it goes beyond the typically false versions of "Hollywood" reality (in which the good guy always wins). There is the expectation that Jimmy will not kill Dave. There is the expectation that Sean, who knows Jimmy killed Dave, but cannot prove it, will somehow find a way to administer justice. Perplexing is the feeling that Dave's death somehow released him from his demons, and that he is, in reality, better off dead. All these situations work together to show how the trauma of violence can become a way of life, accepted by a community that has and continues to live with some version of violence, all becoming the victimized, and accepting the use of that violence to bring order out of chaos. The scene of the parade at the end of this film illustrates the reality of the situation well. Dave is dead, his wife Celeste is, as Redmon says, "left fractured by the events that took place during the night [before], events that resulted in the loss of her husband and her son's father" (327). Sean and Jimmy, and the rest of the neighborhood, are laughing and smiling, enjoying the parade as if the events of the past week, even the past 25 years, are forgotten, or have been accepted as just another part of their everyday reality.

Redmon suggests that the final scene, in which the sidewalks of the neighborhood are filled with residents, and a parade makes its way through the streets, a scene that seems to provide restoration of order for the community, works in the reverse with the appearance of Dave's wife, Celeste, and their son Michael (327). Celeste is now left with her guilt leading to the murder of her husband, and their son Michael has now lost his innocence and will carry the guilt of his mother and the burden of his father, continuing the traumatic effects of violence. Jimmy's violence has not restored order. The death of Dave has not restored order. And, there is a tension between Jimmy and Sean that creates a foreshadowing of violent events to come.

This ending, seemingly the scene of a community back to "normal," is also ambiguous, leaving viewers with a false view of contentment and the question: Who will be the next victim? A similar question was being asked by Catholic parents in the area concerning the safety of their children from pedophile priests. Eastwood has again put violence and victimization within a plausible context, in this case, an entire community suffering the trauma of cyclical violence.

WORKS CITED

Allison, Deborah. 2003. "Clint Eastwood." *Senses of Cinema.* July. Accessed 1 August 2009.

Billy Jack. 1971. Directed by Tom Laughlin, performances by Tom Laughlin, Delores Taylor, and Clark Howat, National Student Film Corporation.

Brockes, Emma. 2009. "A Life in Writing: Dennis Lehane." *The Guardian.* 24 January. Accessed 6 June 2011.

Cape Fear. 1991. Directed by Martin Scorsese, performances by Robert De Niro, Nick Nolte, and Jessica Lange, Amblin Entertainment.

Casablanca. 1943. Directed by Michael Curtiz, performances by Humphrey Bogart, Ingrid Bergman, and Paul Henreid, Warner Bros.

Chamberlin, Carlos James. 2004. "It Came from the Mystic." *Senses of Cinema* 30. 12 Feb. 2004. Accessed 6 June 2011.

Cooper, Rand Richards. 2003. "Unforgiven in Boston." *Commonweal* 130:19: 25–26.

Covey, Russell D. 2009. "Criminal Madness: Cultural Iconography and Insanity." *Stanford Law Review* 61.6: 1375–1378.
Death Wish. 1974. Directed by Michael Winner, performances by Charles Bronson, Hope Lange, and Vincent Gardenia, Dino De Laurentiis Company.
Dirty Harry. 1971. Directed by Don Siegel, performances by Clint Eastwood, Andrew Robinson, and Harry Guardino, Warner Bros.
Eastwood, Clint. 2003. "Clint Eastwood." *Biography*, Arts and Entertainment Network. 20th Century Fox.
Ebert, Roger. 2003. "*Mystic River.*" *Rogerebert.com.* 8 October. Accessed 12 October 2012.
Falling Down. 1993. Directed by Joel Schumacher, performances by Michael Douglas, Robert Duvall, and Barbara Hershey, Alcor Films.
Get Carter. 1971. Directed by Mike Hodges, performances by Michael Caine, Ian Hendry, and Britt Ekland, Metro-Goldwyn-Mayer British Studios.
Goodfellas. 1990. Directed by Martin Scorsese, performances by Robert De Niro, Ray Liotta, and Joe Pesci, Warner Bros.
Honkytonk Man. 1982. Directed by Clint Eastwood, performances by Clint Eastwood, Kyle Eastwood, and John McIntire, Malpaso Company.
Housel, Rebecca, ed. 2006. Introduction. "And Spielberg said, 'Let there be light.'" *From Camera Lens to Critical Lens: A Collection of Best Essays on Film Adaptation.* Newcastle-upon-Tyne: Cambridge Scholars Press. XI–XII.
Hutcheon, Linda. 2006. *A Theory of Adaptation.* London: Routledge.
Javier, Rafael Art, William G. Herron, and Louis Primavera. 1998. "Violence and the Media: A Psychological Analysis." *International Journal of Instructional Media* 25.4: 339. Accessed 22 May 2011.
Maynard, Katherine, Jarod Kearney, and James Guimond. 2011. *Revenge Versus Legality.* New York: Birkbeck Law Press.
Million Dollar Baby. 2004. Directed by Clint Eastwood, performances by Hillary Swank, Clint Eastwood, and Morgan Freeman, Warner Bros.
Mystic River. 2003. Directed by Clint Eastwood, performances by Sean Penn, Tim Robbins, and Kevin Bacon, Warner Bros. Pictures.
Papamichael, Stella. 2003. "Clint Eastwood: Mystic River." BBC. October. Accessed 6 June 2011.
Parkinson, Michael. 2003. "Clint Eastwood." *The Guardian.* 7 October. Accessed 6 June 2011.
A Perfect World. 1993. Directed by Clint Eastwood, performances by Kevin Costner, Clint Eastwood, and Laura Dern, Warner Bros.
Pike, Holden. 2003. "Brian Helgeland on *Mystic River.*" *Creative Screenwriting* 10.5. 21 Sept. 2003. Accessed 6 June 2011.
Pulp Fiction. 1994. Directed by Quentin Tarantino, performances by John Travolta, Uma Thurman, and Samuel Jackson, Miramax.
Ray, Robert B. "2000. The Field of Literature and Film." Ed. James Naremore. New Brunswick: Rutgers University Press. 38–53.
Richards, Linda. 2001. "Dennis Lehane." *January Magazine.* March. Accessed 6 June 2011.
Rothermel, Dennis. 2007. "Mystical Moral Miasma in *Mystic River.*" *Clint Eastwood, Actor and Director.* Ed. Leonard Engle. Salt Lake City: University of Utah Press. 218–241.
Scorsese, Martin. 2003. "Clint Eastwood." *Biography*, Arts and Entertainment Network. 20th Century Fox.
Straw Dogs. 1971. Directed by Sam Peckinpah, performances by Dustin Hoffman, Susan George, and Peter Vaughan, ABC Pictures.
Wink, Walter. 2007. "Facing the Myth of Redemptive Violence." *Christian Peacemaker Teams.* 16 November. Accessed 21 May 2012.

Moral Injury and Civilian Authority in the War Films of Clint Eastwood

KATHLEEN A. BROWN *and* BRETT WESTBROOK

In a 1985 interview, Clint Eastwood discussed *Kelly's Heroes* (1970), a movie set during World War II that he was in 15 years earlier in which a group of disaffected service men make off with a lot of gold: "It was a very fine anti-militaristic script, one that said some important things about the war, about this propensity that man has to destroy himself" (Wilson and Eastwood 47). In the final edit, the scenes that "pull a picture together," as Eastwood saw it, that "humanize it" were all cut as more and more action scenes were spliced in (Eastwood 51). These could have been the moments particularly in an action genre such as war films, that "set the debate in philosophical terms" (Wilson and Eastwood 47). As the combatants pause and reflect, the impact that war has on the men, what killing does to them begins to emerge. In this way, a bit of non-expository philosophizing offsets the flash/bang of combat, creating narrative equilibrium. In *Kelly's Heroes*, however, action and reflection were out of balance. As a result, the picture "had lost its soul" (47).

For screenwriter Troy Kennedy Martin, as well, the film was "a tougher thing that was softened" (Cooke 50). Perhaps most telling is the radical change made to the scene in the minefield. On their way to Berlin to rob the bank, the men wander into a minefield. The tension and the deaths in this scene contrast sharply, even jarringly, with the jocular banter and camaraderie earlier in the film. Two of the men detonate mines; others must crawl to the bodies to check for a pulse and retrieve dog tags and munitions hoping to avoid the same fate. Before they can all safely exit the minefield, the enemy hears the explosions and bears down on the trapped men. According to Martin, as originally filmed, the "enemy" was composed of the elderly and youth forming a scraggly, un-uniformed "Home Guard" unit. Horrified by the deaths of their comrades and almost deranged with fear, the men mow down these effectively non-combatants in a sort of "blood craze," leaving the would-be bank robbers "absolutely shattered, completely demoralized." The scene that might have brought out some of the human response to killing, however, was cut for the softening: "So of course that was all changed, they had to be modern Nazis and they all had to have great machine guns" (Cooke 49).

Eastwood's lament over the scenes left on the cutting room floor predicts the soulful contemplation that would shape the two films he would make about one of the most mythologized battles of World War II: *Flags of Our Fathers* (2006) and *Letters from Iwo Jima* (2006). With Eastwood producing, the scenes that humanize these films were, of course, left intact. The fighting men in both movies ponder "the whole deal about *why* and the philosophies of war" (Avery 51), as Eastwood put it. How the characters, Americans and Japanese, behave in the chaos and duress of combat, what they value, what they regret—their humanity, in other words—reveal the ways in which members of the armed services are put at risk for what is known as moral injury.

Beginning in 1991 with his groundbreaking article "Learning About Combat Stress from Homer's *Iliad*," longtime Veterans Administration psychologist Jonathan Shay has developed an important understanding of how the toxic combat experiences described by the veterans in his care resulted in moral injury. As Shay describes it, moral injury is "present when (1) there has been a betrayal of what's right (2) by someone who holds legitimate authority (3) in a high-stakes situation" (Shay, 2011, 183). As a clinician, Shay is—of course—deeply concerned with the question of prevention: why it is that service members are subject to this particularly devastating injury in the first place. What conditions obtain that put military men and women at risk for moral injury? Who is responsible for those conditions? How can these circumstances be avoided in the first place? Drawing on three Eastwood films set during ongoing combat—*Kelly's Heroes* (1970), *Flags of Our Fathers*, and *Letters from Iwo Jima* (both 2006)—this essay explores the ways in which military and civilian authorities put combatants at risk specifically for moral injury: failed military leadership, political manipulation of the military, and the Catch-22 of killing itself. As he so often does, Eastwood strips the genre film—this time the war film—of the familiar and the sentimental to focus on the human beings just trying to stay alive. In doing so, he answers, cinematically at least, some of Shay's questions about the origins of moral injury. Regardless of who is ultimately responsible for the injuries suffered, in these films and historically, Eastwood makes it clear that it is almost always the "enlisted ranks who pay the butcher's bill for military malpractice" (Shay, 2014, 187).

In the 1985 interview, Eastwood claims that *Kelly's Heroes* "had really nice things in the script. Otherwise, I would never have gone to Yugoslavia for six months" (Wilson and Eastwood 53). Calling it "one of the best antiwar stories I've ever seen," Eastwood admired its subtlety and that "it was never preachy" (53). Deeply dissatisfied with the end product of those six months, Eastwood made an 11th-hour appeal to salvage the film, offering to recut it himself, to "put the film back in its proper order" (51) before the critics screened it. The studio executives, eager to make a quick buck, turned him down (51–52). Even if the film lost its soul during post-production, Shay's concept of moral injury still helps to explain why soldiers in the United States Army during war time, can rationalize deserting their post so they can rob a bank.

Military leadership malpractice, according to Shay, "demotivates vast swathes of troops," and can separate "whole units from loyalty to the chain of command" (2014, 183). In *Kelly's Heroes*, dereliction starts at the top levels, seeps through the middle ranks and then oozes on down to the non-coms until it finally corrodes an entire unit, taking it out of the war effort entirely. At the top of the chain of command in the film sits the aptly-named, Patton-esque General Colt (a cigar-chomping Carroll O'Connor), an officer utterly removed from the men for whom he bears responsibility. His physical location is distant from the front itself. While his men endure shelling, meager rations, and all the deprivations of war, Colt is living the life of Riley with satin sheets, good food, and hot baths in a chateau formerly occupied by the Germans. Far from having his own boots on the muddy, rutted ground with his men, Colt merely flies over the battlefield, convinced he is thus well-briefed. The removal is so complete that he refuses to even think in terms of actual military tactics, dismissing silly talk from his obsequious aides about the importance of protecting an Army's flanks along with piddly details like supplies. In lieu of strategy, Colt seems to believe that positive thinking will carry the day: "What we need is fighting spirit! The will to win!" When Kelly (Eastwood) and his men manage to break a hole in the enemy's flank on their way to the gold, Colt never asks who, how, or why. Instead, the General sees in the deser-tion, dereliction of duty, and planned theft by a portion of his command the gung-ho drive he needs to fulfill his "date with destiny," getting to Berlin ahead of everyone else. He pauses in his headlong rush to glory only to hand out random medals to the men, a farcical and token nod to their valor. The General's vanity even provides cover for the group's escape after the heist. Big Joe (Telly Savalas) tells the newly-liberated villagers that De Gaulle is coming and the excited French folk distract General Colt, who seems to expect such adulation, while Kelly and his heroes slip out of town.

Shay argues that "leaders," such as Colt, "have a privileged role in defin-ing the meaning, purpose, and ethical context of privation and effort" that helps protect service members from both physical and moral injury. Part of that role requires that a "leader shares privation and danger with the troops." The leader's own commitment is contagious, in turn motivating the troops "to endurance that is beyond the grasp of a safe, comfortable citizen" (2001, 6). Leaders must also "subordinate their own interest to those of the person or persons in their care," an aspect of what Shay calls the "fiduciary responsibility" borne by the leadership (2014, 186). Clearly, Colt misses the opportunity to be a leader focused on his men and their shared mission. He sacrificed that opportunity on the altar of an egomaniacal "appointment with destiny" as he helps himself to German Scotch, warm and dry in a villa far behind enemy lines, blithely launching platitudes about "the fighting spirit." At least Colt is marginally connected to the overall war effort, even if only for his own glorification. The General's nephew, Captain Maitland (Hal Buckley), on the other hand, has completely abandoned his command, leaving his men vulnerable to the changes brought about by moral injury.

When the film opens, a sergeant known only as Big Joe desperately tries to save his men from a never-ending bombardment—by their own forces: "Mulligan, your bombs are coming down on our heads! I don't know where the Krauts are! Just lift your goddamned barrage!" Big Joe has to appeal to another non-commissioned officer for respite from the friendly fire when his own commanding officer, Captain Maitland, is unresponsive and self-interested. As Big Joe reminds his CO, the men have been "been rained on, pushed on, bombed on, mortared on by Mulligan all the way from the Normandy Beachhead"; they need relief, soft beds, booze, and "passionate broads." Although the nephew of a general, someone who might be able to call in a few chits, Maitland does nothing to protect his men, even from physical injury. He merely responds that he is "aware of the problem" and returns to more important matters. Just as General Colt remains focused on personal glory, Maitland's less grandiose focus is on a yacht that he intends to liberate for himself. He devotes more attention to the boat than to his men, checking the motor and wondering whether the vessel will fit into the hold of a B-17. More to Shay's point about fiduciary responsibility, the Captain is willing to divert military resources to his little project, directing the engineers to extract the vessel from the barn, while his men shift for themselves. When Maitland heads off to Paris to stash the spoils and "get some things for the general," the Sergeant is at a loss, reminding the Captain, "You're supposed to be in charge of this outfit." Noting that Big Joe is doing "such a good job," the Captain sees no reason to actually take up his fiduciary duty toward his men, though he does take care to warn them—without a trace of irony—that "the penalty for looting is death." When Little Joe (Stuart Margolin) asks Big Joe how Maitland "gets away with it," the answer is obvious, "The General's his uncle, that's how." If officers "create the service ethos and its culture," the ethos created by the General and which infects the Captain is that war is waged in service of self, whether a General's glory or a Captain's looted boat.

The only officer in the film who actually leads his men, shares their privations, and is invested in their well-being is Big Joe, a non-commissioned officer. He is an effective leader, one whom the men respect and listen to, not the least because Big Joe listens to his men. However, it is with Big Joe's sense of his own mission within the greater war effort that the damaging effects of moral injury can be seen. As Shay points out, moral injury changes someone because it "deteriorates their character; their ideals, ambitions, and attachments begin to change and shrink" (2001, 5). As Big Joe tries to end Mulligan's unending barrage, Kelly brings in a captured German officer of high rank— a likely source of needed intelligence on the enemy's position (since neither Mulligan nor anyone in authority seems to know where the Germans actually are). Big Joe, however, asks the German only about the town of Nancy, whether there are hotels and "broads." The officer voluntarily offers intelligence about a planned German counter attack, but the Sergeant cuts him off: "We've got enough troubles of our own. To the right, General Patton. To the left, the British Army. To the rear, our own goddamned artillery. Besides all that, it's raining. And the good thing about the weather is it keeps our Air Corps from blowing us to hell because it's too lousy to fly." Constantly placed in danger by their own forces and filling in for an officer who simply abdicated his position, Big Joe understandably feels abandoned in the midst of war. In such circumstances, his mission, as he sees it, has shrunk from active participation in the larger war effort (e.g. reporting intelligence about a counter attack), to a much smaller goal: "I got a job to do and that is to get you guys to Berlin alive." Big Joe resists the bank robbery, not because it is a significant breach of military conduct, but because it threatens his narrowly-defined mission—necessarily self-defined in the absence of leadership.

Others characters are equally disaffected. Oddball (an insouciant Donald Sutherland) commands three Sherman tanks because he never reported his commanding officer's death on account of being "decapitated by an .88." He has zero grief to spare, however, for his CO's demise: "But don't say you're sorry. He's been trying to get us killed ever since we landed at Omaha Beach." Kelly himself, according to the Yossarian-like Supply Sergeant Crapgame (Don Rickles), whose business it is to know everything, "used to be a lieutenant. Pretty good one, too, until he was ordered to attack the wrong hill. Wiped out a half a company of G.I.s. Somebody had to get the blame, and he got picked." The men respond to military indifference, neglect, and exploitation with an understandable devotion to their own best interests, an example set by their chain of command. Even Big Joe comes around, conceding the ultimate futility: "All we do is we fight and we die. We don't get anything out of it." That he even has a sense that they *should* get something out of the war effort is itself a reflection of the ethos created by his commanding officers through their failure to provide principled leadership.

Without the humanity that Eastwood was willing to go to Yugoslavia for, the movie devolves into broad comedy; all of the characters—officers and enlisted men—are simply cartoonish. Carroll O'Connor played General Colt, to the hilt—bombastic, ego-driven, ultimately just a caricature. Maitland, though more understated, is similarly flat. Both characters are played for shtick, as Colt races around, chewing both the scenery and his cigar while handing out medals willy-nilly. Standard generic characters like the venal Crap game and the louche Oddball are merely funny once action replaced questions about the why of war. The one can scare up munitions, brandy and a quote on the price of gold without moving from behind his desk, while Oddball's men live in a gypsy camp, holding themselves "in reserve in case the Krauts mount a counteroffensive which threatens Paris or maybe even New York." Barbra Worely, writing in the *Austin Statesman*, observed that 1970 was a "very IN year for 'the-war-is-hell; but-let's-get-a-good-laugh-out-of-it anyway' movie." Three and a half decades later, Jim Keogh writing for the (Massachusetts) *Telegram and Gazette* noted that in films like *Kelly's Heroes*, war is just a "glorified backdrop for a caper, like *Ocean's Eleven* in fatigues." While Shay's concept of moral injury pulls into focus the corrosive effect of leadership malfeasance, the generally comedic nature of the final print, the softening that so dismayed screenwriter Troy Kennedy Martin, masks the ways in which the failures of military leadership lead to "passive obstructionism, goldbricking, and petty theft, to outright desertion" (2014, 183).

In the 1985 interview, even 15 years after the fact, Eastwood still sounded wistful, if modest: "I had no control over that thing—not that I have any better taste than anybody else—but I would have liked to have done that movie with a little more control" (Wilson and Eastwood 52). With his next combat films, almost 40 years later, Eastwood had that control with *Flags of Our Fathers* and *Letters from Iwo Jima*. Eastwood had, of course, been involved in war-related films between *Kelly's Heroes* and the Iwo Jima films. One could construe *The Beguiled* (1971), *Firefox* (1982), and *Heartbreak Ridge* (1986) as war films, but each of these films move the wars they mention to the periphery. The Civil War is simply a convenient setting in *The Beguiled*. While the main character in *Firefox* seems (at least at first) to suffer from PTSD, the main point of the film is his stealing a plane. *Heartbreak Ridge* is more a better-late-than-never romance movie rather than a true war movie. The one brief bit of combat showcases the anemic unit's new-found "maniless" rather than a comment about war. *Flags of Our Fathers* and *Letters from Iwo Jima* reverse this trend.

These two films about the Battle of Iwo Jima provided Eastwood with subject matter much more significant than the caper in *Kelly's Heroes*. In the sense that the battle occurred, Eastwood was adapting history. *Letters from Iwo Jima* draws from three such sources: Kakehashi, Kumiko. 2007a. *Letters from Iwo Jima: The Japanese Eyewitness Stories That Inspired Clint Eastwood's Film* (London: Weidenfeld & Nicolson); Kakehashi, Kumiko. 2007b. *So Sad to Fall in Battle: An Account of War Based on General Tadamichi Kurayashi's Letters from Iwo Jima* (New York: Ballantine Books); and a collection of Kuribayashi's letters to his children: Yoshida, Tsuyuko, ed. 2007. *Picture Letters from the Commander in Chief* (San Francisco: VIZ Media). In addition, both films are adaptations of non-fiction books: *Flags of Our Fathers* (2000) by James Brady, son of a medic who served on Iwo Jima, and *Letters from Iwo Jima* (2005), by Kumiko Kakehashi. The two films would, then, necessarily intersect with a historical, military, and cultural narrative of the battle that is under constant revision. Eastwood had to make choices about what to include and what to leave out of the precursor texts as well as out of that cultural narrative. The possibility certainly existed for Eastwood to produce a standard World War II drama, a more thoughtful *Saving Private Ryan*, for example. Instead, his choices emphasize not only the terrible damage inflicted on the men who fight and die in the trenches, but also how it is that they come to be the ones who pay the butcher's bill in the first place.

In *Letters from Iwo Jima*, the counterpoint to the egomaniac General Colt and the thieving Captain Maitland is General Tadamichi Kuribayashi (Ken Watanabe), a career soldier, dedicated to the military mission and well aware of his fiduciary responsibility toward the men who serve under him. Unlike General Colt and Captain Maitland, who do not share "privation and danger with the troops" (2201, 6) they lead, Kuribayashi lives as his men do. In fact, the cook (to his great consternation) is under instructions that "all officers will have the same meal rations as their men." Leadership decisions such as these promote unit cohesion, the sense that everyone—leadership, line officers and conscripts—are all in this battle together. In her book *Letters from Iwo Jima*, Kumiko Kakehashi details the several ways in which the historical Kuribayashi lived in the same conditions as his men, including a strict rationing of water (28–29), eating dried vegetables, and refusing gifts of food. He even shared the cigarettes he received "as a gracious gift from the Emperor," slipping them "into the pockets of the hardworking troops, sharing them out" (31). Officers, too, were required to follow Kuribayashi's example. Kakehashi cites the General's bulletin, "Important Points from the Division Chief," mandated the following: "Officers must pay attention to what the soldiers eat. It is forbidden to prepare food for the officers separately or to be indifferent to the provisions of meal for the soldiers" (29–30).

Standing in contrast to Kuribayashi's principled, dedicated leadership are his line officers. While not in the least clownish as in *Kelly's Heroes*, these officers do not follow their General's example, eroding the unit cohesion—and thus the combat strength—that he took such pains to build. Kuribayashi, historically and cinematically, abandoned the standard island defense which concentrated troops and fire power on the beach, instead utilizing existing terrain, adding caves, connecting tunnels, and moving artillery up to ridge level. This defensive posture was without precedent in the Japanese military. When his tradition-bound officers resist, the General lectures them on their own recent disastrous military history: "How long did our guns last along the beaches of Saipan and Guam? Will you please show me just how effective the beach pillboxes at Tarawa were?"

Just as the line officers resist Kuribayashi's plans for defense, further up the chain of command, the leaders of the Japanese Army and Navy further compromise Kuribayashi's leadership through their failure to coordinate with each other in any way for the island's defense. Navy Admiral Ohsugi (Nobumasa Sakagami) cites the established separation of duties, that the island is under Navy control "until the enemy lands," but the Army alone is responsible for all land-based defense. The implication is clear: for the Navy maintaining control of resources and command of the island—not the actual defense of the island—is the first priority. Such power struggles between branches of the military interfere with what should be a shared military mission, effectively reducing Japanese readiness to fight engendered by unit cohesion. Just as he lectured his line officers, an appalled Kuribayashi excoriates the top level brass: "This is a real war! You are aware of that, aren't you?" In the same way that the line officers mindlessly insist on a traditional island defense, these military leaders place "institutional and career considerations above the lives of the soldiers under their responsibility" (Shay, 1994, 16), a "betrayal of trust" at the highest levels of the military that puts men at risk for moral injury, for their very lives.

The General, however central to the Japanese defense of Iwo Jima, does not sit at the very top of the chain of command. Like the enlisted men and non-coms in *Kelly's Heroes*, Kuribayashi, too, suffers a betrayal of what's right, by those in authority, in a situation of extreme danger. The Japanese High Command, in the film and in the historical record, had not provisioned Kuribayashi with the sufficient resources for the island's defense. Promised air support shrank to "41 Zekes and 13 bombers," with 66 planes rededicated to the defense of Saipan. Kuribayashi trusts that, with so little airpower, he will naturally "have to rely on support from the Combined Fleet then." That plan for defense proved a fleeting hope as well, the Japanese armada having been destroyed in the South Pacific along with the planes. The imperial command keeps this information from the General they chose to defend Iwo Jima. He learned about it only second-hand, through Baron Nishi (Tsuyoshi Ihara).

Just as the individual leader bears a responsibility toward the service members under his command, Shay sees the entire military complex as responsible for what happens to all those who fight, from GI to General: "The vast and distant military and civilian structure that provides a modern soldier with his orders, arms, ammunition, food water, information, training, and fire support is ultimately a moral structure, a *fiduciary*, a trustee holding the life and safety of that soldier" (Shay, 1994, 15). While Eastwood's film makes clear that Japanese military command virtually abandoned its fiduciary responsibility, the historical record reveals the depth of that betrayal. According to Kakehashi, "Prime Minister Tôjô had bombastically described Saipan as 'impregnable,' but that did not keep him from abandoning it only ten days after the Americans had landed. The policy of the Imperial General Headquarters toward Iwo Jima was to chop and change in similar fashion. They had decided that Iwo Jima would be lost even before the American invasion began" (25). For all of the men on Iwo Jima, from the lowliest conscript, to career officers, to the General in command, and despite the noble efforts of Tadamichi Kuribayashi, that military structure failed—catastrophically. Of the entire Japanese force on the island, 95 percent died: from dysentery, bullets, shrapnel, napalm, flame throwers. Eastwood's choices for his adaptation foreground the individuals who fight, not some vast, distant structure. In this way, he maintains focus on the human element that was deleted from *Kelly's Heroes*.

Letters from Iwo Jima is a singular film—the story of the famous battle told from the Japanese point of view, through the eyes of sympathetic characters. With an equal focus on the human element in wartime, *Flags of Our Fathers* tells the story of the same battle from an American point of view. That point of view is necessarily complicated by the ways in which Associated Press photographer Joe Rosenthal's famous photograph was, even as the battle raged, to shape and cement a narrative of that action, a narrative that continues to unspool even today. Any movie about Iwo Jima must necessarily interact with that loaded, constructed history, especially a film by a cinematic figure such as Clint Eastwood, whose stature commands attention for every movie he makes. On one level, Eastwood adapted *Flags of Our Fathers* by James Brady, son of Navy Medic John Brady who served on Iwo Jima. On another, however, he adapted—in a sense—that entire cultural narrative. Every choice he made about what to include and what to exclude from the source text's 357 pages, responded (purposively or not) to that history in all its forms: the bond tour, John Wayne's *The Sands of Iwo Jima* (Allan Dwan, 1949), to the Marine Corps War Memorial with its 60-foot flagpole and 16-foot long M-1 rifle dedicated in 1954. Eastwood's cinematic version of that narrative differs sharply from others, notably John Wayne's *Sands of Iwo Jima*, most particularly in its focus on the individual service members once they are off the battlefield and (supposedly) safe from harm. According to former Marine Lieutenant David Morris, this shift places an emphasis on "the exploitation of the common fighting man by the government" (Morris 99) by both military and civilian leaders for the sake of the war industry itself. The way the military and civilian structure eagerly exploits the human-ness of the three service members identified as flag-raisers is a betrayal of what's right at the most profound level.

The events leading up to Joe Rosenthal's instantly recognizable photograph began on day four of the 36-day long battle as then Undersecretary of the Navy James Forrestal (Michael Cumpsty) watched the action from the beach. When he saw the American flag unfurl on top of Mt. Suribachi, he grasped what it meant for the Stars and Stripes to fly over Japanese soil and wanted the souvenir for himself: "I want that flag, Holland. Mark my words, raising that son-of-a-bitch means a Marine Corps for the next 500 years. I want that flag." Forrestal's capricious demand risked the lives of the men to whom he held a fiduciary responsibility as the Undersecretary of the Navy. Historically, Forrestal may have suffered from some form of PTSD himself. After the War, he was diagnosed with "severe depression of the type seen in operational fatigue during the war," eventually committing suicide, at least according to official reports (Akashah and Tennant 90). Diegetically, as the fight to control Suribachi continued, the men made their way back up the hill, removed the first flag, and hoisted a second at the command of Colonel Chandler Johnson (Robert Patrick) who had no love lost for politicians: "Fuck that. That flag belongs to the men in this battalion. That son-of-a-bitch thinks that our men died taking this ground so we could hand over our flag to some politician to pin to his wall? He's out of his goddamn mind! Get me that flag, and find another one to replace it." As the men struggle under fire to raise the much larger flag, Joe Rosenthal (Ned Eisenberg) happened to turn around and, without even looking through the view finder, took the photograph that ultimately changed everything for John Bradley (Ryan Phillippe), René Gangon (Jesse Bradford), and Ira Hayes (Adam Beach).

Once published in some 200 U.S. newspapers, the power of Rosenthal's image was obvious. The photograph could be just the golden ticket the government needed as the U.S. wearied of a war endlessly consuming their husbands, sons, and brothers in lands far away. For this, the actual men in the photograph had to be identified, not as easy as it might seem given the grainy quality of the image and the men's reluctance to be labeled "hero." To get those names, military and civilian leaders were adept at strong-arm tactics. Marine Sergeant Keyes Beech (John Benjamin Hickey) threatens René Gagnon with (possibly) his life: "It's a damn shame, 'cause I promised the Major you'd know who it was. Fact, you not knowing throws a doubt on you being one of the flag-raisers yourself. Since no one wants to be embarrassed, the moment you land they'll turn you around, ship you off to Okinawa in time to meet your buddies on the beach." This threat is real given the 6,800 deaths and 24,000 casualties by battle's end. The brutal combat scenes (replete with decapitations and death by flame-thrower) testify, cinematically, to that threat as well. The threat works and Gagnon fingers James Brady and Ira Hayes. Bud Gerber (John Slattery) of the Treasury Department then threatens the reluctant heroes with the imaginary consequences of their refusal to participate in the proposed bond tour, twisting their desire to return to their units to his own end: "You want to go back to your buddies? Well, stuff some rocks in your pockets before you get on the plane because that's all we got left to throw at the Japanese. And don't be surprised if your plane doesn't make it off the runway because the fuel dumps are empty." Not just the battle, but the entire war will be lost if they insist they refuse to play hero on the bond tour: "We make a deal with the Japanese, we give whatever they want and we come home, because you've seen them fight, and they sure as shit ain't giving up."

Adept at wringing the big bucks out of human suffering, Gerber is arguably the least likable character in the movie, embodying all of the chronic cynicism that powered the war bond tour. The mothers of fallen soldiers are just as subject to his predatory manipulations as combat-hardened service members. Gerber is frank about his intentions, at least to Ira Hayes: "You present each mother with a flag, they say a few words. People will shit money, it'll be so moving." When the men resist being paraded about as the "Heroes of Iwo Jima" and lying to "Gold Star Mothers" about who was in the picture, Gerber shovels on the blame and guilt to force their participation: "People on the street corners, they looked at this picture and they took hope. Don't ask me why, I think it's a crappy picture myself. You can't even see your faces. But it said we can win this war, are winning this war, we just need you to dig a little deeper. They want to give us that money. No, they want to give it to you. But you, you don't want to ask for it. You don't want to give them hope. You want to explain about this person and that flag. Well, that's your choice. Because if we admit we made a mistake, that's all anybody'll talk about and that will be that." Ultimately, facts do not matter to Gerber, only the power to get people to buy more bonds: "You know what, I don't give a shit, you're in the picture, you raised the flag, that's the story we're selling, boys." Like the veterans Shay and others work with the flag raisers were "exploited and betrayed by people holding the right professional credentials, in fulfillment of their institutional positions" (Shay and Munroe, 392). Consciously practicing coercion and deception to control the flag-raisers, the military structure transforms the men from human beings into mere tokens of a ginned-up patriotism, manifesting a clear disrespect for their very humanity. As movie critic Mark Holcomb puts it: "war is waged by flesh-and-blood people, and expecting soldiers to function as symbols is just one more shitty, impossible job we force on them" ("War Movie: But Which War?").

Just as with *Letters from Iwo Jima*, that part of the historical record not included in *Flags of Our Fathers* reveals the depth of betrayal at the hands of the military political machine. Within a month of its publication, the Treasury Department adopted Rosenthal's image of the flag raising as the symbol of the Seventh War Loan. "They might've called it the 'We're Flat Fucking Broke and Can't Even Afford Bullets So We're Begging for Your Pennies' bond drive," the cinematic Gerber asserts, "but it didn't have quite the ring." The historical record, however, indicates that selling bonds was not the only way of financing the war. Although willing to conscript young men to kill and die for their country in the war effort, Congress was entirely unwilling to conscript wealth, as the *New York Times* put it in "Conscription of Wealth," through taxation or even government take-over of war industries (78). Men, yes. Corporate wealth, no. Despite Gerber's cinematic and dramatic claims that the Treasury was out of money—"Tanks aren't being built. Machine guns, bazookas, hand grenades, zip"—that soldiers would be reduced to throwing rocks at the Japanese, funds were available without a successful bond drive.

The flag raisers were knowingly being lied to. In fact the Treasury Department had access to all the money needed to fund the war. Henry Morgenthau (1891–1967), Secretary of the Treasury, had a deal in place with the Federal Reserve to "assure that an ample supply of funds is available at all times for financing the war effort" according to the *New York Times in* "Tax Rise Hinted by Morgenthau" (35). In other words, the Fed agreed to buy any war bonds not purchased by the United States citizenry. With the Federal Reserve deal in place, as historian William L. O'Neill points out, selling bonds was, in reality, a vehicle for propagandizing the war. Morgenthau "wanted bonds sold widely and in such a way as to make Americans 'war-minded.' He believed this was even more important than helping finance defense purchases. To sell bonds was to sell the war" to those sacrificing their sons, their husbands, their fathers. For the purposes of "selling," then, "bond drives were aimed at the average American rather than wealthy investors" who wielded political clout (O'Neill 138). Despite the popular perception that everyone had to dig even deeper than they already had to fund the war to a final victory, the "degree of American mobilization fell short not because men and women were unwilling to sacrifice more, but because leaders shrank from the prospect" (O'Neill 142). Even the source text falls in line with this past of the narrative. Noting that the tour "occupied a cherished place in American tradition" (281), calls the bond tour "a gargantuan feat of popular democracy" (282).

Rosenthal's photograph, which ran originally without a caption, continued its life as a propaganda vehicle even after the war was over, sucking in the three named flag raisers, despite already emerging doubts about who was who. The story of who was where when began to unravel shortly after demobilization and the end of the draft. According to *Omaha World Herald* reporter Michael Hansen, the family of Harlon Block received a letter from Ira Hayes stating that their son, not Hank Hansen, was in the photo. They sent the note to their Congressman; there was an investigation, Block was listed as a flag raiser, and Hansen's name was stricken from the record. The Blocks demanded the material from that investigation and were turned down, according to Hansen. The new official version was enforced with Orwellian rigor. Although Mrs. Hansen, whose son was killed on Iwo Jima, stumped with the others to sell war bonds, the Marines excluded her and her family from the unveiling of the Iwo Jima memorial in 1954. The Blocks, however, were in attendance.

Despite these and other doubts outlined in the *World Herald* article, the propaganda machine geared up again to use the flag raisers to flog the next conflict, the Cold War. In 1949, Republic Studios was prepared to sink $1,000,000, almost $10 million today, into a John Wayne vehicle about the war in the Pacific. The studio's desire to sell the film by using the flag raisers fit neatly into plans the U.S. military had to win support of Americans for a large peacetime standing military (Grandstaff 303). According to James Bradley, the Marines "moved shrewdly and efficiently. They contacted Ira, René, and John in turn, informing each of them that the other two had agreed to participate. Thus each man was given to understand that if he backed out, he would ruin the entire movie" (321). The Marines' lies allowed them to leverage the men's sense of loyalty and duty to promote the Corps, to provide for the continuation of the institution itself. The three flag raisers, historically and cinematically, experienced the "interpersonal coercion, and institutional exploitation, deceit and betrayal" described by the veterans Shay treats (Shay and Munroe 392). The moral world that should have been constructed by the military and civilian structure failed catastrophically for the flag raisers, and their families, leaving them diminished and bereft.

"All killing," according to theologian Robert Emmet Meagher, "kills something in the killer." In fact, "there is no such thing as killing without dying" (xviii). U.S. Army Lt. Col. Douglas Pryer agrees, claiming that an entrenched myth of war "is that we can kill without being killed ourselves." The fatalities of state-sponsored, armed conflict, he argues, include not just those who are in the ground, but combat "just as surely kills the souls of warriors who, having marched off to war and moral injury, [return] home, heads held high while music plays and their loved ones cheer, yet feeling inside they are forever lost" (134). Eastwood's *Flags of Our Fathers* represents cinematically men whose lives are wrecked by combat and by the way those combat experiences are exploited. Ira Hayes, dead by the age of 32, essentially

drinks himself to death. John Bradley, thinking always of, desperately search-
ing for Iggy, regrets that he is so disconnected from his son. And René
Gagnon, who believed in the promises made by glad-handing businessmen
parasitizing his fame, is quickly abandoned, bewildered, lost. Jonathan Shay,
propelled on a mission by the veterans he serves to see that more young people are not wrecked by war, provides a blueprint for how to prevent moral
injury, the first part of which is "neither new nor surprising: the surest path
to casualty reduction is swiftly and skillfully to win the fights that the nation
sends troops into" (2002, 205). For a mental health practitioner like Shay,
however, there is only one truly effective way to make absolutely certain that
no more lives are lost, no more souls are killed: the "primary prevention of
combat PTSD requires elimination of the source of the injury, which is to
say, elimination of combat" (1994, 196). *Flags of Our Fathers* and *Letters from
Iwo Jima* make clear in ways that challenge the very limits of the genre, that
civilian and military leaders bear a fiduciary responsibility toward the men
who fight. It is a society, however, that bears the final responsibility for sending men and women into combat, for demanding that they will still be the
ones to pay the butcher's bill.

WORKS CITED

Akashah, Mary, and David Tennant. 1980. "Madness and Politics: The Case of James Forre-
stal." *Proceedings of the Oklahoma Academy of Science* 60: 89–92.
"Banks Ready to Meet Any Emergency." 1941. *Pittsburgh Press*, 9 Dec., p. 34.
The Beguiled. 1971. Directed by Don Siegel, performances by Clint Eastwood, Geraldine Page,
and Elizabeth Hartman, Malpaso Company.
Bradley, James, with Ron Powers. 2006. *Flags of Our Fathers*. Bantam Movie Tie-In Trade
Paperback ed. New York: Bantam.
"Conscription of Wealth." 1940. *New York Times*, 8 Sept., p. 78.
Cooke, Lez. 2007. *Troy Kennedy Martin*. Manchester: Manchester University Press.
Eastwood, Clint. 2011. Interview. By Paul Nelson. *Conversations with Clint: Paul Nelson's Lost
Interviews with Clint Eastwood 1979–1983*, edited by Ken Avery. New York: Continuum.
Eldridge, Robert D. 2014. *Iwo Jima and the Bonin Islands in U.S. Japan Relations: American
Strategy, Japanese Territory, and the Islanders In-Between*. Marine Corp University Press.
Firefox. 1982. Directed by Clint Eastwood, performances by Clint Eastwood, Freddie Jones,
and David Huffman, Malpaso Company.
Flags of Our Fathers. 2006. Directed by Clint Eastwood, performances by Ryan Phillippe,
Barry Pepper, and Joseph Cross, DreamWorks.
Grandstaff, Mark R. 1996. "Making the Military American: Advertising, Reform and the
Demise of an Antistanding Military Tradition, 1945–1955." *Journal of Military History*
60: 2:pp. 299–323.
Hansen, Matthew. 2014. "New Mystery Arises from Iconic Iwo Jima Image: History Buffs'
Analysis of the Famous World War II Photo Challenges a Long-Assumed Truth." *Omaha
World-Herald*, 23 Nov. dataomaha.com/media/news/2014/iwo-jima/. Accessed 23 June
2016.
Heartbreak Ridge. 1986. Directed by Clint Eastwood, performances by Clint Eastwood, Mar-
sha Mason, and Everett McGill, Jay Weston Productions.
Holcomb, Mark. 2006. "War Movie: But Which War? *Flags of Our Fathers* Is about WWII,
but It's Also About a More Contemporary War." *Las Vegas Weekly*, 19 Oct.
"Iwo Heroes Speak at Rally Here." 1945. *Arizona Republic*, 8 June, p. 1.

Janis, Irving L. 1963. "Group Identification under Conditions of External Danger." *British Journal of Medical Psychology*, 36:3: 227–38.

Kakehashi, Kumiko. 2007a. *Letters from Iwo Jima: The Japanese Eyewitness Stories That Inspired Clint Eastwood's Film*. International ed. London: Weidenfeld & Nicolson.

_____. 2007b. *So Sad to Fall in Battle: An Account of War Based on General Tadamichi Kurayashi's Letters from Iwo Jima*. New York: Ballantine Books.

Kelly's Heroes. 1970. Directed by Brian G. Hutton, performances by Clint Eastwood, Telly Savalas, and Don Rickles, MGM.

Letters from Iwo Jima. 2006. Directed by Clint Eastwood, performances by Ken Watanabe, Kazunari Niomiya, and Tsuyoshi Ihara, Dreamworks.

Litz, Brett, et al. 2009. "Moral Injury and Moral Repair in War Veterans: A Preliminary Model and Intervention Strategy." *Clinical Psychology Review* 29:8: 695–706.

Meagher, Robert Emmet. 2014. *Killing from the Inside Out: Moral Injury and Just War*. Eugene, OR: Cascade Books.

Morris, David J. 2007. "The Image as History: Clint Eastwood's Unmaking of an American Myth." *Virginia Quarterly Review* 83:2: 94–107.

O'Neill, William L. 1993. *A Democracy at War: America's Fight at Home and Abroad in World War II*. New York: The Free Press.

Pryer, Douglas A. 2015. Review of *On Killing from the Inside Out: Moral Injury and Just War*. *Military Review* 95:2: 133–34.

Sands of Iwo Jima. 1949. Directed by Allan Dwan, performances by John Wayne, John Agar, and Adele Mara, Republic Pictures.

Saving Private Ryan. 1998. Directed by Steven Spielberg, performances by Tom Hanks, Matt Damon, and Tom Sizemore, Dreamworks.

Shay, Jonathan. 1991. "Learning About Combat Stress from Homer's *Iliad*." *Journal of Traumatic Stress* 4:4: 562–79.

_____. 1994. *Achilles in Vietnam: Combat Trauma and the Undoing of Character*. New York: Atheneum.

_____. 2001. "Trust: Touchstone for a Practical Military Ethos." *Spirit, Blood, and Treasure: The American Cost of Battle in the 21st Century*, edited by Donald E. Vandergriff. Novato, CA: Presidio Press, 3–17.

_____. 2002. *Odysseus in America: Combat Trauma and the Trials of Homecoming*. New York: Scribner.

_____. 2006. "The Pen and the Dollar Bill: Two Philosophical Stage Props." *The National Academies of Sciences, Engineering, Medicine*, 13 Feb., www.nationalacademies.org/hmd/~/media/4B043D25DBDA42318421EBAFCBDCDBD3.ashx. Accessed 27 Aug. 2016.

_____. 2009. "The Trials of Homecoming: Odysseus Returns from Iraq/Afghanistan." *Smith College Studies in Social Work* 79:3–4: 286–98.

_____. 2011. "Casualties." *Daedalus, the Journal of the American Academy of Arts and Sciences* 140:3: 179–88.

_____. 2014. "Moral Injury." *Psychoanalytic Psychology* 31:2: 182–91.

Shay, Jonathan, and James Munroe. 1998. "Group and Milieu Therapy for Veterans with Complex Post-Traumatic Stress Disorder." *Posttraumatic Stress Disorder: A Comprehensive Text*, edited by Philip A. Saigh and J. Douglas Bremner. Boston: Allyn & Bacon, 391–413.

"Tax Rise Hinted by Morgenthau." 1941. *New York Times*, 9 Dec., p. 35.

Wilson, Michael Henry, and Clint Eastwood. 2010. *Eastwood on Eastwood*. Rev. English ed. Paris: Cahiers du Cinéma.

Belated Casualties
Delayed Stress Disorder in Gran Torino

JAMES F. SCOTT

In *Tribe* (2016), an extended meditation on "homecoming and belong-ing," Sebastian Junger persuasively argues that "social resilience," which he describes as "society's ability to recover from hardship" (102), is the under-appreciated variable that affects and conditions what is clinically described as PTSD—post-traumatic stress disorder. Without questioning the vivid real-ity of post-traumatic stress, Junger contextualizes the psychic malady of many war veterans by noting that these wounded warriors are troubled not so much by the initial trauma of the battlefield as by their sense of alienation and estrangement from the society that sent them to war. This refinement of a valuable concept applies in a particular way to Clint Eastwood's presentation of Walt Kowalski in *Gran Torino* (2008).

Like his compatriots who would later come home from the killing fields of Vietnam, Afghanistan, and Iraq, Eastwood's protagonist brings his scarred soul back from the "policing action" in Korea to a family and a nation that is simply bewildered by him, implicitly denying what Junger calls his "need of some way to vent his feelings to the wider community" (122). Hence we find him nearly half a century later, living in embittered isolation and still displaying what students of post-traumatic stress disorder describe as "a psy-chic numbing," an "unresponsiveness to affective stimuli" (Peterson, et al., 1991, 22). Frozen in anger and frustration, he resembles the PTSD victims described by Rachel Yehuda, whose patients, she says, have lost all sense of intimacy and tenderness from having lived too long with "interpersonal vio-lence, … graphic scenes of death," and the "imminent threat of subsequent attack" (2002, 108). Though the trauma of battle is nowhere foregrounded in *Gran Torino*, Kowalski's alienation from home and family is decisively evident. In keeping with Junger's analysis, Kowalski is among the war veterans who "realize that the tribe they were actually fighting for wasn't their country, it was their unit" (110). Ironically, his conflicted relationship to an immigrant Hmong family affords him an opportunity to recover the sense of "belonging" he could not find in his own bloodlines or in his native city. This incongruous turn of the plot invites us to explore what Engel and Gourlie (2012) call Eastwood's "new mythology," in which community comes to include his Asian neighbors and where "older orthodoxies of religion and state" will have to be renegotiated in light of a transformed cultural paradigm (275).

Although *Gran Torino* has attracted considerable scholarly interest (not all of it favorable), relatively few commentators have made as much of Kowalski's war experience as one might expect. In *The Silvering Screen* (2011) Sally Chivers calls the film a "vengeful fantasy" (114), while Christopher Traficante (2012) sees Eastwood's troubled protagonist as no more than "a rogue figure at the heart of the contemporary vigilante film" (111). Gourlie and Engel (2012) speak of the "unspecified ways" in which Kowalski's psychological distress "would probably count as post-traumatic stress disorder" but quickly pass on after mentioning his "heavy burden of guilt" and his telltale "postures of self-defense against multiple assaults" (269–270). While he might sometimes be "obnoxious enough to make Archie Bunker seem like a model of working class virtue" (Sterritt, 2014, 200), it's a mistake to assume his hostility to neighbors, friends, and family is somehow an uncaused cause. Kowalski is a victim as much as a vigilante, deeply disturbed by a war experience from which he has never recovered and more recently bedeviled by the loss of his spouse. This latter trauma, together with his precipitously declining health, brings him to the pitch of frustration and fury we first see at the memorial service for his wife. Even before his first encounter with his unwelcome Hmong neighbors, who quickly become a focal point of his social alienation, Walt Kowalski is already a haunted and rage-ridden man.

Like *Unforgiven* (1992), another tale of unresolved guilt, *Gran Torino* opens with the burial of a loved one, his wife Dorothy of many years who has brought the protagonist whatever peace he has enjoyed and whatever purpose he has managed to thread into his life. The memorial service should be a moment of communal feeling, an opportunity for the bereaved to acknowledge the hurt of his loss, but also to find in friends and family a secure tie to the wider social network that must now sustain him. It is also a moment when his personal faith, the spirituality represented for Kowalski by the Roman Catholic Church, should mediate his reintegration into society. But the ceremony does nothing to assuage Kowalski's grief or repair his alienation from his blood family.

In this scene we see Kowalski standing alone by his wife's casket, connected by a slow pan to her smiling face in an old photograph, but entirely removed from his children and grandchildren. He speaks only to Al (John

Johns), a friend and drinking companion, the one person to approach the casket and receive Kowalski's thanks for an expression of sympathy. Kowalski seems almost contemptuous of his grandchildren, particularly his grand-daughter, Ashley (Dreama Walker), whose giggling during the ceremony clearly offends him and whose bare midriff and conspicuous navel ring prompt him to emit a hostile grunt. He also glares at her while she plays with her cell phone, apparently checking messages or sending tweets. His sons show no affection for their father, speaking of him only as an angry old man who poses problems that somehow they have to deal with. "Why don't you have him move in with you?" is clearly meant as a joke between the two brothers, not a loving effort to find a new home for an elderly parent. Nor is the ritual itself in any way satisfying. Though the priest has had some kind of personal relationship with the deceased, his sermon sounds pre-packaged, full of irrelevant clichés like "What is this thing called life?" When Fr. Janovich (Christopher Carley) goes on to say that "death is sweet for those of us who know the salvation that awaits," we are not sure whether this special cadre of mourners he refers to would actually include Kowalski. Small wonder that he soon dismisses the priest as an "overeducated virgin" whose offer to hear his Confession is curtly rebuffed.

The companion scene at Kowalski's home that follows the memorial service confirms the theme of alienation, marking the protagonist as a stranger in his own house, unable to relate to friends or relatives. His direct rebuke to Fr. Janovich is of a piece with his reluctance to talk to his sons or even to make eye contact with other guests as he paces from room to room, floor to floor, and from inside to the porch or garage. His grandsons in the cellar are seen pawing through his military keepsakes with no feeling for their specialness, and Ashley is interested in her grandfather only because of what she might inherit from him. When she suggests that she would welcome the chance to own his "cool car"—the 1972 Gran Torino, which he cares for meticulously, he responds by spitting on the floor and closing the door behind him. We never learn the full backstory of Kowalski's estrangement from his family, but clearly this relationship is damaged beyond repair. Much later he will admit to Fr. Janovich, "I was never close to my two sons. I didn't know them, I didn't know how." Unfamiliar with the details of Kowalski's war experience, we don't immediately see the link between his anger, his extreme introversion, his estrangement from his supposed caregivers, and the xenophobia that spurs him to insult his Hmong neighbors.

No doubt as to Kowalski's racial bias. His psychic growth was frozen in the early 1950s, when it was not unusual to hear Koreans referred to as "gooks," and when relatively few public figures found fault with the internment of Japanese-American citizens during the World War II period, a decade earlier. In fact, prior to the liberalizing Immigration and Nationality Act of 1965,

Asians of all stripes had been discouraged from citizenship by ethno-racial quotas that limited their eligibility to settle permanently in the USA. We should also factor in Kowalski's resentment of the poverty culture that has overtaken the urban core of Detroit. His house, with its proudly displayed flag and well-swept front porch, is almost something from a time warp, as anachronistic as the classic automobile he so deeply prizes. What was once a tidy working-class neighborhood has become run-down, jobless, gang-infested, and seemingly threatened by a faceless racialized "other." Working from these preconceptions, Kowalski's immediate impulse is to keep the Hmong family out of his house and off of his lawn, even if they mean him no harm and are not the true source of his unease. Nor does he understand the ritual blood-letting of a ceremonial fowl, which he observes from his porch and pronounces "barbarian." How could these people ever be "Americans"? The irony is that this pariah culture will turn out to be the agent of Kowalski's redemption just as he accidentally becomes the engine of their further progress towards integration into the national culture of the USA.

In spite of Kowalski's scorn for his neighbors' cultural habits, our privileged look inside their home lets us see that the extended family of the Lors is everything the Kowalski family is not. Incongruously, Kowalski is burying his wife at approximately the same moment that the Lors are celebrating the birth of a child. This is a community event, engaging at least three generations, creating mountains of food, stimulating lively conversation, and drawing both the family and its guests into a religious ritual that is the equivalent of a christening. In the broadly Daoist spirituality of the Hmong, this ceremony, presided over by a shaman, urges the spirit of the child to "come home and not wander anymore," thus assuring that the newborn will have a coherent identity, a personhood that will be drawn from the ancestral realm to enflesh itself in a new generation. The compact grouping of celebrants in the living room of the Lor home emphasizes cohesiveness and the interdependence of the family, not just the nuclear unit, but the cousins, the aunts, and the in-laws. Considering, as contemporary scholars do, that the Hmong people were recently "displaced from China, relegated to the Lao Highlands, persecuted across the Mekong into Thailand, and repatriated to nations such as the United States," their dogged loyalty to tradition and ancestry is fully intelligible as a source of stability and direction. At this same gathering, however, we can also see the fracture points of the new Hmong life world, which for the first time is feeling the impact of the American majority culture. Much to the chagrin of the elderly matriarch (who also wishes that "old white men," like Kowalski, would get out of the neighborhood), the surrounding culture has already begun to affect traditional gender roles, seriously destabilizing both male and female behavior models. Under the influence of public schools, Sue has become much more bookish than the traditional Hmong maiden, while her younger brother, Thao (Bee Vang) swings wildly between female housekeeping or gardening and gang-oriented delinquency.

Thao's behavior in *Gran Torino* answers perfectly to the revised paradigm of assimilation theory that has been circulating since the 1990s, when Alejandro Portes and Ruben Rumbaut did their ground-breaking research on second generation immigrants, particularly migrants from non-white cultures. This research mounted a powerful challenges to "classical" immigration theory and the myth of the American "melting pot" (2001). Instead of a benign and almost inevitably positive outcome of the assimilative process, Portes and Rumbaut postulated a potentially negative assimilation whereby non-white youth would be denied socioeconomic opportunity on racial grounds. What results under these circumstances, according to Nazli Kibria and her colleagues in *Race and Immigration* (2014), is a "dysfunctional pattern of integration into disadvantaged urban minority cultures that are marked by an adversarial outlook of rejection and rebellion against mainstream norms and values" (120). In other words, what results from this worst-case scenario is a perverse form of assimilation in which the new, relatively unwelcome, immigrants "melt" into a criminal underclass given to theft, drug-dealing, and gang warfare. And this outcome, they conclude, may coexist in the same neighborhood, and even in the same family, with a much more positive result, where "upward socioeconomic mobility is concurrent with strong ethnic involvement. Here the second generation continues to identify and be involved with the ethnic communities of their immigrant parents, even as they learn American ways" (120). Or, as Sue Lor (Ahney Her), Thao's older sister, frames it for Walt Kowalski, "the girls go to college and the guys go to jail."

Thao seems jailhouse bound when he is drawn towards the Hmong gang, which behaves very much like the negatively assimilated newcomers described in *Race and Immigration*. They take their inspiration from the black and Mexican gangs that vie for control of Kowalski's Detroit neighborhood, adopting their dress, cultivating their surly attitudes, marking their territory as sites of criminal power. The Lors scorn them but seem powerless to keep them from influencing young Thao. "He's really smart," Sue tells Kowalski, "but doesn't know what direction to go." Why Hmong masculinity is more problematic than its gendered opposite is a question beyond the scope of this paper, but in Thao's case the absence of positive role models together with the high profile presence and cocksure tone of Spider's (Doua Moua) gang are surely the decisive factors. Their effort to recruit Thao into the criminal cadre is what drives the plot of *Gran Torino* and ultimately invites the sacrificial intervention of Walk Kowalski.

The back-to-back "recruitment scenes," where Thao is pulled towards delinquency, build inevitably upon a conversation during the celebration of the newborn in the Lor household. As Thao is shown cleaning plates and rinsing dishes for the washer, it is remarked that he is unmanly, consenting to perform "women's work." This theme is immediately picked up in a scene on the street when Spider's gang cruises slowly past him in a late model car and invites him to "come chill with us." At this moment Thao is completely at odds with his surroundings. In a montage of close-ups and wide-angle shots we see a typical urban ghetto, featuring drab high-rise apartments, a sagging cyclone fence, vacant lots overgrown with weeds and long grass, board fencing defaced by gang graffiti. That Thao is trying to read a book while negotiating this landscape adds an almost comic detail. Spider's gang—which apparently consists of several more of the Lors' cousins—represents itself as "family," the muscle and firepower that will protect Thao from a hostile Mexican gang that is also cruising the neighborhood. "We just bailed your ass out," says one would-be friend, proud that his semi-automatic weapon has put to rout the carload of Mexicans who came armed with no more than a small caliber pistol. Though Thao resists this invitation, it is renewed in the visit to the Lor home that immediately follows. This scene finds the young man cultivating a garden, while his older sister sits on the front porch reading. The gang drives Sue off the porch, then concentrates more forcefully on pushing Thao towards the rite of passage that will make him a "brother" in Spider's criminal "family." Thao must show his manly spirit by stealing the Gran Torino.

In "Stealing Freedom" (2015), Heitmann and Uhlman cite the Gran Torino as a uniquely appropriate symbol of white cultural hegemony and thus an ideal target of the Hmong gang's subversive behavior. Thinking of the automobile as a trope of "autonomous individualism," they maintain that the prospective theft of the classic car "challenges white male privilege" and mocks the mastery that a supremely affluent American bourgeoisie claimed for itself in the decades immediately after World War II (86–87). From this standpoint, it's significant that Kowalski never drives the Torino, but fetishizes it as an icon to signify a world that is gone. If Thao successfully steals the car for Spider, he will not only net something of presumed cash value but also perform an act of ethnic defiance, as if forcing the white patriarchs of a bygone era to yield the road to the delinquent brown teenagers of today. The symbolic import of this act heightens the significance of two later events, when Thao is invited to drive Kowalski's car and finally, at the end of the film, when he inherits it as his personal property. On this present occasion, his incompetence as a thief saves him from the probably disastrous consequences of success.

Thao's grand theft fails almost comically, amid telltale noise and general confusion. But Kowalski almost matches Thao's ineptitude by falling flat on his face as he attempts to capture the burglar. It's not even clear that he realizes the intruder is his young neighbor from next door. Sprawled on the garage floor and spitting up blood (a consequence of his tubercular condition), Kowalski demonstrates that his soldiering days are mostly behind him, though he can still talk about "piling up bodies like sandbags." Fortunately for everyone, Thao flees the premises without doing harm to Kowalski, as he might easily have done. This allows Kowalski the time to refurbish his warrior persona when Spider's gang later returns to the Lor home in an effort to entice Thao into another test of his male prowess. When the Lor family actively resists the gang, the altercation spills over onto Kowalski's lawn, prompting him to grab his rifle and drive the street thugs out of the neighborhood. On this more public stage, Kowalski emerges as a hero to the Lors, credited with "saving" Thao from the street gang that otherwise would have sucked him out of his home. Shortly thereafter, Kowalski intervenes again on behalf of Sue Lor, when she is molested by a small band of black teenagers. These events pull Kowalski into an unsolicited relationship with his Hmong neighbors. Ironically, this bond with the Lor family is what allows the wounded warrior a measure of moral redemption.

To understand the dynamics of Kowalski's relationship to the Lors, we should glance again at Junger's analysis of the difficulties combat veterans encounter when they attempt to reintegrate themselves into the social network they supposedly went into battle to protect and defend. Many veterans, including Eastwood's protagonist, share the sentiments Junger recalls from Siegfried Sassoon, the war weary British soldier from World War I, who upon returning home on sick leave, sadly mused, "In bitter safety I awake, unfriended" (78). The irony here is that the sense of alienation overwhelms the positive feeling of safety. In his "tribalistic" construction of the social contract, Junger argues that, "veterans need to feel they are just as necessary and productive back in society as they were on the battlefield" (74). One of his most meaningful analogies is to "Iroquois warriors (who) would return to a community that still needed them to hunt and fish and participate in the fabric of everyday life. There was no transition when they came home because—much like in Israel—the battlefield was an extension of society, and vice versa" (74). The circumstance that the Iroquois share with the Israelis, according to Junger, is a sense of "shared public meaning (which) gives soldiers a context for their losses and their sacrifice that is acknowledged by most of the society" (97). Fr. Janovich may have a point when he urges Kowalski to seek "forgiveness," since he is indeed a guilty man, but even more certainly he needs relevance, like Junger's veterans who want to feel "they are just as necessary and productive back in society as they were on the battlefield" (102). This is the role he carves out for himself as mentor to Thao and as guardian spirit of his troubled neighborhood.

The action in *Gran Torino* takes a decisive turn in companion scenes where Kowalski celebrates his birthday first with his son and then, quite reluctantly, with the Lors. The encounter with his blood family is a fiasco. Though perhaps well-meaning, or at least persuaded of their obligation to be nice to an ageing parent, Mitch and his wife approach Kowalski with a birthday cake and two gifts, each vying with the other as inappropriate presents. Junger makes the point eloquently that stress-ridden combat veterans resent being treated as misfits and outliers, worthy of sympathy or the status of victimhood, but not social peers, welcome in day-to-day encounters with family, friends, and working companions. "All the praise in the world," he insists, "doesn't mean anything if you're not recognized by society as someone who can contribute valuable labor" (100). This question is of redoubled importance when the geriatric factor is added, as is the case when the stress-victim is an older adult, coping with diminished physical skills. The younger Kowalskis come to the parent's door with one agenda in mind—to hasten his departure from the public world. As transitional objects, they offer a bulky telephone with a monstrously large display screen, as if intended to make phone numbers legible from low-flying drones. The other present is a strange-looking device for grasping ahold of things that are beyond reach, even though it's nowhere suggested that he has trouble reaching anything. They neglect to ask about his health, which is obviously failing, or his social life, which would be worth inquiring into, in spite of the sensitivity of the topic. Or they could simply invite him to dinner. Quickly, the true purpose of the visit reveals itself—the proposal to move him out of his home and into assisted living. Whether or not this is a bread-and-butter question or something that has to do with his personal safety, it's clear he feels more comfortable in his own quarters, proud of his flag and his carefully pruned yard. He also enjoys the close companionship of his dog, the only positive force in his life before Sue Lor draws him into the Hmong family.

Kowalski's less formal encounter with Sue leads him to join the Lors for a barbeque that becomes more dramatic when Sue realizes this is his birthday. In spite of his doubts about "gook food," he finds himself enjoying a meal far better prepared than anything likely to emerge from his own kitchen. Surprisingly, the family is also well supplied with beer, Kowalski's favorite food group, and a mark of the Lors' drift towards the American mainstream. Though some members of the extended family decisively shun him, he becomes the focal point of several small groups and arouses the attention of the family shaman. She nicely counterpoints the impact of Fr. Janovich, making no demands upon him, but remarking that his "spirit is not at peace." The most interesting moments in the scene come when Kowalski makes his way downstairs to mingle with the young people, who seem more open to him than the older members of the family. Among them is an attractive, outgoing young woman named Youa (Choua Kue), who briefly converses with him and towards whom he shows a faint glimmer of erotic interest. Her queries also draw from him the comment that he is a man who "fixes" things, a reference to a broad skills-set that resonates powerfully through the rest of the film. For now, it means that he's a pretty good handyman, as is seen when he feels compelled to stabilize a wobbly washer/dryer unit. This impromptu birthday party also occasions his becoming better acquainted with Thao and beginning to act as his advisor. Astonishingly, his first advice is romantic, urging the shy young man to pursue Youa, the young woman he himself had felt drawn to.

Not long after the social adventure of the birthday party, we find Kowalski mingling with his neighbors when he gathers with Sue, Thao, and Youa at an impromptu barbecue where he performs as a chef, in charge of feeding his new "family." What's more, his prompting has persuaded Thao to arrange a dinner date with Youa, facilitated by Kowalski's proposal that the young man borrow the Gran Torino. At this time, we also see Kowalski turning Thao into a kind of apprentice, gradually passing along to the marginalized adolescent some of the competencies that have caused the older man to describe himself as a fixer. It starts with a tour of the Kowalski tool shed and quickly graduates to serious on-the-job training. Under Kowalski's supervision, Thao repairs a roof, clears large swatches of brush and bramble, uproots a recalcitrant tree stump, and looks on appreciatively as his mentor rehabilitates a dilapidated electric fan. Together, they become a neighborhood handyman service, scheduling small jobs that would otherwise be left undone. Not only do both men add to their personal self-esteem, we can see that several down-at-the-heels houses actually begin to look better. Thao's apprenticeship successfully concludes when Kowalski introduces him to Mr. Kennedy, a construction contractor, who promises to find him "something to do."

These promising developments, however, soon take a darker turn, disallowing Kowalski the golden twilight that might have seemed in the offing. The Hmong gang is unwilling to release Thao to the world of respectable work and more than ready to punish Kowalski for meddling in their affairs. The gang represents the sinister side of the warrior culture that is a crucial part of Hmong history. In fact, most recently, Hmong warriors had been comrades in arms with the Americans in Southeast Asia during the Vietnam years (see Hamilton-Merritt, 1993, esp. 69–94, 225–229), as Sue points out to Kowalski in one of their front porch conversations. But the street toughs of *Gran Torino* are a grotesque parody of this warrior class, akin to what Junger calls the "skinwalkers," borrowing a metaphor from the Navajo. Junger sees these ghastly revenants as an alienated remnant of a warrior class, without discipline, direction, or loyalty, literally "untribed," and detached from history: Their "ultimate act of disaffiliation (is) violence against their own people" (113). In *Gran Torino*, the "disaffiliated" gang visits its nihilistic wrath upon Thao and Sue Lor, the best fruit of the new Hmong generation.

The melodrama that concludes *Gran Torino* is admittedly hyper-intense and understandably has not pleased every critic. But for all of its over-the-top mayhem the finale is carefully crafted. Eastwood gradually escalates the level of violence till we reach a point where the valences are reversed and circumstances demand heroism in a new key. The brutal burning of Thao's face elicits from Kowalski the classical macho response that takes its cue from the shoot-out at the OK Corral. Kowalski briefly triumphs, but his satisfaction is short-lived. Now the gang attacks the whole Lor family, strafing the house with automatic weapons fire, while beating and sexually assaulting Sue. When Kowalski takes stock of the situation in his noir-lit living room, he knows that he must craft a new strategy. And it is a strategy that unwittingly releases him from his troubled past.

In *Myths of Masculinity* (1993), William Doty calls for a revisiting of the male hero, which would diminish the stature of Mars while striving to "reintegrate" Apollo and Dionysos (see 138–154; 172–188). His new millennium version of "heroic masculinity" requires more interiority, more femininity, more leaning towards the lunar over the solar, in terms Carl Jung would feel comfortable with. Quoting Athene, in Homer's *Iliad*, Doty dismisses the god of war, as "a thing of fury, evil wrought" (138), preferring instead the discipline of the martial arts, which emphasize control and confidence, a man's power "to transform his blind rage, ... to commit himself, to handle tensions, and to make difficult decisions" (142), Like Apollo, the new male will embody clarity and precision, but combine it with the energy and spontaneity of Dionysos, lord of the dance. He will, above all, avoid "the ethical dualism by which evil is denied in oneself and projected outward upon shadow figures" (194). Doty concludes that "a new heroism on this model would strengthen the planetary, not the individual ego, it would involve not merely fighting the demons of constricting institutionalism but those of the egoic denial of others" (197). Kowalski may fall short of becoming this utopic male icon, but his moral growth in the climactic scene of *Gran Torino* is certainly in the direction Doty recommends.

The sacrificial resolution of *Gran Torino* begins in Kowalski's darkened living room, where Walt and Fr. Janovich gather to lick their wounds, after they have failed to deter the brutal assault upon Sue (01:29:30–01:33:20). Each implicitly acknowledges misjudgment, the priest misplacing his faith in a bureaucratic solution (summon the police), Kowalski delusively supposing that his personal bluster and threat would intimidate the criminal gang. Kowalski's pain-ridden face and slumped posture suggest a defeated man, though the arrival of Fr. Janovich jars him into renewed engagement with the problem that's "never going to go away." In spite of his predictable reservations about the use of force, the priest admits, "I'd want vengeance," and realizes the Lors expect retaliatory violence against the gang, with Thao standing "shoulder to shoulder with you (Kowalski) until they're dead." Though this is a grim moment, the scene records Kowalski's first steps towards resocialization, as he offers his uninvited guest a beer and suggests that he call him "Walt." After both men agree that, "nothing's fair," Kowalski promises to "think of something—and whatever it is, they won't have a chance."

By the time Kowalski meets Thao the following morning, he has his strategy in place. Recognizing the futility of a firefight, though this is what "honor" seems to demand, he is determined to save Thao at the expense of himself. Almost providentially, his sacrifice on behalf of Thao and the Lor family forces him to make the confession he could never make to Fr. Janovich in the churchly ritual of Penance. This whole-hearted commitment to his friend and his immediate community finally allows him to exorcise the demons he has held within him for three decades.

The verbal explosion that erupts as Kowalski locks Thao in the basement completes an exchange the Korean veteran has been trying to have with Fr. Janovich since the priest's second visit to his home. On that occasion the cleric, attempting to be empathetic, spoke of the moral burden soldiers feel when "being ordered to kill, killing to save yourself, killing to save others, being ordered to do appalling things." Kowalski acknowledges the problematics of combat and his general discomfort in dealing with "a thousand screaming gooks." But then he adds cryptically, "The things that haunt a man the most are the things he **isn't ordered** to do." In other words, the brutalities he undertakes spontaneously, on his own initiative. These are foregrounded in his final conversation with Thao, when the want-to-be warrior asks, "How many men did you kill in Korea?" Evasively, Kowalski responds, "You don't want to know," then adds, "It's goddamn awful. Not a day goes by that I don't think about it." He then recalls more precisely one horrific encounter with "Some scared little gook just like you, who wanted to just give up, that's all. I shot him right in the face with that rifle you're holding." The final irony, of course, is that Kowalski was awarded a Silver Star for "valor," in a situation where he reflexively responded to extreme circumstances with primal fear. As he now goes to his death, Kowalski has the satisfaction of knowing he has saved a life to compensate for the one he had taken carelessly many years before. And by duping the gang into murdering him in front of a whole neighborhood full of witnesses, he has assured that they will be removed to prison and the neighborhood will be significantly more safe, not only for the Lors but for the whole multi-ethnic community, to which he is now irrevocably bonded. Significantly, the dying Kowalski also holds in his hand the insignia of his military service, as if he had finally rejoined "his unit."

Appropriately, *Gran Torino* draws towards a close with a second funeral scene that counterpoints the memorial service for Dorothy Kowalski. The ceremonies that mark her husband's passing, however, are significantly different, reflecting the changes Kowalski himself brought about in his life. We're in the same church and Fr. Janovich is again presiding over the service. But now, much to the surprise of his sons and grandchildren, the service is attended by the Lors, most conspicuously by Sue and Thao, both of whom are wearing traditional Hmong dress, appropriate for ceremonial mourning. Their solemn respectfulness contrasts sharply with the distracted behavior of Kowalski's blood family at the earlier funeral. The troubled warrior has rejoined his "tribe," but the new tribe that is defining the Motor City in the 21st century is poly-lingual and multi-ethnic, including not simply the Lor family, but the Asian physician who attends to Kowalski in his last illness and Officer Chang (Stephen Kue)who speaks to Thao in his native language as he seeks to comfort him at the scene of Kowalski's murder.

The property bequest is of a piece with the memorial service. It's fitting that Thao should inherit the Gran Torino, since he—far more than the progeny Kowalski actually fathered—is truly the dead man's spiritual son. Thao also inherits Kowalski's dog, though the beloved pet (and Walt's most trusted confidante) is not mentioned at the reading of the will. This transfer of property is particularly significant, because Kowalski was once convinced that the Lors ate dog meat. The last shots of the film show Thao at the wheel of his new vehicle with the dog beside him in the passenger seat. Nor are they circling the streets of an urban slum, like the cultural introverts of the Hmong gang, for whom power meant intimidating other inmates of the ghetto, as tragically entrapped as they themselves. Like other newly-minted Americans before him, clear back to the settlers that Boone led through Cumberland Gap, Thao is on the open road, with a picturesque lake to his right and an unencumbered thoroughfare before him. Quite literally, Kowalski's supportive presence has created for him safe passage to a wider world and a future open to possibility. Driving an iconic automobile, he embodies something of Detroit itself, hobbled by debt and an archaic infrastructure, but populous, powerful, and seeded with young people who might be poised to make a new beginning.

Gran Torino is a fable of recovery, the saga of an elderly action hero who paradoxically restores himself through self-denial. But it is also a social parable, built upon trust, honesty, and the capacity to learn. Though steeped in his libertarian convictions, chiefly the injunction to "leave everyone alone," Eastwood at some level is also what David Sterritt (2014) calls "a communitarian," sensitive to "the hazards of unchecked individualism" and committed to "communitarian ideals of mutual understanding and support" (225). Walt Kowalski in *Gran Torino* harks back to characters like the protagonist of *The Outlaw Josey Wales* (1976), who loses his blood family to the partisan fury of the Civil War, but builds a new one from a small cadre of people entirely unlike him, including an untribed Indian that he accidentally meets on the road. Both Josey and Walt, horribly scarred by violence, regain a measure of psychic health by finding new friends to come home to and a new way to "belong."

WORKS CITED

Bowman, Cara, Nazli Kibrea, and Megan O'Leary. 2014. *Race and Immigration*. Cambridge: Polity Press.

Chiu, Monica, Mark Pfeifer, and Kau Yang. *2013. Diversity in Diaspora: Hmong Americans in the Twenty-First Century*. Honolulu: Hawaii University Press.

Chivers, Sally. 2011. *The Silvering Screen: Old Age and Disability in the Cinema*. Toronto: Toronto University Press.

Cornell, Drucilla. 2009. *Clint Eastwood and Issues of American Masculinity*. New York: Fordham University Press.

Doty, William D. 1993. *Myths of Masculinity*. New York: Crossroad.

Engel, Leonard, and John Gourlie. 2012. "Gran Torino: Showdown in Detroit: Shrimp, Cowboys, and a New Mythology" 266–275. *New Essays on Clint Eastwood*, ed. Leonard Engel. Salt Lake City: Utah University Press.

Gran Torino. 2008. Directed by Clint Eastwood, performances by Clint Eastwood, Bee Vang, and Christopher Carley, Matten Productions.

Hamilton-Merritt, Jane. 1993. *Tragic Mountains: The Hmong, the Americans, and the Secret War for Laos, 1942–92*. Bloomington: Indiana University Press.

Heitmann, John, and James Uhlman. 2015. "Stealing Freedom: Auto Theft and Autonomous Individualism in American Film." *Journal of Popular Culture* 48: 86–101.

Junger, Sebastain. 2016. *Tribe: On Homecoming and Belonging*. New York: Hachette Book Group.

Kibrea, Nazli, Cara Bowman, and Megan O'Leary. 2014. *Race and Immigration*. Cambridge: Polity Press.

The Outlaw Josey Wales. Directed by Clint Eastwood, performances by Clint Eastwood, Sondra Locke, and Chief Dan George, Warner Bros., 1976.

Peterson, Kirtland, et al. 1991. *Post-Traumatic Stress Disorder: A Clinician's Guide*. New York: Plenum Press.

Portes, Alejandro, and Ruben Rumbaut. 2001. *Legacies: The Story of the Second Immigrant Generation*. Berkeley: California University Press.

Redding, Art. 2014. "A Finish Worthy of the Start: The Poetics of Age and Masculinity in Clint Eastwood's *Gran Torino*." *Film Criticism* 38 (Sept.): 2–23.

Stein, Louise. 2012. "Beyond *Gran Torino's* Guns: Hmong Cultural Warriors Performing Genders." *Positions* 20: 763–792.

Sterritt, David. 2014. *The Cinema of Clint Eastwood: Chronicles of America*. London: Wallflower Press.

Traficante, Christopher. 2012. "From Victim to Vigilante: Anomie and Misanthrophy in Gran Torino." *Screen Education* 66: 111–116.

Unforgiven. 1992. Directed by Clint Eastwood, performances by Clint Eastwood, Gene Hackman, and Morgan Freeman, Warner Bros.

Yehuda, Rachel. 2002. "Post-Traumatic Stress Disorder," *New England Journal of Medicine* 346:2: 108–114.

National PTSD in *Invictus*

Laurence Raw

Recently the London *Guardian* newspaper published an article high-lighting the progress the England rugby union team made winning three matches to nil in a recent contest against Australia after earlier being knocked out in the qualifying rounds of the World Cup. This was the first time ever that an English side had triumphed by that margin on Australian soil. Jeremy Snape, the psychologist involved in the transformation, described the way he persuaded the players to reflect "on the things that underpin success," rather than being influenced "by the emotional turbulence of winning and losing." This kind of thought "creates connections and structures in the brain which, if reinforced repeatedly, create a kind of broadband connection between thought and success or failure." Some prefer to remain "closed" by internalizing their "anxieties or limitations rather than take a risk in exploring something new." Others value team success before personal glory and "enjoy the struggle, the sacrifice and the challenge more"; this is "exactly where the fun is" (qtd. in Foster). Personal worries should be shared with the group, and the process of resolving them becomes a means to reinforce that group's collective strength, depending as much on the unconscious as well as the conscious mind.

On the other hand every athlete has to cope with performance problems that might be attributable to injuries, illness or emotional imbalance. If such problems remain in the mind or body, they can become insoluble; the more we try to resolve them through counseling or medicines, the more we can be overwhelmed by a mix of frustration and anxiety leading to PTSD in which the event (i.e., the moment when we first lost our ability to perform at our peak) is transformed into a traumatic experience. The former cricketer Graeme Fowler described his mental struggles after having lost his fulltime job as a coach: "Nothing mattered. I didn't care about anything—family, my life, nothing. And when I thought about it, I realised I didn't want to be alive.

Everything was hopeless, pointless, worthless…. For the first time in my life [after coaching] I hadn't analysed anything. It was as if my head stopped working. All I felt was like I was at the bottom of a well" (2).

The relationship between performance, sport and PTSD has been addressed in several films. John Hefin's made for television comedy *Grand Slam* (1978) focuses on the experiences of a party of Welsh rugby union supporters visiting Paris for an important match against France. The plot invokes familiar stereotypes associated with the sport—drunkenness, excessive aggression—but also examines how the team's on-the-field performance helps the supporters of a long-colonized nation to reassert their national and personal identity. Winning the match (and the Five Nations championship of Europe, which annually pits national rugby teams from England, Scotland, Ireland, Wales and France) functions as a cure for the trauma wrought by seven centuries of English colonization. Even if the team loses—which they eventually do—the supporters can enjoy a brief moment of wellness as they sing songs in Welsh both before and after the match has concluded. The Thai film *Cheerleader Queens* (2003) treads a similar thematic path, as three gay men learn how to deal with the trauma of social exclusion by joining the school rugby team and transforming it into a winning unit. *Walk Like a Man* (2008) follows the same storyline. In this Australian-made documentary, the struggle and ultimate success of two gay rugby union teams, one from Sydney, the other from San Francisco, overcome prejudice, inhabitation and self doubt so as to participate in the Bingham Cup Final, a biannual tournament held for the above purpose. In both cases, these films track psychologist Jeremy Snape's suggestions and enjoy the struggle and sacrifice of participating successfully in a contact sport commonly associated with aggressive heterosexuality, and thereby revealing its capacity to acknowledge sexual difference.

The documentary *Murderball* (2005) follows the opposite narrative path. The film focuses on the fortunes of the American wheelchair rugby team, who compensate for their disabilities by sustaining images of aggressive masculinity both on and off the playing area. The same message is reinforced in a brief sequence during Martin Scorsese's *The Departed* (2006). Colin Sullivan (Matt Damon) is shown participating in a rugby game, after which he takes pains to assert his aggressive masculinity. *Forever Strong* (2008), another American-made rugby film, shows the central character undergoing a process of psychological evolution through involvement with the Highland rugby team in Arizona. He begins the film as a rebellious inmate of a juvenile prison; by the end he has learned the value of teamwork. In all three films, rugby exists as a means to realize some form of masculinity that might otherwise be lost, if only perceptually.

Perhaps the best-known film with a rugby theme is Clint Eastwood's *Invictus* (2009), charting South Africa's triumph in the World Cup of 1995 through the lives of President Nelson Mandela (Morgan Freeman) and national team captain François Pienaar (Matt Damon)—which forms the subject of this contribution. The PTSD informing the plot is both individual and collective: in the post-apartheid era both Afrikaner and black members of society try to heal the hurt caused by decades of racial segregation. That process is exacerbated by mistrust on both sides. It is chiefly due to Mandela that change occurs; like Snape he encourages Pienaar and his Afrikaner teammates to consider what success means both on and off the rugby field. The cycle of fear that separates the two races needs to be broken; this can only be accomplished if they are prepared to listen to one another. Past mistakes need to be acknowledged and new strategies of toleration and community developed instead. The emotional journey required is not easy and often fraught with difficulties, both for Mandela and the rugby players, but their struggle is rewarded as they beat the New Zealand All Blacks in the World Cup final and assert their identity as a newly-united nation. *Invictus* offers a good example of how sporting endeavor is intimately related to wider issues of psychology and community. Those who suffer from it might not think that they do, but the legacy of apartheid has a profound effect on their personal identities. Director Eastwood asks us to reflect on the condition: is PTSD a disorder, an illness, a mental condition, or a combination of all three? Such distinctions might be insignificant: what matters more is that we find ways of dealing with them by learning how to care for ourselves as well as our fellow human beings.

One can learn self-care in any number of ways. In writing a review for *The Evil Hours: A Bibliography of Post-Traumatic Stress Disorder* (2015), Ben Shephard remarks that sufferers should "try anything—yoga, horse-back riding, mountaineering—until you find what helps you. In his [Morris'] own case, it seems as though the writing process has been the main curative agent" (7). In my case, writing this article in the midst of serious illness has held considerable personal significance. I have come to understand that I am a team member; my colleagues comprising all those people who support me emotionally in all walks of life, whether through face-to-face or virtual encounters. I was never a great rugby player, but have been a fan ever since my childhood, when I played audio cassette recordings of England matches recorded live off the television while holidaying on the Italian Riviera. *Invictus* offers a unique chance to show how sporting passions can be integrated into a much wider process of dealing with mental trauma as expressed through PTSD.

What distinguishes most fictitious texts about South Africa from those of other territories, especially in the apartheid era, is the writers' responsibility to their societies, whether Afrikaner or black. As the government-sponsored Truth and Reconciliation Commission continued its investigations in the late nineties, one independent exhibition catalog suggested that "[all] Artistic and cultural concerns in many ways engage with, yet are distant from the legal-political concerns that will arise [from the Commission's work]. Betrayal, sadism, mourning, loss, confession, memory, reparation, longing, these are the persistent themes of the arts. The Commission will be examining the legal and political implications of these same themes. Through the arts we can explore who we are, and what we do to one another" (qtd. in Van Dongen 126).

J.M. Coetzee's Booker Prize–winning novel *Disgrace* (1999) depicts a world riven with violence: the arrogant Afrikaner treats women, learners, and blacks as second class citizens, but now the blacks respond in kind. There are no racial distinctions between "us" and "them," or "self" and "other"— everyone, it seems, is striving to construct new identities. They find it impossible to communicate with one another—not only do they speak different languages (Afrikaans, Ndebele, Sotho, Swazi), but even when they employ a common tongue (English) they willfully neglect to listen to one another. Anthony Schneider's recently-published novel *Repercussions* (2016) explains why; ever since the sixties South African society has been riven with secrecy, betrayal, and the sufferings of people—Afrikaans as well as black—discovering the personal costs of political commitment. In a survey of post-apartheid literature Vilashini Cooppan suggests that many authors have re-negotiated their pasts, whether individual or collective—for example, in Antjie Krog's *Country of My Skull* (1998), a mélange of journalistic observation, poetry, memoir and oral history. As an Afrikaner she tries to empathize with her black counterparts, but social distinctions keep getting in the way (Cooppan 53). Achmat Dangor's *Bitter Fruit* (2001) explains that there can be no easy burial of the traumatic past, despite the work of the Truth and Reconciliation Commission. While the Afrikaner privileged might feel exonerated by its findings, others might end up affected by PTSD. The novel's characters occupy different positions determined by race, gender, and history: each tries to deal with trauma in their own way.

Eastwood's attempt to render this process cinematically was not easy. In an interview ahead of *Invictus*' British premiere in early 2010, Morgan Freeman revealed that he had tried to film Nelson Mandela's autobiography *Long Walk to Freedom* (1995), which hitherto had been unrealized due to difficulties of cinematic adaptation. *Invictus* came about when he teamed up with producer Mace Neufeld on the rugby project, based on the book by John Carlin (originally titled *Playing the Enemy* but renamed *Invictus* after the film's release), and obtained approval from Mandela. Eastwood agreed to direct, having previously dealt with trauma and PTSD in *Grand Torino* (2008) (Hiscock). In the earlier film the focus centers overwhelmingly on the central character Walt Kowalski (Eastwood), a PTSD sufferer whose turbulent mind is revealed through behavioral incongruities. The basic premise of *Invictus* is very different: we all know why the South African people react as they do, but we witness the ways in which individuals try to cope with life in the post-apartheid era. The difficulties are depicted in an early sequence set in the presidential security offices where the chief bodyguard Jason Tshabalala (Tony Kgoroge) holds court among his sharp-suited black associates. The door opens to reveal some Afrikaners, their close-cropped hair and no-nonsense gray outfits giving them a threatening air. Jason starts in his chair, while his black colleagues go for their guns anticipating trouble. The white leader Henrick (Matt Stern) takes something out of his pocket; it turns out to be his ID, which he presents to his new boss Jason. The atmosphere is reminiscent of that described in Coetzee's *Disgrace*: so much animosity exists between the two races that they cannot hold a conversation. Jason thinks he is going to be arrested while Hendrick has become so accustomed to throwing his weight about that he automatically appears arrogant. The memory of violence is never far away among erstwhile captors and their victims.

Eastwood employs this sequence to suggest the consequences of collective PTSD; as the action unfolds, he concentrates more on individuals. The Afrikaners have not been accustomed to failure: when the South African rugby team loses to England in a pre–World Cup match, the Afrikaners treat it as a national disgrace with the players wearing "the hallowed green and gold" letting the country down. Their reaction draws on contemporary notions of masculinity, which according to Brian Baker, show one-time strong figures being rendered largely irrelevant in a globalized universe. James Bond has a peripheral role in the British Secret Service, while members of the U.S. Army in Kathryn Bigelow's *The Hurt Locker* (2008) prove themselves unable to cope with increasingly complex military circumstances, prompting them to question their physical and mental capabilities (Baker 27, 32). The fact that Afrikaners now have to take orders in *Invictus* prompts them to reflect on their identities in similar manner, as shown in a sequence in the Springbok dressing-room when Pienaar distributes copies of the black National Anthem to his teammates, all of whom save one are Afrikaners. They respond by crumpling the papers into balls and throwing them into the trash. Such behavior might seem unimportant (most rugby teams pride themselves on their aggression), but it denotes detachment from the team's immediate environment produced by the need to cope with an extreme emotional state. Furthermore, this reaction is among the diagnostic criteria for PTSD (Sutton 218).

In Carlin's factual account of this incident, the Springboks' reaction was not just due to resentment; many of the players "feared the prospect of the Afrikaner fans jeering the new national anthem … or unfurling the hated old orange, blue, and white flag. The millions watching in the black townships would feel humiliated and outraged" (17; ch. 1). Pienaar did not distribute the sheets; Carlin says that task was undertaken by another Afrikaner, Anne Munnik, who was highly intimidated by the task, especially when the players reacted to the suggestion with "giggles and laughter and innuendos and teasing" (8; ch. 13). *Invictus* offers an interesting historical contrast to the rugby match represented in the film *A Dry White Season* (1989). Released a year before political moves began to eliminate apartheid, Euzhan Palcy's drama shows a group of Afrikaner learners at an exclusive private school enjoying a match under the benevolent tutelage of former international player Ben du Toit (Donald Sutherland). The image is one of complacency, of perpetual Afrikaner privilege and hegemony. The fact that his hegemony had been dismantled so rapidly explains why Springbok losses on the international stage were felt so keenly. The significance of Springbok's success to the Afrikaners was paramount, and that fact was routinely represented in film. *Bakgat II* [*Wonderful 2*] (2010), a teen comedy whose central character Wimpie Koekemoer (Ivan Botha) is reminded by his fiancée, Katrien (Cherie van der Merwe), that "we South Africans don't give up hope," especially while playing rugby teams where everyone is expected to "put [their] bodies on the line," and dedicate themselves to three maxims: "Like one. As a team. Unite."

Mandela comes to power on these very premises. He promises equal rights for all even though poverty is still rife, especially in the townships of South Africa's big cities. The chronic inequalities between the two races are underlined in a sequence where the camera contrasts the privileged rugby-playing environment of an Afrikaner private school with the primitive soccer game played by black youths nearby. The Afrikaner boys interrupt their game, come to the wire fence separating them from the blacks and collectively wince. The blacks have a similar view of rugby; it is "a white sport, and especially the sport of … apartheid's master race" (Carlin 7; ch. 1).

Such negative constructions of rugby contrast starkly with the sport's transformative potential as represented in films of similar subject-matter. As long ago as 1949 the Ealing comedy *A Run for Your Money* used the occasion of the annual England versus Wales match to depict the misadventures of two greenhorn Welshmen (Donald Houston, Meredith Edwards) traveling to London on a rare weekend away from their mining communities. Free from the often monotonous life of the pit, church and male voice choirs, they drink to excess, have casual love-affairs and narrowly miss losing all their money before catching the train home. Frank Marshall's *Alive* (1993) tells the true story of the Uruguayan rugby team, the victims of an air-crash in the Andes in 1972. While traveling on the aircraft they are just another group of testosterone-filled youths throwing a ball around and smoking in designated no-smoking areas. The experience of survival for fifty days in sub-zero temperatures teaches them how to deal with PTSD through group endeavors, as well as understanding their individual limitations. The team is everything—just like Highland Rugby Club in *Forever Strong*, whose group mantra contains three golden rules: "I will do nothing to embarrass myself, my team, or my family." In South Africa rugby's negative connotations among blacks persist to this day. Writing in *The Guardian* immediately prior to the 2015 World Cup, Siya Mnyanda (a rugby player himself) accused the national selectors of refusing to take concrete steps to mirror the country's demographic make-up: "we have grown impatient with the pace of change. Witness the recent unrest at universities" (Mnyanda).

With such resentment in their minds, it is hardly surprising that Jason should react so skeptically to Mandela's policies. The only means to cope with them is to cultivate a "comfortable numbness"—another dissociative state securing release from psychological pain through emotionlessness. This detail is another example of how the screenplay departs from the book so as to stress the PTSD experienced by the characters. Carlin claims, "The truth was that black South Afrikaners were, for the most part, sufficiently shrewd and sufficiently patient to know that Rome would not be built in a day. They trusted their government to deliver but understood that to drive the whites into the sea would not do any good" (14; ch. 12). Eastwood's film emphasizes this understanding through performance. The black bodyguards' faces assume a mask of indifference as they learn about the Springboks' mixed fortunes leading up to the World Cup; their mood can be summed up by the words of one PTSD sufferer who believed that comfortable numbness "makes everything go away and I can be at peace for the moment. I want my mind to release everything and I want to just be numb to everything" (qtd. in Sutton 207).

When Mandela assumes power he is faced with an Afrikaner population who react violently to change, like caged animals deprived of their strength yet trying to maintain power. The blacks adopt more passive coping mechanisms that are no less internally traumatic, even though they seldom reveal their feelings openly. I can empathize with both strategies: sometimes sheer frustration produces violent reactions, as on one occasion when I yanked a hotel closet door off its hinges while under stress; or it can render me silent as I sit alone in my workroom neither talking to nor reacting to anyone. In *Invictus* Mandela understands the magnitude of his task as he tries to make everyone understand how rugby is "a human calculation" removing the cycle of fear that divides Afrikaner from black. His job is rendered more complicated by his daughter Zindzi's (Bonnie Henna's) refusal to embrace a policy of reconciliation in the belief that he is ignoring black interests. The sheer strain of Mandela's daily life emerges in one sequence as he emerges from the presidential compound for his daily pre-dawn walk. Hendrick asks him about his family; Mandela responds with a non-committal answer and turns abruptly back to the compound, his walk uncompleted. It is left to Jason to explain that this is a taboo subject: Mandela has developed a "comfortable numbness" to try and make his familial problems disappear, for a brief period of time at least.

This reaction might seem surprising for someone who spent 18 of his 27 years of imprisonment in the Robben Island jail, and who learned how to cope with solitariness by embracing the ideas set forth in W.H. Henley's poem "Invictus" that provides the film's title:

> I thank whatever gods may be
> For my unconquerable soul [...]
> I have not winced nor cried aloud.
> Under the bludgeonings of chance
> My head is bloody, but unbowed [...]
> It matters not how strait the gate
> How charged with punishments the scroll,
> I am the master of my fate
> I am the captain of my soul [56–57].

From one point of view Mandela is not master of his fate as he allows his personal feelings about his family to affect his daily rituals. Curtailing the walk might be interpreted as an act of weakness, a sign of edginess as PTSD gets the better of him. From another perspective Mandela's reaction denotes a compassionate mind responding to a traumatic memory, as he imagines himself talking to a friend who might be worried and offering words of encouragement while trying to understand the source of that worry. If we can respond to personal traumas in similar fashion and subsequently get on with our lives, we are on the way to dealing with PTSD (Williams 346). Mandela understands that this mental adjustment will not only restore him to the position of "captain of [his] soul" but will inspire him to offer the Springboks similar words of encouragement so that they might deal with their own traumas.

Mandela understands the importance of walking the talk, so to speak. It is all very well devising slogans such as "One Team, One Country," but he has to set an example to others by bringing them together, asking them to reflect on what constitutes success and devise their own collective means of achieving their aims. They might not always succeed, but as the sports psychologist Snape suggests, the struggle to achieve that goal will change them permanently. In Carlin's book Mandela has to deal with the hard-headed Afrikaner president of the South African Rugby Union, Louis Luyt, who "hated being told what to do by anyone, let alone a black man" (ch. 13, 1). Nonetheless he found the task comparatively straightforward, especially as he had previously encountered Pienaar and explained his intention to "use sport for the purpose of nation-building and promoting all the ideas, which we think will lead to peace and stability in our country" (9; ch. 12). By the time Mandela encountered Luyt, Pienaar had already reported to the South African Rugby Union what had happened in his personal meeting. Hence Luyt was more inclined to listen to the president's suggestions. Mandela follows a three-point plan for emotional and psychological learning, as outlined in the first person by Susan Jeffers: "i) the only way to feel about myself is to go out ... and do it; ii) not only am I going to experience fear whenever I'm on unfamiliar territory, but so is everyone else; and iii) pushing through fear is less frightening than living with the underlying fear that comes from a feeling of helplessness" (21–25).

Eastwood omits these largely conversational sequences in favor of dramatic set pieces designed to make similar thematic points. In one of them the Springboks travel to coach black township boys; none of the Afrikaners relish the task, as they are penetrating a soccer-mad enclave and fear an adverse reaction from the locals. Pienaar invites them to bear Mandela's dictum in mind ("times change, we need to change as well"), but no one really believes them. Eastwood cuts to a point of view shot from inside the coach looking outwards, as the players reflect on the poverty-stricken landscape— surely they don't have the power to make a difference. What follows proves pleasantly unexpected for everyone involved, as the black boys espy Chester Williams (McNeill Hendricks), the Springboks' talented wing and the only non–Afrikaner member of the team, and repeatedly chant his name. The subsequent action unfolds in a series of dissolves as the Springboks teach the boys how to pass, to jump in the lineout and form scrums; this is the first time that many of the boys have played with an oval ball. What proves to be a revelatory afternoon ends with the boys shouting, "Bokke! Bokke!" (the Springbok chant) in unison. Small beginnings produce unexpected ends— soon a South African Airlines (SAA) jet departs Johannesburg airport with the legend "Go Chester!" emblazoned on its side. By breaking through their innate fears and discovering the innate pleasures of coaching beginners, the Springboks discover a shared love of sport. Three hours of energetic practice provides the inspiration for a renewed commitment to changing attitudes in a rapidly changing environment.

In a further Mandela-inspired scheme—included in both book and film—the Springboks have a day in Robben Island prison, with the centerpiece being a visit to Mandela's former cell bearing the legend 46664 (his prison number) on the door. It is a small, bare space except for a chair and a view of the yard outside where the inmates pass their time playing sport or reflecting on their own. Eastwood's film shows Pienaar closing the cell door and looking out of the window; as he does so we hear Mandela reciting "Invictus" in voiceover while the screen dissolves to a mental image of the politician reading on his chair. Pienaar glances out of the window once more, and glimpses prisoners chopping wood outside. Carlin's book extends this sequence by describing how the inmates singing a song in their local language; James Small, one of the Springbok players, burst into tears (11–12; ch. 14). The team has once again confronted the fears that contributed to so much misunderstanding in the past. Placed in the position of the other, they have learned to negotiate what stress counselor Colin Lago terms the "power distance" separating the two races and thereby realized how uncertainty avoidance prevented them from coming to terms with the past (46). For the first time they understand how apartheid destroyed innocent lives through incarceration.

No one is exempt from the healing process, not even Mandela. At the end of one Springbok training session, he shakes the hand of every team-member and addresses them by name. The film shows his bodyguards—Afrikaner and black alike—marveling at the care taken over this task, which concludes with him giving Pienaar a copy of "Invictus" and receiving a Springbok cap in return. This is a highly symbolic moment, as Mandela makes a public acknowledgment of the potential of community in which everyone, irrespective of racial difference, dedicates themselves to the national future. Carlin's book describes the occasion thus: "[It] redefined the Springboks' feelings for their president and their country. Describing the scene ... [their manager Morné] du Plessis was almost lost for words. "I looked at the players ... and they were like young boys, waving, so full of this ... excitement. These guys had all seen a million helicopters before but Mandela ... well, he had won their hearts" (4; ch. 14). From now the World Cup will not be just a festival of rugby but a unique opportunity to deal with the nation's collective PTSD by enabling everyone to express their emotions, soothe or calm themselves (by pushing through fear), reaching out to members of other races and thereby transmitting positive messages (Sutton 268). The sequence re-enacted one of Mandela's basic tenets as set down during his prison-term: "I have cherished the ideal of a democratic and free society in which all persons live together and with equal opportunities. It is an ideal which I hope to live for and to achieve" (qtd. in Younge 4). The fact that Mandela succeeded so spectacularly with Springboks was due to what fellow-activist Desmond Tutu termed "incredible empathy.... He said of the Afrikaners you can very well understand how they must be feeling" (Tutu 5). This form of collective reconciliation is also close to Eastwood's heart; in 2010 he joined fellow-director David Lynch and British comedian Russell Brand in launching Operation Warrior Wellness, an initiative designed to encourage PTSD victims to practice transcendental meditation in group therapy sessions. While *Invictus* does not go that far, it nonetheless underlines the importance of everyone achieving "a relaxed sense of oneness" (McGreal).

The film culminates with the dramatic set-piece of the World Cup final between the Springboks and the New Zealand All Blacks. Several previous rugby films experienced difficulty trying to portray the action sequences convincingly: *Grand Slam* deals with this issue by incorporating news footage of Wales playing France interspersed with cameo appearances by some of the team's leading lights—Gareth Edwards, Phil Bennett, Gerald Davies. The actors' role in the action is restricted to that of spectators cheering the Welsh on during the match and reasserting their national identity by singing the Welsh National Anthem once the Parc des Princes stadium has emptied. *Cheerleader Queens* shows its youthful protagonists actually involved in a game, but compensates for their technical shortcomings through incessant rock-beat on the soundtrack. *Forever Strong* adopts a similar strategy, with the music replaced with the guttural grunts of the players struggling for the ball in open play. In *Invictus* Eastwood does not use Damon very much in the action (if he had been injured, there would have been unnecessary delays in wrapping up the production [Hiscock]). Instead he restages the match using professional rugby players from South Africa, interspersed with the comments of an omnipresent stadium announcer (Mark Rickard).

Eastwood is less interested in the game and more on the spectators' reactions as they learn to deal with their collective PTSD. Pienaar's family are all there; his mother (Penny Downie), father (Patrick Lyster), and their black maid Eunice (Sibongile Nojila). Earlier on in the film Mr. Pienaar had voiced contempt for the blacks, a predictable reaction from a family described by Mandela (in the book) as "churchgoing rugby fanatics who related to their superabundant black neighbors with a mixture of disdain, ignorance, and fear" (Carlin 81; ch. 12). The film shows him caught up by the fervor as he applauds Chester Williams for his on-field efforts. When the Springboks level the scores, Mrs. Pienaar embraces Eunice in joy—a testament to rugby's capacity to bring people together. The Afrikaner and black bodyguards experience a similarly epiphanic moment at the game's end, as they embrace one another in delight. Their reactions are intercut with a minor subplot (that doesn't exist in the book) where two Johannesburg cops (Jackie Greenewald, Murray Todd) shoo a black township boy (Kgosi Mongake) away while they listen to the radio commentary on the match. As time passes and excitement mounts, the boy sidles closer and closer to the officers' car so that he can listen as well. By the final whistle he stands right next to them; one officer gives him a grateful hug for sharing the victory. This moment gives added poignancy to the Rugby World Cup theme "A World in Union" that soars aloft on the soundtrack as the Springboks receive their medals.

The Springbok team experiences similar moments of revelation, as Pienaar shouts "Who's the fittest team on the field?" and subsequently calls the players into a huddle and urges them to make a special effort to stop the All Blacks, especially their star player Jonah Lomu (Zak Feaunati). They understand—perhaps for the first time—the importance of what sports performance coach Dave Alred has termed "leadership rules," whereby a captain forges a culture of consensus and courtesy while being ready to introduce anything designed to improve performance on the field, even if it seemed outwardly unrelated to the game of rugby (197, 203). In Eastwood's film the success of this latter strategy is shown in the huddle, where everyone links arms in a circle and remains silent for a few moments, simply looking into one another's faces and drawing strength from one another's resolute expressions.

There is only one potentially traumatic moment that threatens the celebratory ritual as a low-flying aircraft flies over the packed stadium prior to the beginning of the match. The bodyguards exchange apprehensive glances in anticipation of a terrorist attack designed to scupper Mandela's best-laid plans. Their worries prove unfounded as everyone reads the legend "Good Luck Bokke" painted on the undercarriage. The sequence offers another object lesson in how to deal with PTSD: rather than expecting the worst of the future, it is liberating to embrace the moment and "*say yes*. There is something about physically accepting an idea that helps to create acceptance [of the unknown].... You'll notice you feel something positive.... It gives you the sense that everything will be all right" (Jeffers 154–55).

Mandela's efforts to change the country have met with limited success. In 2015 learners at the University of Cape Town demanded the removal of the statue of white imperialist Cecil Rhodes that stood in the center of the campus. Kolela Mangcu, a staff member at the same institution, explained why: "There has been a failure [since 1995] to really engage with the raw emotions of people's experience. A thing like the Rhodes statue triggers the raw feeling of alienation" (qtd. in David Smith 10). The word "alienation" indicates that the psychological trauma of apartheid still remains, preventing young blacks from participating in the multicultural consensus that seemed so strong in those heady days following the World Cup final.

PTSD has historically been associated with military conflict; during World War II it was termed "shell shock" or "combat neurosis." The current usage came into being as a means of describing the traumas experienced by troops returning from Vietnam. Many current publications focus almost exclusively on this area: as I researched this article I encountered a text outlining the effect of transformational leadership designed to stimulate motivation amongst everyone, even those suffering from PTSD (Baker 28). This model is both person-centered and sympathetic, encouraging "integration of capabilities of leader and follower" and thereby strengthening community values both in the field and in civilian life (Baker 114). The only problem with this framework is that it ignores what psychologist Daniel Smith terms "the monkey mind" that keeps "flipping and jumping and flinging feces at the walls [of the brain] and swinging from loose neurons like howlers from vines" (Daniel Smith ch. 3). The mind can induce psychosomatic illness by paralyzing us both physically and mentally, and rendering us resistant to everything. The best means to negotiate this kind of PTSD-related trauma is to admit the anxiety and convert it into energy (Daniel Smith, ch. 3). *Invictus* makes an important contribution to this issue by showing the origins of PTSD; a phenomenon best explained by drawing on a four-part model proposed by Smith (ch. 1). The post–1994 era was one of extreme *uncertainty* in which nobody knew what would happen in the future. The absence of structures causes *withdrawal*: no one wants to share their opinions for fear of being considered week or (worse still) deviating from their established racial stereotypes. With no one courageous enough to express their inner selves, this leads to *blowback*, where no one believes anything they are told. Hence the Springboks' decision to throw copies of the black National Anthem into the trash, in the mistaken assumption that Mandela is trying to colonize them just as they did to the black under apartheid. In this kind of environment it is hardly surprising that everyone should feel *locked in*. Mandela spent 27 years being physically incarcerated in Robben Island; his people are likewise imprisoned in a mental jail of PTSD.

The only way to deal with this condition is to create alternative narratives based on empathy rather than isolation. We need to ask questions of ourselves as well as others such as "What are you thinking?" and "Why do you feel anxious?" If more radical measures are required (for example, Mandela's decision to reverse the apartheid narrative by placing the Springboks in the position of the Other in Robben Island), they need to be undertaken sympathetically, with a view to understanding past traumas more deeply. Through reflection Pienaar comes to understand that dealing with the nation's collective PTSD as well as his own mental struggles is entirely in his own hands. They need to undertake mental tasks analogous to the prison inmates' physical tasks by digging new psychological trenches and keep digging them.

The cure for PTSD is not just mental but needs to be reinforced in all areas of life—in the workplace and at home. Hence Mandela's assignments are highly similar to those strategies proposed at the beginning of this article by Snape. The Springboks are encouraged to make a collective effort wherein everyone's voice counts, especially that of Chester Williams, the only black player in the side. Relationships have to change as well: Pienaar's parents take their maid Eunice to the World Cup Final; black and white bodyguards communally acknowledge the Springboks' victory. Future initiatives should be determined through similar collaborations, in which *process* assumes as much importance as *outcomes*.

In truth *Invictus* can be read superficially as a familiar Hollywood narrative of the underdogs triumphing against impossible odds, as Carlin's book notes: "Many a Hollywood scriptwriter would have had them [Mandela and Pienaar] giving each other a hug…. Instead the two just looked at each other and laughed" (4; ch. 19). It is to Eastwood's credit that he reworks the convention and invests it with a psychological depth arising from his awareness of people's struggles to deal with life-changing traumas in all walks of life. Until I had my illness I was an adaptation scholar, focusing almost exclusively on adaptation as a process whereby source-texts are transformed into target texts, mostly in the cinema and on television. Films like *Invictus* persuaded me to broaden my definition of "adaptation" as the outcome of a process of cognitive therapy, more accurately defined as a process of self-understanding based on a revaluation of the self as well as one's relationship to others. The adaptive process of looking inwards and outwards is not easy, depending substantially on the support of others. Yet the consequences can prove momentous, as we share the Springboks' and Mandela's delight in acquiring new insights that might encourage us towards a better world. PTSD might be traumatic, but dealing with it can prove revelatory.

Works Cited

Alred, Dave. 2016. *The Pressure Principle: Handle Stress, Harness Energy, and Perform Where It Counts.* London: Penguin Life.

Alive. 1993. Directed by Frank Marshall, performances by Ethan Hawke, Vincent Spane, and Josh Hamilton, Film Andes S.A.,.

Baker, Brian. 2015. *Contemporary Masculinities in Fiction, Film and Television.* New York: Bloomsbury Academic.

Baker, Karin A. 2016. *The Effect of Post-Traumatic Stress Disorder (PTSD) on Military Leaderships: An Historical Perspective—War Neurosis in World War I, Combat Stress in World War II, Combat Stress in Vietnam.* Progressive Management.

Bakgat II. 2010. Directed by Henk Pretorius, performances by Ivan Botha, Cherie van der Merwe, and Altus Theart, Film Factory.

Carlin, John. 2009. *In2003.* Directed by Poj Arnon, performances by Wongthep Khunarattanrat, Watcharachai Sataphitak, ThaiFilm.

Coetzee, J.M. 1999. *Disgrace.* London: Secker and Warburg.

Cooppan, Vilashini. 2012. "Affecting Politics: Post-Apartheid Fiction and the Limits of Trauma." *Trauma, Memory, and Narrative in the Contemporary South African Novel: Essays.* Ed. Edward Mengel and Michela Borzaga. 47–65. Amsterdam: Rodopi.

Dangor, Achmat. 2001. *Bitter Fruit.* London: Atlantic.

The Departed. 2006. Directed by Martin Scorsese, performances by Leonardo DiCaprio, Matt Damon, Jack Nicholson, Warner Bros.

Disgrace. 2008. Directed by Steve Jacobs, performances by John Malkovich, Natalie Becker, Jessica Haynes, Fortissimo Films.

A Dry White Season. 1989. Directed by Euzhan Palcy, performances by Donald Sutherland, Susan Sarandon, Marlon Brando, Davros Films.

Forever Strong. 2008. Directed by Ryan Little, performances by Sean Faris, Penn Badgley, Gary Cole, Go Films.

Foster, Richard. 2016. "What Does a Sports Psychologist Do?" *The Guardian,* 1 July. Accessed 6 July 2016.

Fowler, Graeme. 2016. *Absolutely Foxed.* New York: Simon & Schuster.

Gran Torino. 2008. Directed by Clint Eastwood, performances by Eastwood, Bee Vang, Christopher Carley, Matten Productions.

Grand Slam. 1978. Directed by John Hefin, performances by Hugh Griffith, Windsor Davies, Siôn Probert. BBC Wales.

Henley, W.H. 1888. "Invictus." *A Book of Verse*. 56–57. D. Nutt.

Hiscock, John. 2010. "Matt Damon and Morgan Freeman Interview." *Daily Telegraph*, 28 Jan. Accessed 8 July 2016.

The Hurt Locker. 2008. Directed by Kathryn Bigelow, performances by Jeremy Renner, Anthony Mackie, Brian Geraghty, Vintage Pictures.

Invictus. 2009. Directed by Clint Eastwood, performances by Morgan Freeman, Matt Damon, Tony Kgoroge, Warner Bros.

Jeffers, Susan. 1987. *Feel the Fear and Do it Anyway*. Vermillion.

Krog, Antjie. 1998. *Country of My Skull: Guilt, Sorrow, and the Limits of Forgiveness in the New South Africa*. New York: Broadway.

Lago, Colin. 1996. *Race, Culture and Counselling*. New York: Open University Press.

Mandela, Nelson. 1995. *Long Walk to Freedom*. Boston: Little, Brown.

McGreal, Chris. 2010. "David Lynch Tackles Post-traumatic Stress with Transcendental Meditation." *The Guardian*, 13 Dec. Accessed 10 July 2016.

Morris, David J. 2015. *The Evil Hours: A Biography of Post-Traumatic Stress Disorder*. Boston: Houghton Mifflin Harcourt.

Mnyanda, Siya. 2015. "Why I Won't Support the Springboks at the Rugby World Cup." *The Guardian Africa Network*, 17 Sept. Accessed 9 July 2015.

Murderball. 2005. Directed by Henry Alex Rubin, Dana Adam Shapiro, performances by Joe Soares, Keith Cavill, Mark Zupan, Paramount.

Le Placard. 2001. Directed by Francis Veber, performances by Daniel Auteuil, Gérard Depardieu, Michel Aumont, Gaumont.

A Run for Your Money. 1949. Directed by Charles Frend, performances by Donald Houston, Alec Guinness, Moira Lister. Ealing.

Schneider, Anthony. 2013. *Repercussions*. Sag Harbor: Permanent Press.

Shephard, Ben. 2015. "After a Fight." *TLS* 17 July: 7.

Smith, Daniel. *Monkey Mind: A Memoir of Anxiety*. New York: Simon & Schuster, 2012.

Smith, David. 2015. "Rhodes Protest Leads to 'Identity' Debate." *Guardian Weekly* 191.8 (20–27 Mar.).

Sutton, Jan. 2007. *Healing the Hurt Within: Understanding Self-Injury and Self-Harm, and Heal the Emotional Wounds*. 3rd ed. Oxford: How to Books.

Tutu, Desmond. 2013. "Jail Embitters Some, but It Ennobled Him." *Guardian Weekly* 190.1 (13–19 Dec.): 5.

Van Dongen, Els. 2001. "Trauma, Remembrance and Art in South Africa: An Impression." *Medische Anthropologie* 13.1: 121–32.

Walk Like a Man. 2008. Directed by Jim Morgison, Patricia Zagarella, performances by Annah-Ruth Dominis, Pete Dubois, and Sean Dmyterko, Special Broadcasting Service.

Williams, Chris. 2012. *Overcoming Anxiety, Stress and Panic: A Five Areas Approach*. London: CRC Press.

Younge, Gary. 2013. "Never a Revolutionary, Always a Radical." *Guardian Weekly* 190.1 (13–19 Dec.): 1, 4.

"He's here and he's there"
Projecting Recovery in
American Sniper *and* Sully

ALLEN H. REDMON

Clint Eastwood's two directorial efforts, *American Sniper* (2014) and *Sully* (2016), each feature trauma in explicit ways. *American Sniper* tells the story of Chris Kyle, widely recognized as the deadliest sniper in United States' military history, and his struggle to return home after his wartime experiences. *Sully* explores the psychological aftermath of Captain Chesley "Sully" Sullenberger's forced water landing on the Hudson River in New York City, which became necessary after the plane experienced dual engine failure at low altitude shortly after takeoff. Most audience members arrive at the theater expecting to see a story that involves trauma. Both films are, after all, based on true stories, and true stories that gained considerable media attention. James Berardinelli (2016) begins his review of *Sully* commenting on the way the news outlets played "The Miracle on the Hudson" as it came to be tagged on a continuous loop for days after the event occurred. As *Sully*'s script openly admits in several places, the news of flight 1549 provided a sense of celebration and relief to a city and a nation that needed it. Chris Kyle's story gained wide coverage after Kyle was killed at the hand of a fellow soldier he was trying to help. Those who missed the media coverage of these stories as they unfolded in real-time were given every chance to anticipate each film's focus on trauma. The trailer for *American Sniper* played portions of the opening scene that staged Kyle (Bradley Cooper) having to decide if he should fire on a woman and child. The scene captures the complexities and moral dilemmas most assume exist in modern warfare, which encourages one to see the film as an exploration of the psychological impact of having to make these sorts of choices. *Sully* bills itself in a similar way. Prerelease materials attempted to attract audiences with a promise to tell the half of the story not reported in the media.

Eastwood reveals in the first 90 seconds of *Sully* that the uncirculated story of flight 1549 involved the trauma Sully (Tom Hanks) experienced after his heroic water landing. The film opens with an alternate ending to flight 1549, one that has the plane crash into a building in New York City rather than land safely on the Hudson. The counter-story is quickly revealed to be a nightmare, a reimagining born in the mind of Sully. In this way, the film admits from the start that it is as interested in telling a story of trauma as it is circulating another story of heroism. The rest of the film documents how Sully moves from traumatic event, to traumatic response, to recovery. Interestingly, *American Sniper* follows the same narrative course. The early parts of the film reveal a traumatic event in Kyle's life, albeit not the one the trailer or those expecting to watch the story of a soldier might expect. The middle parts of the film show Kyle's response to that event. The latter parts show Kyle's recovery. Approached in this way, *American Sniper* and *Sully* develop a thematic rather than merely chronological relationship. A close examination of Eastwood's narrative and stylistic choices throughout *American Sniper* and *Sully* reveals that Eastwood makes artistic choices throughout these films that elevate the traumas and some recovery from those traumas above all other details. Both films stage a very specific traumatic journey, one that begins with a traumatic event, that continues with a displacement from both that event and the reality to which they want to return, and that ends with some reconciliation of these two realities. Just as interestingly, Eastwood constructs the plots of these two films so that they perform the recovery they permit their characters. The narrative and stylistic elements find a clarity and coherence at the end of *American Sniper* and *Sully* that Eastwood denies them for much of the film. The eventual resolution of these elements mirrors the resolution in the minds of the films' main characters. In this way, *American Sniper* and *Sully* project *and* perform the full cycle of trauma, moving as they do from early narrative and stylistic leaps to the kind of cinematic certainty and simplicity so common in Eastwood's films. They become in this way two of Eastwood's most thorough examinations of trauma and confessions of the cinema's ability to negotiate such things.

One can trace a clear concern for trauma throughout Eastwood's film. The difference between those projects and these last two is the extent to which these movies were released into societies that have become accustomed to recognizing and discussing post-traumatic stress disorder (PTSD). The causes and symptoms of this "disorder" have become conventional for most educated or media savvy citizens. Films have routinely turned to these conventions to inform their films, so much so that some of these techniques risk becoming cliché. Janet Walker (2001) goes as far as to suggest that "the 1980s and 1990s have seen the development of a 'trauma cinema' … a group of films, each of which deals with a world-shattering event or events of the past, whether public, personal, or both" (214). Walker further explains that films in this cycle tend to mimic the symptoms of post-traumatic stress, privileging "non-linearity, fragmentation, nonsychronous sound, repetition, rapid editing and strange angles" over more direct techniques (214). Walker suggests that too much uncritical familiarity with such techniques within stories about trauma can actually circumvent any meaningful understanding or empathy. Thomas Elsaesser (2001) aptly extends this suggestion: "the notion of victimhood, the emphasis on history and power(lessness), the anxiety about memory, its ambiguous relation to an inner psychic reality and to an outer, public (or cinematic) representation" can overwhelm active spectatorship (195). An appeal to trauma can circumvent the need for interpretative choices to be made at all unless filmmakers keep in front of their audience the need for ongoing interpretation. Eastwood does just this and he does so most fully in *American Sniper* and *Sully*. The narrative and stylistic choices in *American Sniper* and *Sully* promote rather than pacify active spectatorship. Both films push for what Elsaesser perceptively phrases a recovery of "referentiality," which is to say a recovery of the interpretive work one must perform to discover any sense of "there-ness" (201). Eastwood's *American Sniper* and *Sully* ground their narratives in a *there*, a moment where some stable meaning exists for the character being examined, and the narratives work to bring the character back to this *there* in their present reality, which is to say they work to bring the character *here*. Both films work, therefore, to bring *there here*.

The dissociation in *Sully* and Eastwood's strategy for recovering it is a bit easier to identify than the dissociation in *American Sniper* if only because it is much more tangible. The *there* of Sully does after all exist on the cockpit voice recording (CVR) that will literally be played in the hearing at the end of the film. The CVR plays over a set of images that are not included in the recording, but that serve rather than work against the reality to which Sully has spent to the entire film trying to return. The reality in this final version exists differently than those projected in Sully's earlier flashbacks. The visual and aural elements struggled to cohere in those early retellings. This is especially the case with the opening version, which has the plane crash into the base of building. In this version, Eastwood tolerates a *there* and a *here*, moment that did happen against what might have happened. This tolerance is particularly meaningful, especially in the film, since audiences expect a different ending than the opening gives them. In this way, *Sully* opens with what appears to be two competing binary positions. Only one version of flight 1549 can be true. Either the plane landed safely on the Hudson or it did not. Sully's alternative reality can be a *here*, in the space where one speculates about what has happened; it cannot be a *there*, where the event actually did occur, where some stable meaning exists. Eastwood withholds this *there* from

Sully until the final moments of the film. Only in the final hearing can what Sully remembers and what can be accepted converge.

Eastwood plays with the distinction between *here* and *there* during the scene in a bar that at first feels like something of a non sequitur. Sully enters a bar after a late night run. Somewhat importantly, the narrative structure of the film suggests that the run occurs soon after Sully attempts to answer his wife's question of why he would attempt a water landing knowing all the dangers involved in such a maneuver. His explanation prompts what audiences can recognize upon their own reflection as a kind of dissociated flashback one retelling of the events of January 15, a flashback that will be worth some discussion in a moment. Along the run, which occurs as a response to the explanation he gives his wife, Lori (Laura Linney), Sully sees an F-4 Phantom II aircraft sitting atop an aircraft carrier. His mind ostensibly pulls the story and the camera to an earlier moment in Sully's life when he brought the same type of aircraft to a safe landing after some in-air troubles. With these two memories in the mind of both Sully and the audience, Sully enters the bar and takes a seat on one of the barstools. The bartender, Pete (Michael Rapaport), almost immediately recognizes the celebrated pilot. Pete praises Sully for his landing. He admits to creating a drink to honor his esteemed patron's triumph, "The Sully," a shot of Grey Goose and a splash of water. Pete passes Sully his invention, and Sully graciously takes a sip, clearly uncomfortable with the attention he is receiving. A few seconds later two customers at another end of the bar notice a picture of Sully on the television set above the bar. One of the men points out the happenstance of Sully's presence at the bar and on the bar's television: "Hey, Pete, Sully's here and he's there (gesturing to the set)." The other adds, "Yeah, he's everywhere." The two raise their glasses and erupt into laughter. Sully turns his attention to the television set, which presumably prompts another disassociated flashback of the events of January 15th as Sully conceives them, or at least as he struggles to do so.

Rather than a non sequitur, the patron's comment in the bar about Sully being at once *here* and *there* would seem to be something of a thesis statement for *Sully*, and, as will be discussed shortly, *American Sniper*. Both films deliver stories about characters seemingly stuck in two worlds, or at least stuck between two realities, and stuck in at least two ways. The two main characters, on the one hand, stuck between the reality they experienced and their memory of that experience. At the same time, they are also at once inside and outside their present reality. The former divide fits Dori Laub's (2005) assessment that trauma occurs "*out there*, not as an event related to an experiencing subject ... but ... dissociated from the narrator who has gone through it" (311). The latter also aligns with Laub's expectation: "often, survivors emphasize that they indeed live in two separate worlds, that of their traumatic memories ... and that of the present" (311). In the parlance of this essay, such individuals struggle to bring some *there here*. In the case of *Sully*, the film's accomplished and suddenly celebrated pilot is caught between his experience of flight 1549, his memory of those events, what the media reports, and what the National Transportation Safety Board (NTSB) says about it. Eastwood builds the narrative points in *Sully* around the contests these different positions create. The film opens with Sully's memory, the most traumatic of these positions and, ironically, the only clearly untrue version of the historical event the film relates. Flight 1549 does not crash into the middle of Manhattan no matter how many times Sully mentally simulates that outcome, and he does envision the plane he is piloting crashing into the same building twice—once at the film's opening and a second time following his interview with Katie Couric. At these two points in the film, Sully's mental simulations indicate that he is in the midpoint of the traumatic journey, that space where he suffers from PTSD. Sully's thoughts are the exact kinds of inexact contemplations commonly associated with post-traumatic stress. Eastwood resolves this trauma by correcting this false version with an actual one, one that allows Sully to move into recovery, and to show how film can replicate that recovery as it unites image and sound to produce a coherent and authoritative version of events.

The other two versions of flight 1549 presented before the final hearing in *Sully*, those versions above described as dissociated flashbacks, also exist in the midpoint of the traumatic journey, and become part of the recovery *Sully* ultimately performs. Eastwood presents both flashbacks in a forthright manner. The dark shadows and extreme angles that mark the film's opening sequence have been replaced with more natural light and more standard framing. The only detail that suggests that these two versions are not authoritative is the fact that Sully would seem to be their narrator even though both versions contain details that he could not have known. Eastwood's narrative arrangement suggests that each version exists as a kind of response, once to the National Transportation Safety Board (NTSB) and then to the media. The justification for this interpretation resides primarily in the narrative placement of each mental simulation. The first flashback of sorts occurs directly after the NTSB reports the results of its own computer simulations, which conclude that flight 1549 had enough speed and altitude to make a successful return to LaGuardia and Teterboro airport if need be. The NTSB report clearly shakes Sully. He tells his co-pilot, Jeff (Aaron Eckhart), "somehow that's, that's not how I remember it. It just doesn't seem right." Jeff contends, "That's because it's not right." For the moment, though, what is right, what is *there*, is what the NTSB reports. Eastwood conveys this point by having Sully enter the conversation with Lori as though that report might be the authoritative voice on whether he made the right call in the cockpit. The conflicted pilot and husband wonders what will become of him if he did make the wrong choice, if he unnecessarily endangered the lives of all of his passengers. Lori rejects this idea, pointing to the reports that fill every news channel as evidence that her Sully is a "hero and that every one is going to have to get use to it, including the NTSB." Sully will consider the media's report in the next memory. At this moment, he counters Lori's claim that the media is right by sharing with her the evidence the NTSB presented him earlier that day: "the left engine might have still been idling and the airbus simulations say [he] could have made it back to LaGuardia safely." Lori asks what Sully himself is almost assuredly thinking, "Then why would you do it, Sully? What, land in the water? Wasn't that the most dangerous thing you could have done?"

As a sort of answer to this question, Eastwood's camera unexpectedly cuts to a scene in the airport that the audience comes to understand as an event that occurred on the day of the flight. The details in this flashback would seem to serve as a response to Lori and the NTSB, a point Eastwood reminds his audience at the end of the flashback by returning to Sully, who still sits in the same chair, presumably on the same phone call he was having when the flashback began. None of this is immediately apparent. The viewer has to reconstruct these elements in just the way Sully is, or the plot presumes he is doing. The most interesting aspect of the flashback is the way it quickly denies Sully as the narrator. The flashback contains details he could not have known. For instance, after Sully purchases a sandwich at a shop in the airport, the camera leaves the pilot to focus on two soon-to-be passengers of flight 1549. Sully literally vacates the space the plot projects, which makes explicit the divide between memory and reality in this moment. The choice to leave Sully in this way is made most interesting when one realizes that Eastwood has already revealed these two shoppers as eventual passengers of flight 1549. The audience watched the same news report that Sully watched earlier in the film that had the younger of the two shoppers talking about her experience. By placing these two at the beginning of the flashback, Eastwood reveals what follows as a *here* to be sure, a consideration of what might have happened, but not necessarily a *there*, a definitive version of what took place. This point is emphasized again when the camera finds three additional eventual passengers that Sully could not have seen. A man and his son and nephew run through the airport to try to board flight 1549. They arrive late, but talk the desk clerk into allowing them to board. The event is hardly significant other than what it almost became, namely, the kind of ironic story one tends to learn after a tragedy of someone just making a flight that would eventually crash. Eastwood refuses to submit to the cliché entirely. The inclusion of this detail alerts audiences that Sully's remembrance of January 15th is a remembrance at a distance. The character is both *there* and not *there*. He is above all, here, which is to say in that moment kept from a *there*, at least as such a place is understood as the site where some space that permits the presence of a stable meaning. The script's sudden shift to the air-traffic controller's perspective registers this point again. Sully can imagine what the air-traffic controller was experiencing during the event, but he cannot see that portion of the day's events as the audience does. This first flashback, then, works in the same way the NTSB's report does, providing a report of what might have happened rather than what did happen.

The second flashback does the same thing only the catalyst for this retelling would seem to be the media rather than the NTSB. Several aspects of the scene that immediately precede the second flashback suggest what Sully watches on the television while in the bar drives this second flashback. For one thing, the news report remains on the screen throughout the afore-mentioned bar scene. The television set is the first thing Sully notices when he walks into the bar. The framing of the camera once Sully takes his seat at the bar leaves the television in clear view. The characters make direct reference to the broadcast as already discussed. And, perhaps most telling: the voice from the broadcast forms a sound bridge between Sully in the bar and his imagination of the events of January 15. Most of all, though, the flashback begins with the story being reported on the television. Sully's flashback starts on deck one of the New York Waterway taxis that participated in the rescue. Eastwood ensures his audiences do not miss this fact by including the actual news footage in the final credits of his film. The similarities between the news reports and the shots in the film are especially striking. The fact that various riverside reports find their way into this second mental simulation further supports the idea that what appears in the second flashback is a response to the media. So, too, is the fact that a news report forms a second sound bridge when Sully returns to the bar. The reporter's comment about the impeccable timing of everyone involved provides Sully the link he needs to reconcile *here* and *there*. Sully's entire condition shifts after this scene. He suddenly gains some control over the stories, media and otherwise, that had been engulfing him.

Eastwood's willingness to locate the turn Sully makes in his ability to control the stories about his forced water landing becomes one of the more interesting aspects of *Sully*, and one of the ways that *American Sniper* and *Sully* relate to one another. Both characters begin to leave the middle portion of the traumatic cycle at the moment they begin to control their story. Sully begins to leave his trauma when he finds a response to the NTSB report. Eastwood's solution is interesting, as it seems to counter the solution to trauma most often imagined by trauma scholars. Following Cathy Caruth (1996), for example, one of the clearest indicators of trauma is that the trau-matized subject becomes "possessed by an image or event" (4–5). The idea is that the initial traumatic experience envelops the individual. This is what constitutes post-traumatic stress. E. Ann Kaplan and Ban Wang (2004) follow this very line of thought when they describe trauma as "a debilitating kind memory ... engraved on the body, precisely because the original experience was too overwhelming to be processed by the mind" (5). Kaplan and Wang move beyond this idea only far enough to emphasize the extent to which such traumas exist within cultures as much as the individual. The authors reason, "as trauma implies a shattering of a culture's meaning-making scheme and representational modes, it is, as many critics insist, beyond the reach of representation" (8). And, yet, Kaplan and Wang insist that media representations still have a role to play in the negotiation of such traumas, becoming as they do "a matrix of understanding and experiencing of a world out of joint" (17). Eastwood's *Sully* shows one of the ways film can help subjects negotiate trauma. His main character reclaims control of his story, and, in so doing, gains some vindication with NTSB and verification of what happened (there) with what he remembers happening (here). *Here* and *there* reconcile.

Eastwood stages the movements in this reconciliation during the NTSB hearing at the end of the film. The hearing looks like it will conclude what the first interview did, namely, that flight 1549 could have made it back to LaGuardia or even to another nearby airport. If left unchallenged, Sully's forced water landing was unnecessary and at odds with his experience. The hearing takes a different narrative turn as soon as Sully has a response to the data presented to him. He wonders aloud how many practice runs the pilots took before completing the "simulation" he has just been shown. Sully's stance is that any practice invalidates the simulation. He was never given the chance to simulate what to do when a plane experiences dual engine loss at low altitude. By not allowing any time "for analysis or decision making," Sully insists the NTSB review board has "taken all of the humanity out of the cockpit." New simulations must be run to determine if Sully's reality was necessary or not. The board agrees to add a delay into the simulations, and the results exonerate Sully. Neither pilot makes it to a runway. Both crash before reaching their target, the plane bound for Teterboro in a virtual replay of Sully's worst-case scenario found at the opening of the film.

The failed simulations exonerate Sully, but more importantly they create a path for him to reconcile his memory with the official record. This happens quite literally in the film as the cockpit voice recording (CVR) is played and Sully and Jeff can hear what they might otherwise only remember. Jeff prefaces the playing of the CVR with a question: "now that we've seen what could have happened can we uh listen to what actually did?" This contest between what might have happened (here) and what did happen (there) sits at the center of Eastwood's *Sully*. The earlier flashbacks revealed part of what happened, but they also portrayed some details inaccurately. For instance, the recording played at the hearing does not have Sully say at any point that he will head for LaGuardia. To the contrary, he says from the start that he "may end up in the Hudson." This correction begins to align Sully's memory with the officially recognized events of flight 1549. This alignment starts the formation of an authoritative record, a combining of *here* and *there* in one place. In this way, *Sully* realizes a union of memory, sound, and image that seemed earlier in the film as impossible as the forced water-landing Sully performed. Sully leaves the hearing with one authoritative perspective. *Here* and *there* are one and the same both for the character and, just as importantly, for Eastwood's audience. The filmmaker shows the ways that film can reconcile what appears irreconcilable. It can end the contests between versions of a story, and, in so doing, eliminate the trauma that follows too many versions of the same event from remaining open.

Eastwood celebrates the significance of this resolution during the "quick break" Sully and Jeff take in the hall after hearing the recording. Sully has remained somewhat aloof throughout much of the film. He has been unable, for instance, to maintain telephone conversations with his wife. He says he is too tired to keep talking in one conversation. He simply says, "I have to go" to end another. He has had very little to offer his co-pilot either. His condition would seem to confirm Maureen Turim's (2001) understanding of trauma as something that "invades, troubles and even forecloses by asserting the unresolved pain of events that cumulatively have overwhelmed a subject's ability to cope" (209). Turim contends "one of the effects of trauma is to distance the self not only from one's memory, but also from the experience of others" (210). For much of the film, *Sully* corroborates this account. It is not until the official CVR is heard that Sully makes it back to his co-experiencer. Eastwood draws particular attention to the shift Sully makes by giving the pilot a chance to share his pride for how Jeff went through the experience with him: "You, you were right *there*, with so much distraction and so much at stake. We did this together. We were a team … we did our job." Sully continues to speak in the same spirit of togetherness in the closing moments of the film when he rejects the board's willingness to identify Sully as the reason the story ended the way it did. Sully disagrees: "It wasn't just me. It was all of us. It was Jeff and Donna and Sheila and Doreen, all of the passengers, the rescue workers, and air-traffic control, ferryboat crews, and the scuba cops. We all did it. We survived."

The "we" is particularly important. Sully's ability to locate himself within a community allows him to bring *there here*, to bring his memory of what happened to the present, and to do so in a definitive way. Interestingly, this is the same catalyst Eastwood uses to indicate Chris Kyle's recovery in *American Sniper*. Admittedly, this film follows a different narrative path, a simpler one in many ways, but it reaches the same end-point, at least as it relates to

Kyle's recovery: the traumatized man finds a way through his post-traumatic stress by finding community that allows him to recover his sense of identity and purpose. Unlike in *Sully*, this sense of identity and purpose is not contained on an actual recording, but left in the mind of its hero. The film actually reveals what could only be made known through some confession by leaving the main action of *American Sniper* through a flashback placed very early in the film to identify Kyle's strong sense of identity and purpose. The contents of the flashback constitute Kyle's *there*. His trauma arises from his inability, first, to realize that *there* effectively as sniper, and, then, for a time, at all as a civilian. His recovery occurs, like Sully, when he can combine his *there*, his definitive sense of self and purpose in life, with his *here*, his present circumstances.

The most significant moment in *American Sniper*'s narrative, at least as it relates to the resolution the film ultimately finds for Kyle, occurs in the early moments of the film. The tension from the film's opening scene builds into a dramatic moment that forces Kyle to decide whether to shoot an adolescent boy he believes to be carrying a grenade. The camera zooms in on the trigger of the rifle. A shot fills the soundtrack. At that very moment, a hard cut carries the audience from the adult sniper's rooftop perch in Iraq to a more pastoral scene in Kyle's life. The younger Kyle and his father sit behind a makeshift covering in the woods. The camera finds this moment just after the younger Kyle has fired on a deer. A second cut shows the result of Kyle's gunshot: the animal falls to the ground. Kyle's father, Wayne (Ben Reed), proudly reports what the audience has already seen, "you got him." Eastwood's choice would seem to exist as a bit of mercy. Rather than show the fallen boy, who hardly anyone is ready to see just over three minutes into the film, Eastwood cuts to the image of a fallen deer. Sergei Eisenstein performed a similar shift in *Strike* (1925), albeit for different reasons. The famed Russian director wanted to show real blood on the screen to create the right effect in the audience as they watched the Russian army's slaughter of the unarmed laborers. Eisenstein intercut images of a bull's slaughter with the massacre.

Eastwood's cut is almost certainly for another reason. He will, in fact, later show the killing this explanation would have him avoid showing. Eastwood's cut to this hunt with Kyle's father seems more interested in focusing the film's narrative through this early memory, and those that follow it in the flashback. As to the purpose of this initial aspect of the flashback, Eastwood is able to show in short order the weight of Wayne's influence on his eldest son. The subsequent shots build on this idea in important ways, too. Following the fatal shot of the deer, the camera captures Chris' movements as he runs toward the fallen animal. Just moments before he reaches his kill, the young hunter drops his rifle to the ground. The father immediately commands

Chris to return to his rifle, teaching him that one never leaves one's rifle in the dirt. Wayne then praises his son for his shot, telling him he has "a gift," that he will "make a fine hunter some day." The words are full of unmistakable irony in the moment they are delivered. One could construe the kill shot the camera refused to show in the opening moments of the adult sniper's story as a kind of hunting. Kyle has become a fine hunter. The script does not reject this irony, but it does use the next several moments of the flashback and other moments in the film to emphasize a more substantive interpretation, one that explains Kyle's traumatic event, his traumatic response to that event, and his ability to move through both.

The flashback moves from the woods to a church wherein Chris sits on a pew beside his younger brother and their parents. The soundtrack captures the words of a preacher delivering a message about humanity's limited ability to discern any place in the divine plan. Again, Eastwood fashions a bit of irony in this scene. The preacher talks of God's authority while the screen shows the unquestioned authority of the parents. Chris' mother, Deby (Elise Robertson), corrects Chris' younger brother, Jeff (Luke Sunshine), who sees his sibling flipping through a pocket-sized Bible and asks aloud what it is his brother is doing. Deby demands Jeff's attention, and the foursome return their focus to the speaker in the pulpit. Eastwood frames the scene in such a way that the parents sit in the foreground rather than the preacher, which serves as a succinct way to assign the parents as the highest authority in their sons' lives.

The next scene extends this thought. Eastwood shows the pocket-sized Bible Chris took from the church now sitting on a dresser in the Kyle home. The most interesting aspect of the shot is the way that Wayne's words fill the soundtrack over the image of the Bible. Eastwood's mix of image and sound place Wayne in the position of the preacher in the earlier moment. Wayne's words literally over the Bible turn the father's voice into the "the word of God," at least for Chris, and at least in this moment. The rest of the sequence puts this interpretation to use as well. Wayne explains that there are three types of people in the world. There are the sheep that ignore the evils in the world and, therefore, never learn how to protect themselves. There are the wolves that "prey on the weak." And there are the sheepdogs that "are blessed with the gift of aggression and the overpowering need to protect the flock." Wayne delivers extra praise for this third group, identifying those in this group as "a rare breed that live to confront the wolf." Wayne's "sermon" ends with an admission that he is not raising any sheep, and that he will deal with any of his that become a wolf. During Wayne's homily, Eastwood cuts to a scene from the schoolyard where all three types of people can be seen. A bully punches Chris' little brother in the face. Chris breaks through the crowd to free his brother and to punish "the wolf." Wayne asks Chris, "Did you finish it?" Chris says he did. Wayne says, "Then you know who you are; you know your purpose." The moment has the same tenor as Wayne's praise of Chris' gift as a hunter. In both scenes, Eastwood loads the early parts of this flashback with a clear sense of authority, the kind of authority that remains present throughout one's life. In so doing, Eastwood suggests even in these early moments that Kyle's trauma has more to do with his ability to perform the role his father has assigned him than anything else.

The most interesting aspect of this flashback for those wanting to consider Eastwood's understanding of trauma is the presence of these images so early in the film. The significance of these scenes never dissipates. They are always present. In this way, Kyle's trauma is never as much about absence as it is about displacement of that which has been present. The rest of the flashback extends this line of thought, too. Most of the rest of the flashback shows a Kyle that does not know who he is or what it is he should be doing. Eastwood shows the now older Kyle on the back of a bronco, winning a competition at a rodeo. Kyle immediately empties the achievement of any significance. He admits that the prize offers little more than a belt buckle and chance for sex with his girlfriend. The story rejects even this last award, though, in the next scene when Kyle returns to his trailer only to find his live-in girlfriend with another man. Kyle quite literally has nothing to show for his life. Kyle spends the rest of the night drinking with his brother, at least until a report of another bombed embassy appears on the screen. The next image has him at a recruiter's office.

The narrative sequence implies that military service provides Chris with a way to legitimize the identity and purpose his father awarded him earlier in the flashback. This implication continues to intensify as the sequence has Chris meet his wife, Taya (Sienna Miller), find his place in the Corps as a sniper, watch the World Trade Center collapse on 9/11, and receive his orders for his first tour of duty. It is only at this point that the plot returns to Iraq and to the place in the story the film started. Chris and his unit sit in a briefing that not only explains what will happen as Chris' unit moves through a new part of the city, but what was happening when the film opened. The sequence eventually finds its way back to the moment Eastwood left his opening albeit with some minor and relatively unimportant ellipses. Chris and his partner position themselves atop the roof. The woman and adolescent boy enter the street. The woman hands a grenade to the child. The boy begins to run toward the convoy. Kyle shoots him through the chest. The boy and the grenade fall to the ground. The next image entertains for a brief second that Kyle made the wrong call. The woman runs toward the boy in the way a mother right run to her son only to pass him in order to retrieve the fallen weapon. The coconspirator picks up the grenade, reaches back to hurl it, only to have Kyle shoot her just as she makes her throw. The grenade explodes well short of the convoy. Kyle's command commends him for his shot and the call he made. Kyle's partner tries to commend him as well, but Kyle rejects his praise. The gifted sniper simply looks through his scope at the boy's body.

The placement of the earlier flashback begins to reward those who connect what they see to what Eastwood conveyed there. Without the flashback in place, what follows would move more ambiguously than it does in its current structure. One might misconstrue the acts Kyle performs and must see through his scope at close range as a catalyst to some trauma. The images of the kills certainly create space for an empathetic response from the audience. In the aftermath of the above kill, for instance, the camera not only settles on Kyle's point-of-view through the scope, but sets the crosshairs of the scope at the center of the exit wound that fills the top half of the boy's back. The image is certainly unsettling for those in the audience. One must question the extent to which the image troubles Kyle, though. The sniper has simply done his job. This point is, in fact explicitly conveyed in a later part of the flashback. Taya asks Chris if he ever thinks "about what happens when there's a real person on the other end of that gun?" Chris admits he does not know. He explains that he just hopes he can do his "job when that day comes," and now he has. He has ended the threat against his unit. A sequence of images soon after the above scene shows Kyle's repeated ability to "do his job." In one image, a man literally falls from the sky after Kyle marks him. In another, a man is shot through the head as he attempts to drive a car bomb into a group of Marines. Still another shows Kyle shooting a man as he tries to plant an IED. A final image in this particular sequence shows Kyle killing a man who runs into the street carrying an AK-47. Eastwood's camera centers on an image of Kyle after each kill, and the audience sees what appears to be a more vexed Kyle with each killing.

One could conclude that the killings are beginning to weigh on Kyle, but a moment at the end of this particular sequence suggests another weight. Kyle's counterpart on the Iraqi-side, Mustafa (Sammy Sheik), an Olympic medal-winning marksman, kills one of Kyle's men during a night patrol. Kyle's initial response is one of calculation: he dials in his scope, determined to eliminate this threat as he has so many others. When he hears the position of the enemy sniper, and it is clear that he will have no shot and that the enemy sniper will escape, Kyle conveys the familiar pained response. Kyle has no shot. More men will be lost until he does. This final revelation reorients the earlier expressions. Kyle's concern is less with his role in the killings; it has more to do with his inability to save every man under his watch. Eastwood's placement of the earlier flashback would support this interpretation. Kyle feels an "overpowering need to protect the flock," and he does so with unparalleled proficiency. But his efforts are not perfect. He looses some men. In this way, Kyle would seem to be unable to realize fully his sense of identity and purpose as the sheepdog, and this awareness is, firstly, his trauma event, and, secondly, what traumatizes him most. The script explicitly makes this point, too, in the very next scene. A relief comes to release Kyle from his station. The man asks Kyle how many kills Kyle had that night. The relief cannot believe Kyle's success. He is recording more kills than all of the other snipers combined. Kyle remains unimpressed. He can only see the man he could not save: "Yeah, but they got one of us." The comment highlights Kyle's drive to be the sheepdog, protecting all of his sheep. The pains on his face can more accurately be taken as a reflection of his own sense of failure protecting every soldier under his watch. The words of the script support this interpretation; so, too, does the placement of the earlier interpretation the early flashback.

Subsequent aspects of the script also encourage audiences to see Kyle's trauma as some perceived failure. After Kyle's four tours of duty have come to an end and he is presumably stateside for good, Taya and Chris go to a neighborhood barbeque. During the scene, Kyle sits in the backyard drinking a beer. Children play in the yard as a domesticated dog runs between them. Eventually, the dog playfully pounces on one boy who has fallen to the ground. The dog makes a series of playful snaps at the boy's neck, although almost no one in the yard would deem any of this a threat. Kyle, on the other hand rises from his seat on the porch and rushes toward the dog. He removes his belt, rolls the dog over, and raises his arm to strike the dog. He stops when Taya calls his name. A series of crosscuts indicate the two ways of seeing at work in this scene. The threat is not what Kyle thought it was. More importantly, there is no need for him to play the role of sheepdog in this new life, and he would seem to have no opportunity to return to the war where he could continue to act in that role. Kyle is, quite literally, a man without a sense of identity or purpose in this moment.

Kyle recovers both in the very next scene. Kyle meets with a VA doctor (Robert Clotworthy) after the event at the barbeque. The doctor specifically asks Kyle if he "ever thinks that [he] might have seen things or done some things over *there* that wish you hadn't" (emphasis mine). The decorated Marine rejects this idea with the telling statement "that's not me." The choice of words is particularly interesting, and especially when combined with the earlier flashback. Kyle has been grounded for much of the film in a clear sense of purpose and identity. Everything he did in the war, all that he saw, he did and saw in the role of the sheepdog. In this way, Kyle's service as a sniper was not something he did; rather, it is who he was, or is, depending on the sense of coherence he is experiencing. As a sniper, who he is and what he does are aligned. Kyle's trouble is that he cannot remain a sniper, nor can he perform his job in such a way that every man in his command is saved. The losses Kyle experiences during later tours really focus on this point. Every loss calls Kyle's identity and sense of purpose into question. Kyle explicitly admits each of these points when the doctor asks Kyle to explain his comment "that's not me." Kyle does so by saying, "I was just protecting my guys. They were trying to kill our soldiers, and, uh, I'm willing to meet my Creator and answer for every shot I took." Kyle's trauma springs from a different place, a point he makes just as explicitly: "The thing that, uh, haunts me are all of the guys I couldn't save; I'm willing and able to be there, but I'm not. I'm here. I quit."

The VA doctor offers Kyle a way to return to his role as sheepdog by introducing him to others soldiers needing to be saved. Initially, Kyle simply sits among others who have returned from the war with mutilated bodies. The camera initially focuses on each loss, but eventually settles on the story one soldier tells of how smoking saves his right hand. The shift from the broken bodies to the sustaining stories reorients Kyle in just the way his decision to join the Marines reoriented him. The next scene brings this interpretation to the surface. Chris is watching as a former Marine, Wayne (Dean Wayne) takes target practice. Wayne asks Chris why he "spends all this time with us." Chris makes a joke about wanting the man's boot-collection before simply saying "we take care of each other." Kyle's joke reveals more truth that it at first seems to reveal. Kyle suffers because he did not "take care" of every man in his unit. Eastwood had already made room in his plot for this point. Kyle encounters stateside a man he had saved in country. The man thanks Kyle for saving his life, but Kyle remains completely unaffected by the life in front of him. His thoughts are with those men still in danger or those he could not save. This scene reveals one side of the confession delivered in the joke Chris makes to Wayne's question. The other side is provided by what the audience knows, namely, that Kyle's trauma intensifies when he has no way to assume the role of the sheepdog. Having filled that role in the past is not enough for Kyle. He must remain the sheepdog if he is to answer the role his father assigned him and he accepted as a teen. Kyle finds his way through his trauma most of all by finding a group of men he can help.

The point that Eastwood's narrative makes is that Kyle's recovery is less about filling an absence than it is about bringing a prior sense of presence and purpose to his present. Just before the graphic appears on the screen that tells audiences that Kyle "was killed that day by a veteran he was trying to help," Chris' wife praises him for making it "back." There is a clear sense in which Kyle literally makes it back that seems critically important to the story Eastwood tells. Kyle's triumph as Eastwood frames it is not his ability to leave the horrors of war behind him. Eastwood presents a more fundamental struggle, one that requires Kyle to bring the sense of identity and purpose his father bestows upon him at a pivotal point in life to his present. Kyle's recovery is not realized when someone else tells him his story, but when he reinvents and reanimates a sense of identity and purpose that he might have thought only existed so long as he was a sniper, and even then imperfectly. By agreeing to help the veterans he meets, Kyle has resumed his role as sheepdog. He has found a way to realize the sense of self and purpose given him during the scenes contained in the flashback. He has made it back to that definitive sense of self. He has brought there here, and he has completed the traumatic journey as a result.

In *American Sniper* and *Sully*, Eastwood delivers stories of characters that bring *there*, some stable site of stable meaning, *here*, to their present. The feat adjusts the infamous saying "there is no there there" to proclaim that trauma occurs when there is no *there here*. Recovery occurs when *there* and *here* reconcile. This reconciliation occurs as a journey. It takes time to move from traumatic experience and traumatic response to recovery. *American Sniper* and *Sully* show what that passage of time looks like and how it moves characters into a space of recovery. In this way, these two films do more than just tell the story of characters that move through three stages of trauma; they also reveal the ways in which film can perform these movements. In an introductory article to a special issue of *Screen* on trauma, Susannah Radstone (2001) comments "on the illusory but shocking indexical 'thereness' of the moving visual image" (190). The idea implied throughout that introduction is that film creates a relationship between the image and the spectator that can be (re)constructed into a fuller understanding of trauma and one's ability to move beyond it. One can string the narrative and stylistic choices in *Sully* along a continuum between trauma and recovery that identifies some of the causes of trauma and a means to move through it. One can mark the narrative choices of *American Sniper* in a similar way. By creating two films that can be shown to do more than simply project stories of trauma, Eastwood offers a profound reassessment of benefit that follows the interplay between films and their audiences. Films can form a *there*, some site of trauma that might otherwise be forever lost, that can be brought *here*, to a place of coherence and relevance, through the active engagement of the spectator. In this way, film can project recovery into places where recovery has yet to be experienced. It can find a way for audiences to sit both here and there, and to see how to relate the two spaces together.

WORKS CITED

American Sniper. 2014. Directed by Clint Eastwood, performances by Bradley Cooper, Sienna Miller, and Kyle Gallner, Warner Bros.

Berardinelli, James. 2016. "Sully: A Movie Review." *Reelviews*. 8 September. 4 January 2016. http://www.reelviews.net/reelviews/sully.

Caruth, Cindy. 1991. "Unclaimed Experience: Trauma and the Possibility of History." *Yale French Studies* 79: 181–192.

Elsaesser, Thomas. 2001. "Postmodernism as Mourning Work." *Screen* 42:2: 193–201.

Laub, Dori. 2005. "Traumatic Shutdown of Narrative and Symbolization." *Contemporary Psychoanalysis* 41:2: 307–326.

Kaplan, Ann E., and Ban Wang. 2004. "Introduction: From Traumatic Paralysis to the Force

Field of Modernity." *Trauma and Cinema: Cross-Cultural Explorations*. Hong Kong: Hong Kong University Press.

Radstone, Susannah. 2001. "Trauma and Screen Studies: Opening the Debate." *Screen* 42:2: 188–193.

Strike. 1925. Directed by Sergei Eisenstein, performances by Maksim Shtraukh, Grigori Aleksandrov, and Mikhail Gomorov, First State Film Factory.

Sully. 2016. Directed by Clint Eastwood, performances by Tom Hanks, Aaron Eckhart, and Laura Linney, Flashlight Films.

Turim, Maureen. 2001. "The Trauma of History: Flashbacks upon Flashbacks." *Screen* 42:2: 205–210.

Walker, Janet. 2001. "Trauma Cinema: False Memories and True Experiences," *Screen* 42:2: 211–216.

Conclusion
Eastwood's Perfect World

CHARLES R. HAMILTON
and ALLEN H. REDMON

Clint Eastwood's *A Perfect World* (1993) depicts a world that is far from perfect. The film begins idyllic enough. The first image frames the afternoon sun sitting in the sky. The camera pans from left-to-right across a thick field of tall, green grass. Eventually, it settles on the curious image of a Casper the Friendly Ghost Halloween mask and the film's central character, Butch (Kevin Costner), who appears to be catching a nap in the afternoon sun. A hard cut and repositioning of the camera, which now frames Butch as if it were lying beside him, repositions Butch. Curiously, American currency begins to float through the shot. Butch smiles the way one might in a dream. Those watching the film for the first time or who arrive at the theater not knowing anything about the film's story might expect he is dreaming. The sounds of a bird screeching pull Butch's eyes and the camera skyward. Another hard cut returns the camera to the very first image only this time a bird glides alongside the sun. The film's title appears to the right of the star: *A Perfect World*. A new sound redirects Butch's attention again and the camera connects the reverberations to the image of a helicopter hanging in the sky, seemingly between Butch and the sunlight the audience assumed he was enjoying.

The plot leaves Butch at this moment and the camera literally reverses direction and attention as it pans right-to-left across first an unnamed city and then settles on the house of a woman, Gladys Perry (Jennifer Griffin), and her three children on a Halloween night. The scene accepts the same incongruities found in the opening sequence. The Perry family does not fit in this world any more than the Casper mask, the floating U.S. dollars, or the helicopter fit in the other. While the rest of the world is dressed for Halloween and trick-or-treating, the occupants of the Perry house remain inside. The

175

children protest their non-involvement, especially the son, Phillip (T.J. Lowther). The mother explains their noncooperation by telling her son, "Our religious beliefs lift us to a higher place." Much of what follows throughout the film tests this assertion. Gladys and Phillip will quite literally be in a higher place when the film ends, as they will be inside the helicopter the audience sees in the opening sequence. They only arrive in that place, though, after going through an overtly traumatic experience, one that has Phillip kidnapped by two prison escapees and forced to shoot one of these men in order to protect another family. If there is "a perfect world" in this film, it is not the one placed on the screen; it might be the one watching what transpires on screen, though, depending on the extent to which the film invites conversation and reflection on the traumas it refuses to solve.

Eastwood's *A Perfect World* refuses to realize a perfect world diegetically, in part, because it always places two worlds in opposition to each other. The opening sequence contrasts the tranquility of the first images with the image of a chopper suspended in the air. The plot leaves this aspect of the story before this difference can be resolved, which pits the opening of the story against its beginning and, ultimately, its ending as well. In the same way, the Perry household defies the world around it by not participating in a child's holiday, which establishes the world the Perry's occupy and the one the rest of that community inhabits. The prison-break scene that Eastwood intercuts with his introduction of the Perry household demonstrates the same clash of two world orders. There is the world of pleasantries caught in the exchanges between Larry (Mark Voges) and his co-workers, who let Larry into the prison, and the world of violence and intimidation Terry (Keith Szarabajka), Butch's collaborator in the prison-break, employs to commandeer Larry's help in getting the two convicts out of the penitentiary. Finally, there is the world of order, represented at least initially by the Perry home, and the world of disorder, embodied in Terry's entering that home apparently to rape Gladys.

The most important conflict between two worlds exists within Butch. He is not entirely in the pastoral nor procedural world in the opening sequence; he never knew the normalcy of a home life, which means he can neither fully occupy the world the Perry's populate nor the community around them; and, he is not the mentally disturbed, outright criminal Terry appears to be. Eastwood uses the scene that brings together the two stories that had existed together only through the editing choices of the film to mark this last point. At the moment Terry's attack on Gladys becomes most physical, Butch knocks Terry to the ground. Butch stands at the center of the kitchen still wearing his prison uniform, but also donning a red and black jacket. The choice of costuming is telling. Terry has disrobed from his prison clothes. He wears an entirely pedestrian outfit. Butch, on the other hand, dons both his prison garb and a jacket he has acquired from "the outside." The choice inscribes Butch in dual roles, at once convict and protector. Butch cannot realize either role fully. He remains between them both, which becomes clearest when Butch begins to interact with Phillip. Rather than try to intimidate the boy as Terry does, Butch starts a joke. He tells Phillip to pick up the gun, bring it to him, point it at him, and tell him "stick 'em up." When the boy does as he is told, Butch laughs and says, "Perfect." Butch's perfect world exists somewhere between the realities of what he is and what the play involved with what he wants to be.

Interestingly, Butch is not the only character to exist between worlds. Chief Red Garnett (Clint Eastwood) occupies the same intermediary place in his world, which the plot establishes in a number of ways during Garnett's first scene, but, most importantly through its juxtaposition of Butch and Garnett's story both in the present and in the past. In terms of the present concurrence, the plot juxtaposes Butch and Red's stories through editing. The plot cuts from the Perry home to Red's office directly after Butch decides to kidnap Phillip. Red is on the phone at his desk as he looks through Butch's file. The Chief tries to pacify the governor, who is on the phone, and the criminologist, Sally Gerber (Laura Dern), who the governor asked to participate in the manhunt Red will direct. The script emphasizes the newness of such an arrangement. Sally admits to Red that her involvement in such cases is "a relatively new procedure." The hope is that "an understanding of the particular behavioral case history" can be an "aid to apprehension." Red rejects the new science Sally represents. He prefers older methods that include good instincts, technology, and "a lot of coffee."

In terms of a past correspondence between Butch and Red, the script establishes Red's prior interactions with Butch with a late conversation between Red and Sally. Red admits to having interfered with the sentencing the adolescent Butch received after taking a stolen car for a "joy-ride" in the country where Red served as sheriff. Worried about the life that awaited Butch given the cruelty and criminal background of his father, Red convinced the judge to send the boy to Gatesville Juvenile Detention Center. Red explains, "Gatesville isn't so bad. I know kids there who've straightened up. One even became a priest." Red insists to Sally that it was the right thing to do to create some distance between Butch and his father, to send him to Gatesville, which is just what happened. The only complication is that the outcome Red expected did not occur. Butch did not gain any real separation from his father, presumably because the father had already traumatized his son.

Eastwood reveals Butch's inability to distance himself from his father in the pivotal scene involving Butch, Phillip, Mack (Wayne Dehart), Lottie (Mary Alice), and their grandson, Cleveland (Kevin Jamal Woods). This scene occurs almost directly after Red's confession and its suggestion that Butch's father beat him as a child. The timely delivery of this information explains the reactions Butch has to Mack's rough, physical treatment of his grandson. Butch restrains himself from acting on the first instance of physical harm. Mack slaps Cleveland on the side of his head after the boy does not respond to Mack's request to get a thermos from the tractor. Butch's face gains a new expression. It appears that he is at once still at the breakfast table with the family that gave him shelter the night before and in some distant household full of abuse. Butch loses control the next time Mack slaps Cleveland. Butch punches Mack in the face, throws him to the ground, and chokes him before finally pointing a gun in his face. Butch asks, "What did you want to go and hit Clev for? He didn't move fast enough for you? Is that it?... You make me sick to my stomach." Audiences have every reason to suspect that Butch is talking as much to his father as he is talking to Mack. This suspicion continues to grow into a near certainty as Butch forces Mack to take Cleveland in his arms and tell his grandson that he loves him. The action seems a more fitting response to Butch's troubled and uncertain past than it does anything occurring in the present.

The moment fits what Bessel A. van der Kolk and Alexander C. McFarlane (1996) describe as the "tyranny of the past," the reemergence of some traumatic event that "comes to taint all other experiences, spoiling appreciation of the present" (4). Butch loses the ability to learn from his experience, a point made most apparent when Lottie tells Butch that she knows he is a good man. Butch responds, "No, I ain't a good man. I ain't the worst either. I'm just a breed apart." Unable to fully distance himself from his traumatic past with his father, Butch allows all of those he encounters who exhibit anything close to his father's behavior to become an extension of that relationship. Butch exhibits the characteristics of one suffering from chronic PTSD, which has an individual relive the past with an "immediate sensory and emotional intensity that makes [one] feel as if the event were occurring all over again" (8).

Eastwood ensures audiences recognize the two worlds Butch fills in this moment, at once in the past with his father, and in the present with Mack and his family, by having Butch restart the record player that spins a Zydeco dance song as he prepares to shoot Mack. Lottie begins to pray the Lord's Prayer, though, which disrupts Butch perhaps as much for how it inserts an unexpected voice into the ritual he is trying to perform as anything else. In an effort to silence that voice or any other, Butch reaches back for a roll of tape. He tapes the mouths of Lottie, Cleveland, and Mack before reaching back for the gun he had set on the floor to manage the tape. To his surprise, Phillip has taken the gun. The still young boy unexpectedly shoots Butch in the side. The shot returns Butch to the present just enough that he forgets his earlier designs and thanks Mack and his family for their "hospitality."

Phillip's action proves Judith Herman's (1997) opinion that faced with "human vulnerability in the natural world and with the capacity for evil in human nature" people have to take sides (7). One can either be on the side of the perpetrator or the victim: "it is morally impossible to remain neutral" (7). One can either develop an understanding of the trauma that sees the victimization of the subject or that takes the side of the perpetrator. *A Perfect World* seems especially aware of this point. Each of the films discussed in this volume (and many of those not) demonstrate an attentiveness of this idea. As to the films in this collection, the contributors to this volume have shown how these films arrive at a place by the end of their running where the traumatized can be more fully recognized and considered, where the causes of those traumas can be more fully expressed, and, at least in the later films, some way through those traumas can be imagined. *A Perfect World* exists, like its principle characters, somewhere in between these categories. The film identifies a series of personal traumas, and, in the case of Red, a personal trauma develops into an institutional one. Red and Butch's traumas fill the first two categories: their personal traumas can be seen and some new appreciation for what causes those traumas can be comprehended. The extent to which Eastwood's *A Perfect World* reaches the final category, some space where one can move through their trauma, institutional or otherwise, is yet to be determined. The audience will decide if the film reaches that ideal or not.

Eastwood's *A Perfect World* ends at least visually where it started, with Butch lying in a grassy field with money floating around him and a helicopter hanging above him. The audience is much more aware at the end of the film than they were when it began. Butch lies in the field the way he does after an FBI sniper unnecessarily shoots him. Were this a news report, the media would almost certainly ignore or at least reconfigure many of the details included in Eastwood's film to emphasize either the mistake that had been made or the necessity of the shot. There would be very little middle ground, very little space for some new consideration or understanding. Butch's concern and kindness for Phillip would almost certainly be lost or cast simply as the kind of bond that oftentimes arises between a captor and his captive. Red's guilt over the life he may have helped ruin would be acknowledged as an interesting intersection of two unrelated moments of a long and successful career if they were acknowledged at all. The traumas identified and examined would, in short, be erased. To return to Herman, this erasure or forgetting is just what the perpetrator demands happen: "the perpetrator does everything in his power to promote forgetting" (8). When others try to remember, the perpetrator will first try to deny the alleged atrocities ever happened. If that does not work, it will insist that the victim is unreliable or prone to hyperbole or, better, responsible for what befell her. When these strategies begin to fall flat, the perpetrator will simply declare it time "to forget the past and move on" (8).

For Herman, the only way to break this cycle is to create a social environment that "affirms and protects the victim and that that joins victim and witness [...which every citizen stands to be...] in a common alliance" (9). Herman concludes, "In the absence of strong political movements for [...the victim...], the active process of bearing witness inevitably gives way to the active process of forgetting" (9). Herman supports this view by pointing to the history of trauma studies, which, from her view, has oscillated between moments of acknowledgment and "amnesia" (7). The late 19th century saw a willingness to study hysteria and to understand those who suffer from this disorder. At the end of the First World War, theorists investigated "shell shock," a study that continued through the end of the Vietnam War. In more recent years, theorists have explored the traumas connected with sexual and domestic violence. In each case, vital insights are fashioned, quite literally, fit to the times, and then forgotten. For Herman, the only thing that will forgo this cycle is a political movement that frustrates the tendency to forget.

Some 20 years after Herman wrote her opinion, one might feel just as comfortable claiming that the reach and range of the 21st-century media can break the cycle to forget, or at least sustain the political movement that can do so. Past forms of media already demonstrated an ability to shape public perception even if that power tended to demarcate the parameters of an issue rather than promote a discussion about it. The media's rather limited portrayal of how one might respond to the Vietnam War is a clear case-in-point. Networks set before the American public the images of the war they wanted to show each night. For the most part, these images focused on one of two aspects of the war, depending on which network one watched. One could either witness scenes of peace marches and protests against the war, or observe pictures of National Guard troops policing college campuses and curtailing "un-patriotic" protests. The networks decided which images to emphasize. The public similarly fell into one of two camps as a result: one could either support the troops and the country against the threat of communism or one could join the ranks of the protesters. Media rarely imagined any middle ground.

This tendency to divide and limit the number of positions surrounding an important social issue like war was not something new. Media had performed in a similar way throughout the 20th century, a point Maxwell McCombs (2014) exposes in his book *Setting the Agenda: The Mass Media and Public Opinion*. News reports from World War I and World War II appeared in a range of formats—either in print by way of newspapers, over the air by way of radio, or on screen by way of newsreels that would play during the previews or intermissions in movie theaters, but the message was largely the same. The media projected patriotic messages meant to encourage the populace that was supporting the war efforts. The perceived range of media reports could each promote the same message, in part, because the number of voices involved in determining what was fit to print, broadcast, or project was relatively limited. The executives of these outlets had control of the messages they circulated, and they knew it. McCombs illustrates this point when he quotes former executive of the *New York Times,* Max Frankel, as he describes the power of the paper at its height: "It is the 'house organ' of the smartest, most talented, and most influential Americans at the height of American power. And while its editorial opinions or the views of individual columnists and critics can be despised or dismissed, the paper's daily package of news cannot. It frames the intellectual and emotional agenda of serious Americans" (ix–x). In short, a media source like the *Times* can and has set the political agenda of the American public. The best one could do in those times was to be aware of power the media held. American humorist Will Rogers' satirical (but appropriate) comment might have shown the most clear-headed response: "All I know is what I read in the newspapers."

Times have certainly changed as they relate to media. Today's media creates space for a wider range of topics to be considered and a variety of voices to be heard. Sarah Newman (2016) demonstrates this point in her blog "How Media Shapes Our View of Post-Traumatic Stress Disorder," which describes the ways in which media sets the agenda "in what the general population and lawmakers associate with PTSD." Newman finds that the vast majority of legislative proposals between 1989 and 2009 focused on either military populations (91.4 percent) or identified combat experience as the cause of PTSD (81.7 percent). This willingness for lawmakers to regard PTSD as a military disorder exists despite the fact that more and more clinicians recognize PTSD symptoms in the civilian population. Newman suggests that this reality exists, in part, because of how PTSD gets covered in the media. She cites a study by researchers at Drexel University, "which reviewed 35 years of articles on PTSD published in the *New York Times*—from 1980, the year PTSD was added to the Diagnostic and Statistical Manual of Mental Disorders, to 2015." The Drexel study identifies 871 cases of PTSD being reported over that time. Most of the reports were, as one might expect, related to the military, with 20 percent of those reports being related to veterans of Afghanistan and Iraq. The *Times* did report on civilian traumas, things like sexual assault, natural disasters, or car crashes, but with much less frequency, and rarely with any attention to anything more than the symptoms associated with PTSD. Newman laments "stories of survival or prevention" are rarely printed.

The danger in this kind of singular emphasis is that it narrows the discussion on PTSD. The fact that scholars are studying public representations of PTSD or bloggers are writing about PTSD can certainly help broaden the public conversation on issues the commercial media might prefer to bind. These efforts can only go so far in changing social and political opinion. The researchers involved in the Drexel study concluded that despite broader media attention on PTSD, "results suggest that public awareness of PTSD has increased, but may be incomplete, inaccurate, and perpetuate PTSD stigma at individual- and institutional-levels" (636). One has to wonder the impact a study like the present one, a study that traces the steady and staunch examination of PTSD by one of the world's most influential filmmakers can have.

Eastwood's perfect world is not realized in the film by that name; in fact, it may not be realized in any of the films he has made, at least not those that feature trauma. The perfection of any of these worlds depends on the work the audience may or may not do after seeing his films. Eastwood creates films that withstand scrutiny under the most sophisticated discussions of PTSD, but even without placing those films in that dialog, audiences can see in the stories he presents the sympathy and understanding he extends characters that experience trauma. When set in the conversation this collection creates, one extends these sympathies and understandings in unexpected places. The character's decisions to turn to violence in *The Outlaw Josey Wales* (1976) or *Pale Rider* (1985), for instance, can be viewed less for their violence and more as signs of trauma, and an inability to have any other response to it. The heroes of *White Hunter, Black Heart* (1990) or *Blood Work* (2002) develop new dimensions. The hope in *Hereafter* (2010) or *Sully* (2016) becomes more pronounced. The insights may not be entirely new, but their reasons have them gain a new sense of urgency. Eastwood's films are as much about the world the audience occupies as they are about the world captured on film. The imperfections of his world become an opportunity for audiences to address the flaws in theirs. His films do not do the work society needs done, but they do help society see what work needs to be done and give them a reason to do it. Eastwood's films set the parameters for the conversations needed to initiate or support that work. The extent to which Eastwood's perfect world materializes prompts those conversations if nothing else.

WORKS CITED

A Perfect World. 1993. Directed by Clint Eastwood, performances by Clint Eastwood, Kevin Costner, and Laura Dern, Warner Bros.

Blood Work. 2002. Directed by Clint Eastwood, performances by Clint Eastwood, Jeff Daniels, and Anjelica Huston, Warner Bros.

Hereafter. 2010. Directed by Clint Eastwood, performances by Matt Damon, Cecile De France, and Richard Kind, Warner Bros.

Herman, Judith. 1997. *Trauma and Recovery*. New York: Basic Books.

McCombs, Maxwell. 2014. *Setting the Agenda: The Mass Media and Public Opinion.* 2nd ed., Kindle ed. Cambridge: Polity Press.

Newman, Sarah. 2016. "How Media Shapes Our View of Post-Traumatic Stress Disorder." *World of Psychology,* June 10, http;//psychcentral.com/blog/archives/2106/06/10/how-media-shapes-our-view-of-post-traumatic-stress-disorder/. Accessed 31 Dec. 2016.

The Outlaw Josey Wales. 1976. Directed by Clint Eastwood, performances by Clint Eastwood, Sondra Locke, and Chief Dan George, Warner Bros.

Pale Rider. 1985. Directed by Clint Eastwood, performances by Clint Eastwood, Michael Moriarty, and Carrie Snodgress, Warner Bros.

Purtle, Jonathan, Katherine Lynn, and Mashal Malik. 2016. "Calculating the Toll of Trauma in the Headlines: Portrayals of Posttraumatic Stress Disorder in the *New York Times* (1980–2015)." *American Journal of Orthopsychiatry,* 632–638.

Sully. 2016. Directed by Clint Eastwood, performances by Tom Hanks, Aaron Eckhart, and Laura Linney, Flashlight Films.

van der Kolk, and Alexander C. McFarlane. 1996. *Traumatic Stress: The Effects of Overwhelming Experience on Mind, Body, and Society.* New York: The Guilford Press.

White Hunter, Black Heart. 1990. Directed by Clint Eastwood, performances by Clint Eastwood, Jeff Fahey, and Charlotte Cornwell, Malpaso Productions.

About the Contributors

Kathleen A. **Brown** is an associate professor of history at St. Edward's University, where she teaches courses on film history, war and militarism, and movements for social change. A Presidential Excellence Grant from St. Edward's University Funded the Research for her essay in this collection.

Mária I. **Cipriani** is an adjunct assistant professor of English, American studies, and media studies, who teaches courses at the City University of New York and the State University of New York. She has worked as a psychotherapist specializing in trauma, LGBTQIA stressors, and gender identity since 1996.

Andrew **Grossman** is the editor of the collection *Queer Asian Cinema* (Harrington Park Press, 2000), an editor of and regular contributor to *Bright Lights Film Journal*, and a columnist for *PopMatters*. He has contributed essays to a number of critical works, including *Movies in the Age of Obama* (Rowman & Littlefield, 2015).

Charles R. **Hamilton** is a professor of English at Northeast Texas Community College, where he teaches literature and composition courses, and an adjunct professor at Texas A&M University–Central Texas, where he teaches courses in liberal studies and communications. He is also the chair of the Adaptation: Literature, Film, and Culture Area for the Southwest Popular/American Culture Association.

Coady **Lapierre** is the counseling and psychology chair and a member of the Distinguished Graduate Faculty at Texas A&M University–Central Texas. He has published on the treatment of trauma and combat-related mental health issues since the 9/11 attacks and he has helped create and implement programs used by the U.S. Army to address consequences of combat deployment on military families.

Fernando Gabriel **Pagnoni Berns** is a graduate teaching assistant in the Facultad de Filosofía y Letras at the Universidad de Buenos Aires (Argentina). He teaches seminars on international horror film and has published essays on a variety of topics in a number of edited collections.

Laurence **Raw** teaches in the Department of English at Baskent University, Ankara, Turkey. He has published extensively in the field of film adaptations and performance and has several books on the topic, including *Adapting Henry James to the*

Screen (Scarecrow, 2006), *The Adaptation of History* (McFarland, 2013) and *Translation, Adaptation and Transformation* (Bloomsbury, 2012).

Allen H. **Redmon** is a professor of English and film studies at Texas A&M University–Central Texas. His research on Carl Theodor Dreyer, Clint Eastwood, and Quentin Tarantino looks at the ways they undermine the violence their films tolerate (if not celebrate). He is the author of *Constructing the Coens* (Rowman & Littlefield, 2015).

Canela Ailén **Rodriguez Fontao** is a lecturer specializing in horror television and cinema. She has contributed to essays *Cine y Revolución en America Latina* (Ediciones Imago Mundi, 2014), *Bullying in Popular Culture* (McFarland, 2015), and *Deconstructing Dads* (Lexington, 2015).

James F. **Scott** is a professor emeritus and lifelong academic who divides his time between teaching, writing, and video production. His work in documentary film includes a series of productions for local and regional PBS, among them *William Clark* (2009). He is the author of an introduction to film aesthetics, *Film* (Holt, Rinehart and Winston, 1975).

Alison S. **Wallace** is a captain in the United States Army. She teaches composition and literature at the United States Military Academy at West Point. Her studies focus on psychological traumas and horrors ranging from the Victorian Gothic period to present day texts and films.

Sydney Sian **Walmsley** is a visiting instructor of literature at Charleston Southern University, where she teaches freshman courses on writing and other courses on metafiction, post-colonial fiction, and magic realism. Her research interests include the criminalization of homosexuality, pop-culture, sports-fandom, and fiction.

Brett **Westbrook** is an independent scholar. Her publications include essays on masculinity and on ghosts in the novels of James Lee Burke. Her writing on Clint Eastwood includes essays on masculinity and on gender relations.

Index